INTERNATIONAL DEVELOPMENT IN PRACTICE

Governing Infrastructure Regulators in Fragile Environments

Principles and Implementation Manual

WORLD BANK GROUP

Contents

Figure

Tables

Preface

Two billion people now live in countries where development outcomes are affected by fragility. Fragile states tend to be characterized by weak governments and institutions, low levels of trust, and the inability to deliver core services to their citizens. To help infrastructure investments succeed in an already difficult environment, while also reducing costs for enforcement and monitoring, governments may initially opt to lower barriers for market entry by keeping general regulation at a minimum.

However, while it is crucial for fragile states to address critical short-term infrastructure needs, they should also rebuild their capacity to create and administer good regulation—and promote the establishment of a coherent and high-quality regulatory system reaching beyond and across specific public-private partnership (PPP) solutions. There are several very pertinent reasons for strengthening capacity to manage the regulatory system early in the state building process, including bolstering state legitimacy and improving conditions for the private sector. Academic post-conflict literature often refers to a "golden hour" after major crises, wars, and instabilities when existing governance structures are left weak and local patronage networks are disrupted. This is the moment when regulatory agencies, particularly those that require institutional autonomy to prevent local capture, are best generated—simply put, when local veto players and rent-seekers lack the capacity to distort the process.

Good regulatory practices can make or break policies. Studies show a strong correlation between regulatory quality and economic growth, improved governance and higher incomes. Eliminating cumbersome procedures and red tape, while sometimes necessary, is usually not enough to achieve sustainable regulatory reform. Optimizing the technical capacities of sectoral regulators to control utility delivery efficiently is also important.

These are some of the regulatory governance challenges that governments must address to ensure a high-quality and reliable regulatory environment for investments in infrastructure sectors. Equally important is the central government's capacity to establish and maintain a coherent and accountable governance structure for regulators across sectors. Without such capacity, experience has shown that "independent regulators" become unaccountable islands of expertise, which can contribute to significant uncertainties both for potential investors and regulated entities. These challenges become particularly pertinent in the case of fragile states,[1] with limited capacity to adjust and correct regulatory regimes that have been poorly designed from the outset.

This manual was prepared to develop and strengthen good practices in this field. The target audience includes policymakers and regulators in developing countries, other reform stakeholders, World Bank technical teams, and other experts.

The project was developed and managed by the World Bank's Regulatory Policy and Management Team (initially located in the World Bank's Global Governance Practice, subsequently with the Macroeconomics, Trade and Investment [MTI] Global Practice) in close collaboration with the Public-Private Infrastructure Advisory Facility (PPIAF). Early drafts of the report were prepared by Rex Deighton-Smith and Peter Carroll (Consultants). The project team was led by Peter Ladegaard (Lead Private Sector Specialist, MTI) and consisted of Petter Lundkvist (Regulatory Specialist, MTI) and Christine Shepherd Vermeulen (Consultant, MTI/PPIAF). The PPIAF team consisted of Jemima Sy (Program Manager), Sara Ahmed (Operations Analyst, Global Knowledge), Luciana Guimaraes Drummond e Silva (Global Knowledge Coordinator), Giulia Motolese (Global Knowledge Consultant), Philippe Neves (Senior Infrastructure Specialist), and Svitlana Orekhova (Global Knowledge Consultant).

Valuable comments were received throughout the project from Professor Mark A. Jamison and Professor Sanford V. Berg (Public Utility Research Center, University of Florida). In addition, important guidance and comments were provided by an advisory group of World Bank experts consisting of Catherine Kadennyeka Masinde (Practice Manager, Global Business Regulation, MTI), Ana Bellver (Global Lead for Government Service Delivery, Governance Global Practice [GGP]), Jerome Bezzina (Senior Regulatory Economist, Transport and Digital Development Global Practice), Helene Grandvoinnet (Co-Lead of GGP Fragility, Conflict, and Violence [FCV] working group), Junglim Hahm (Senior Infrastructure Specialist, PPIAF), Asbjorn Haland Wee (Senior Operations Officer, FCV Cross-Cutting Practice), Joanna Kata-Blackman (Senior Operations Officer, International Finance Corporation [IFC]), Tim Kelly (Lead Information and Communications Technologies Policy Specialist, Transport and Digital Development Global Practice), Daniela Henrike Klau-Panhans (Senior Operations Officer, FCV Cross-Cutting Practice), S. Akhtar Mahmood (Lead Private Sector Specialist, Global Business Regulation Unit [GMTBR]), Yogita Mumssen (Senior Infrastructure Economist, Water Global Practice), Fernanda Ruiz Nunez (Senior Economist, PPP Cross-Cutting Practice), Markus Scheuermaier (Senior Operations Officer, IFC), and Heba Shamseldin (Lead Private Sector Specialist, MTI).

The publication was prepared under the overall guidance of Caroline Freund, Director, Trade, Regional Integration, and Investment Climate, Macroeconomics, Trade and Investment, World Bank Group; and Jordan Schwartz, Director, Infrastructure Finance, PPPs and Guarantees, World Bank.

This publication is part of the third phase of PPIAF's *Improving Infrastructure Regulation for Low-Income, Fragile and Low-Capacity Countries Program*, conducted between 2016 and 2018. This program aims to support the development of sustainable regulatory systems and improve the delivery of infrastructure services by building regulators' capacity to design and implement regulatory functions. Phases 1 and 2 developed the content and tools for regulators in developing countries with low regulatory capacity. The resources developed in the first two phases included an updated *Body of Knowledge on Infrastructure Regulation* (BoKIR), identification and analysis of best practices for regulation in low-capacity contexts, a regulatory maturity taxonomy, and a self-assessment tool. These resources were disseminated online to make them more accessible to practitioners.

NOTE

1. For the purposes of this document, "fragile" countries are those included in the World Bank's *Harmonized List of Fragile Situations* (see https://www.worldbank.org/en/topic /fragilityconflictviolence/brief/harmonized-list-of-fragile-situations).

Executive Summary

CONTEXT

Countries exiting situations of fragility face many urgent priorities and almost invariably suffer from substantial infrastructure deficits. During periods of fragility and conflict there is typically very little infrastructure investment, while existing installations are often damaged or destroyed. Immediately after the conflict, especially in poor, rural or peri-urban areas, small-scale providers often emerge to respond to pent-up demand for infrastructure services. While the services they offer, are often expensive and of uncertain quality, they fill a gap because private investment in infrastructure is limited at such times (Schwartz, Hahn, and Bannon 2004).

Building or rebuilding infrastructure on a larger scale that provides high quality services to greater numbers of people at a more affordable rate, requires that countries exiting fragility raise capital to finance the projects; yet they have limited ability to do so. As a result, there is a strong need for private investment. The limited presence of local investors and capital suggests that much of this funding needs to come from foreign sources. Attracting this investment requires that governments ensure an investment climate sufficiently appealing to attract private and foreign investors, who require returns on their capital commensurate with the risks—invariably high in fragile environments. Indeed, research points to a significant correlation between the risk rating of conflict-affected countries and their success in attracting investment in private infrastructure projects (Schwartz, Hahn, and Bannon 2004).

Building a favorable investment climate entails a wide range of factors, with some of the most basic including secure property rights, the enforceability of contracts by an impartial legal system and the free movement of capital. The quality of the regulatory system is also widely recognized as a fundamental element in this equation: research has found that limited regulatory capacity has an adverse impact on economic growth and, in turn, on a range of social issues (see, for example, Chisari, Estache, and Romero 1999; Estache and Rossi 2005; Jalilian, Kirkpatrick, and Parker 2007; Zhang, Parker, and Kirkpatrick 2005). Thus, while fragile states face an immediate need to focus on reconstruction in post-conflict situations, it is just as important for them to address the medium- and long-term objectives of creating an institutional, legal and regulatory environment to attract private investment (Bray 2004).

Appendix B summarizes the literature on the links between regulatory capacity and economic performance, as well as on the more limited, but rapidly growing, research on the connections between regulatory governance (including the governance of regulators) and economic outcomes.

A wide body of literature devoted to infrastructure regulation exists and has helped guide the development of this manual. For example, the reader is encouraged to examine the World Bank's *Body of Knowledge on Infrastructure Regulation*.[1] This provides an excellent summary of most of the literature, as well as links to key texts and documents.

PURPOSE

This purpose of this manual is to contribute to improvements in the quality of infrastructure regulation in countries exiting situations of conflict and fragility. It does so by identifying key principles for the governance of infrastructure *regulatory agencies,* and by suggesting how those principles can be introduced successfully and maintained over time. The introduction of cross-cutting governance principles for regulators is based on the assumption that a uniform set of governance principles can be less costly and complex for governments to implement and enforce, and will provide potential investors with a more consistent and predictable regulatory environment to navigate. Consequently, it is assumed that improvements in governance frameworks for infrastructure regulators will support better and accountable regulatory decision-making, as well as increased investment and overall economic development.

WHO IS THE AUDIENCE?

The manual can be used by policymakers and experts when legislation is being developed to implement the new regulatory arrangements needed to support a new, competitive structure in a key infrastructure industry. The principles and associated strategies can also serve as a frame of reference for subsequent reviews of the progress of the reforms as well as in the context of an *ad hoc* review and reform activity that responds to specific problems. In the latter, it is feasible to address only a subset of the principles.

This publication is accompanied by materials for a 2-day training program, building on the findings of this book. The program targets analysts, practitioners, or key stakeholders concerned with revitalizing and reforming regulatory systems. It presents ideas, concepts, and perspectives designed to improve decision-making. Moreover, modules based on this book are available for online access on the *Body of Knowledge on Infrastructure Regulation* (http://regulationbodyofknowledge.org).

DEFINING "GOVERNANCE OF REGULATORS"

The term "governance" refers to the rules that govern the establishment and operation of an organization. Governance concerns the processes whereby organizations make and implement decisions, including how those decisions can be challenged or appealed. Working to ensure good governance provides a systematic way of certifying that an organization has a clear set of objectives and functions, and that it acts consistently in their pursuit. In other words, ensuring good governance is a systemic way of pursuing good outcomes.

The governance of regulators is one element within the regulatory governance concept. It refers to the processes whereby regulatory agencies are established, and their operations governed. Thus, it is concerned with the means of regulatory design, implementation and enforcement. By systematically enhancing regulatory practices over time, improved governance of regulators strengthens the legitimacy and credibility of both the regulators and the regulation they administer, building trust among the regulated. Definitions of other key concepts used throughout the report can be found in Appendix A.

DEFINING "FRAGILITY"

This guide often uses the term "fragile" to refer to those countries once classified as fragile and conflict affected, as per the World Bank Group's *Harmonized List of Fragile Situations*. Some of the discussion, however, pertains more broadly to "fragile" countries or situations within countries, irrespective of their classification in the "Harmonized List." The discussion and principles presented in this guide would be relevant in all cases of fragility, where there is structurally increased risk of events with extreme consequences. The key drivers of these risks include weak state capacity and poor legitimacy and accountability; societal mistrusts and fractures; poor economic resilience (shocks to income are associated with increases in conflicts); and the lack of capacity to protect firms and families from violence and conflicts.

PRINCIPLES OF THE GOVERNANCE OF REGULATORS

The Guide identifies 10 key principles needed to establish a sound governance structure for an infrastructure regulator, and how the principles can be addressed in fragile contexts. These principles and their application are described in detail in Section B of this guide and are outlined in table ES.1.

Section B of this guide is complemented by five case studies, which examined how these principles manifested in the telecommunications and/or energy sectors[2] in Georgia, Kosovo, Madagascar, Nepal and Rwanda; all countries "exiting" or that have recently "exited" fragile status. The cases were selected based on regional distribution and exhibited a range of fragility drivers—from conflict, both between internal factions (Georgia, Nepal and Rwanda) and between internal and external forces (Kosovo); economic collapse due to a change in economic model, (Georgia, Kosovo, Madagascar) aggravated by high corruption (Georgia and Madagascar); and extreme political upheaval and instability (Madagascar and Nepal); and, social fractures (Kosovo and Rwanda). Tables ES.2 and ES.3 provide overviews of how the energy and telecom regulatory agencies and their related laws and regulation in the case countries, fared against the "best-in-class" ideal of the 10 principles.

The case studies underscored that the principles are mutually reinforcing and inter-related. For example, mandate clarity is important only if the regulator

TABLE ES.1 Ten key principles for governance of regulators

PRINCIPLE	DESCRIPTION
Principle 1—Mandate Clarity	Regulators should have a clearly defined mandate, which consists of its overall purpose or goal, its specific objectives or aims, and the functions it is required to undertake.
Principle 2—Requisite powers	The regulator should have the legal authority necessary to undertake the functions and responsibilities assigned to it.
Principle 3—Independence	For infrastructure regulation, it is important for regulatory decision-making to be independent of political processes.
Principle 4—Decision-making and governing body	Regulators require governance arrangements that ensure they operate effectively, provide for high-quality decision-making, safeguard the agency's regulatory integrity, and deliver the objectives of their mandate.
Principle 5—Funding	The regulator must have access to sufficient resources to allow it to carry out its assigned functions effectively, while funding must be supplied in ways that do not risk distorting the regulator's decisions.
Principle 6—Integrity	As with all public governance, regulatory agencies must demonstrate high standards of integrity.
Principle 7—Predictability	Individual decisions made by regulators should, to a substantial degree, be predictable for regulated entities.
Principle 8—Engagement	Regulators should have established mechanisms for consultation and dialogue with stakeholders as part of achieving their objectives.
Principle 9—Accountability and transparency	Regulators should be accountable to their governments and parliaments, as well as to regulated entities and the public, for their decisions and use of resources.
Principle 10—Performance evaluation	Evaluations of the performance of regulators should consider both their effectiveness in carrying out the functions assigned to them both in legislation and through other directives and the fitness for purpose of the regulatory structures that are in place.

TABLE ES.2 Summary of the regulation related to energy regulatory agencies using the 10 principles

	GEORGIA	KOSOVO	RWANDA	MADAGASCAR	NEPAL
Mandate Clarity	✓	✓✓	✓	✓	✓✓
	High legal clarity, except for its role in competition; less so in practice.	High legal clarity; yet vague on tariffs and strengthening socio-economic cohesion.	High legal clarity but some conflict between objectives and no provision for reviewing laws.	Limited legal clarity partially overcome, but led to uncertainty and limited coordination, exacerbated by low funding.	High level of legal clarity. Practical implementation tough due to low level of role clarity of past body.
Requisite powers	✓	✓✓	✓	✓	✓
	Appropriate powers specified in law; except regarding policy advice and competition.	Appropriate powers specified in law.	Appropriate powers specified in law but limited in practice by the exercise of Presidential authority.	Powers in place though insufficient for setting tariffs, standards, and for dealing with consumer complaints.	Several powers established in new law not yet put into practice, especially regarding tariffs.
Independence	✓	✓✓	✓	✓	✓
	High level of independence in law restricted in practice by funding arrangements.	High level of independence in law restricted in practice by funding arrangements.	High level of independence in law restricted in practice by President's power to appoint chair.	High level of legal independence restricted by civil service Board members and overlapping responsibilities to ministers.	High level of independence in law, subject to constraints. Limited experience of new regulator.

continued

TABLE ES.2, *continued*

	GEORGIA	KOSOVO	RWANDA	MADAGASCAR	NEPAL
Governing body	✓✓	✓	✓	✓	✓✓
	An appropriate structure and decision-making processes.	Appropriate structure and decision-making processes except for appointment of commissioners.	Appropriate structure and decision-making processes; except for appointment of Managing Director.	Partly appropriate structure but Chair is also CEO, and a there is lack of detail regarding some processes.	New law establishes appropriate appointment structure, though grounds for removal too broad.
Funding	✓✓	✓	✓	✓	✓
	Largely self-funding with a cap on fee levels.	Self-funding in law but difficulties caused in the budget approval process.	Largely self-funding with a cap on fee levels but lacks a fund to cover legal costs.	Limited degree of self-funding also limited by lack of budgetary authority and independence.	Law establishes appropriate funding arrangements, but does not specify budget-setting process.
Integrity	✓	✓	✓	NA	✓
	Appropriate legal basis for integrity; practical enforcement limited.	Appropriate legal basis with a code of conduct but not published on its website.	An appropriate legal basis for integrity but seems to lack a code of conduct.	Lack of formal attention to integrity in law and practice, with no code of behavior.	Broadly suitable integrity measures, but lacking appeals process under new NERC Act.
Predictability	✓✓	✓✓	✓	✓	NA
	Increasingly sophisticated body of regulation and plans has increased predictability of decision-making.	Increasingly sophisticated body of regulation and plans has increased predictability of decision-making.	Increasingly sophisticated body of regulation and more predictability of decision-making; but Presidential powers can cause uncertainty.	Increasing but limited degree of predictability, especially for key decisions, for example, tariffs and consumer complaints.	Lack of mechanisms to ensure predictable decision-making. History of corruption, political interference and insufficient funding lead to a lack of predictability.
Engagement	✓✓	✓✓	NA	✓	✓
	A substantial regulatory basis for engagement with high levels of access; largely done in practice.	Substantial regulatory basis for engagement largely complied with in practice.	No regulatory requirements or practice of consultation with stakeholders or the public.	Very limited legal basis for engagement (no formal policy), though in practice a degree of consultation takes place.	New law requires formal engagement on some, but not all key issues. Practice shows relatively consistent approach.
Accountability and transparency	✓✓	✓✓	✓	✓	✓
	Laws provide for high accountability, transparency, appeal rights.	Laws provide for a high degree of accountability and transparency.	Growing accountability and transparency but limited regarding rights of appeal and consultation.	Law provides for several means of accountability but there is a lack of agency transparency.	New law includes several transparency and accountability mechanisms, though gaps exist; actual practice is yet to evolve.
Performance evaluation	NA	NA	✓	NA	NA
	Not prescribed or used.	Not prescribed or used.	Some evaluation required in law; being put into practice.	Not prescribed or used.	Not prescribed or used.

Note: Extent to which each principle has been addressed: ✓✓ = principle fully addressed; ✓ = principle partly addressed; NA = principle not addressed. NERC = Nepal Electricity Regulatory Commission.

TABLE ES.3 Summary of the regulation related to telecommunications regulatory agencies using the 10 principles

	MADAGASCAR	KOSOVO	NEPAL
Role Clarity	✓	✓✓	✓
	A lack of role clarity and funds have severely restricted performance. A current review might remedy these weaknesses.	The law provides a high degree of role clarity for the regulator.	The role is outlined in generally clear detail in the law but in practice some of its functions have been ineffectively implemented, notably in relation to competition.
Requisite powers	✓	✓✓	✓
	While endowed with a wide range of formal powers it cannot set tariffs, lacks power relating to cyber security and, in practice has given little attention to competition or consumer issues.	The formal powers provided by the law are appropriate and adequate.	In law there are appropriate powers but, in practice, they are more limited with considerable government use of a general power to give directives to the agency, and the lack of detailed and transparent procedures for the removal of board members.
Independence	✓	✓	✓
	In law there is considerable independence. In practice it is limited as regards appointment of board members, strategy and finance.	In law there is a reasonable degree of independence. In practice financial procedures substantially limit independence.	In law there is a reasonable degree of independence for the agency but this is limited in practice by the government's use of its power of directive.
Governing body	✓	✓✓	✓
	In law there is an appropriate governing body and key decision processes. In practice, there is considerable ministerial involvement, representative board members and a lack of detail regarding appointment processes.	The law establishes the agency on sound governance principles.	The law establishes the agency on generally sound governance principles, again limited in practice by the government's use or potential use of its power of directive.
Funding	✓	✓	✓
	The agency has a limited degree of financial independence but no authority in relation to setting fees.	Unusually, the National Assembly is to approve the agency's budget although in practice negotiations are with the Ministry of Finance. It has no control over its budget and limited financial autonomy.	The law provides for self-funding and separate accounts. The setting of license fees and royalties has been by a tendering process rather than on the basis of the recovery of regulatory costs.
Integrity	✓	✓	✓
	There is no explicit clause in the statute regarding integrity or the need for a code of behavior.	While the law includes a number of articles aimed at reducing conflicts of interest, it does not require the development of codes of behavior, nor has the agency developed such a code.	The law includes a number of articles aimed at reducing conflicts of interest but does not require a code of behavior and there are no required procedures for removing board members.
Predictability	✓	NA	✓
	Most key decision procedures are outlined, briefly, in the law, with the exception of those in relation to competition and consumer complaints.	The law does not require decision rules to be developed and the agency either has not developed them or made them available on its website, so predictability is limited.	Detailed operational rules based on legislation have been developed and included in new legislation. This could improve decision-making predictability, assuming levels of corruption fall sharply.
Engagement	NA	✓✓	✓
	While there has been a new interest in engagement, there is no policy in this regard and little signs of practical activity to increase effective engagement.	The law establishes an appropriate basis for engagement which seem to be followed in practice, with good feedback processes.	The law has been largely silent regarding engagement, but, in practice, the agency has undertaken on a discretionary basis a relatively high degree of consultation.

continued

TABLE ES.3, *continued*

	MADAGASCAR	KOSOVO	NEPAL
Accountability and transparency	✓	✓	✓
	The law provides a limited basis to achieve accountability to ministries, but not to operators or Parliament, with a marked lack of transparency.	Unusually, the agency is accountable to the National Assembly, not the Government. This breaks the chain of accountability and limits the ability of Governments to ensure accountability. Frequent elections limit the extent to which the Assembly can hold the agency accountable.	The law contains reference to limited, traditional means for accountability and transparency and the agency website contains substantial material to relevant policies, principles, and procedures. However, there is no indication that independent review of decisions is available.
Performance evaluation	NA	✓	NA
	No explicit requirement for performance evaluation, nor is it undertaken in practice.	The law does not explicitly require performance evaluation but provides general powers that could enable it, but it has not been implemented.	The law does not explicitly require performance evaluation.

Note: Extent to which each principle has been addressed: ✓✓ = principle fully addressed; ✓ = principle partly addressed; NA = principle not addressed.

is also able to fully exercise its requisite power; and performance evaluation strengthens the accountability of the regulator. However, despite each country's different circumstances, the case studies illustrated common path constraints, suggesting that the absence of some of the principles, above others, pose an immediate challenge requiring attention at an early stage in designing regulatory frameworks in post-fragile contexts, namely:

- *Mandate Clarity,*
- *Predictability,* and
- *Engagement.*

Assessing and determining the clarity of a regulator's mandate should begin in the immediate post-fragile stage. Specifying a regulator's mandate involves identifying its purpose and objectives and setting out the functions it is required to undertake. These need to be clearly understood so that the regulator can set appropriate priorities and develop strategies to ensure their achievement. Clearly specifying the regulator's mandate is also a precondition for effective evaluation of its performance over time and, in a more general sense, for holding the regulator and its officials accountable for their actions. Doing so involves drafting legislation, which in fragile contexts, due to capacity constraints, can prove challenging. As a work-around, those determining a regulator's mandate could use key elements of legislation from similar jurisdictions and customize them. Particularly in the fragile context, continuous assessment is needed to ensure that the regulator's mandate is feasible.

Related to providing clarity of mandate for the regulator, ensuring the regulator has "requisite powers" that are clearly communicated and understood by relevant stakeholders as well as establishing the regulator's mechanisms for "stakeholder engagement" are important. Developing a regulator with clarity of mission, strength of powers and robust mechanisms for engaging with all relevant stakeholder groups is helpful to guard against possible "regulatory capture," whereby the regulator is beholden to powerful stakeholder groups. This risk of capture may be more prevalent in fragile contexts, where conflict may have erupted along ethnic or cultural lines or there are vested economic interests and risk of well-connected groups overpowering the interests of others.

Further, achieving regulatory "predictability" in post-fragile environments is helpful to ensuring the strength of the regulatory system and creating an environment favorable to outside investment. This may prove challenging, though establishing it should be a high priority. Establishing regulatory functions in law, helping the regulator publish material on how it will carry out its duties, providing regulator staff with clear guidelines so they know how to carry out their duties, and publishing formal written policies are all steps a government can take to help establish regulatory predictability.

IMPLEMENTING REGULATORY GOVERNANCE REFORMS

In addition to giving context to how the principles could work in post-fragile contexts, the case studies surfaced key lessons that helped formulate the strategic advice found in Part C of the guide, which discusses how to manage implementing regulatory governance reforms. These lessons pertain to the broad task of adopting and maintaining a program of reform of the regulation of one or more infrastructure sectors, including the establishment of a regulatory agency in accordance with the principles and include:

1. **The need to develop a regulatory governance policy and reform strategy at an early stage**—The cases indicated that little attention is given to policies necessary for robust regulatory governance. Instead, reforms following fragile situations typically focused on addressing the urgent challenges faced by the sector (asset destruction, financial collapse, etc.) Yet major failings in the regulatory system were frequently key factors frustrating reform initiatives. This suggests that the issue of regulatory policy and governance should be included as a priority item in, for example, post-conflict needs assessment and planning, followed by the adoption and monitoring of relevant indicators of progress, for periodic review by cabinet, or the equivalent. This does not mean that widespread regulatory reform should be undertaken while still in fragility. Rather, a basic policy framework should be put in place as part of post-fragility planning and progress made on specific reforms sequentially, in accordance with the specific needs and circumstances of the individual state in question. In addition to establishing a basic policy framework, a system-wide evaluation of the state of current regulatory management practices, including any existing, underlying regulatory policy, should be undertaken. The evaluation should aim to at least: identify major weaknesses and strengths in regulatory management practices to guide later, relevant reforms; and assign priorities to the areas requiring reform.

   Well directed and substantial donor aid can help bring about relatively rapid regulatory reform, especially in the infrastructure sector. Where this is not made available, or is available only on a much smaller scale, regulatory reform is likely to be far slower and performance on global rankings much poorer. This reflects both the limited regulatory governance capacities available within government administrations and the importance of opposition from entrenched interests and suggests that governments in countries exiting fragile countries should actively seek partnerships to enable the adoption of early regulatory reform efforts, particularly given the importance of such efforts in enabling and maintaining broader reform in the medium term.

2. **The need to assign authority and responsibility for regulatory policy reform to a strong minister at the center of government**—A significant factor in the success of specific regulatory and governance reforms was the

allocation of oversight responsibility and appropriate authority to a senior and influential minister, sometimes the Prime Minister or President, at the center of government. This provided a visible sign of the government's commitment to the reforms, increasing the influence of the officials responsible for implementing the various reforms. This strengthened their role clarity and enhanced the legitimacy and requisite authority of the eventual regulatory framework established.

3. **The need for policy stability**—A key risk in recently reformed sectors is that disappointing regulatory performances lead to frequent changes in the institutional architecture, with recently established regulators subject to major restructuring or even abolished and replaced with new entities. It is important to recognize that the development of regulatory capacity and credibility, and a reputation for having these qualities, takes significant time to generate. This suggests the need to give significant weight to policy stability as a key objective. This, in turn, is likely to imply seeking to work within the existing regulatory architecture to address emerging issues, wherever reasonably possible, rather than undertaking major changes within short periods. Policy stability improves the experience and capacity of the regulator, increases familiarity of market participants to the rules of engagement and therefore, enhances predictability.

4. **The need to take a strategic view of the question of privatization of state enterprises in the context of low-income states with a shallow bench of local private sector and financial markets**—Governments in all countries studied rapidly adopted policies to privatize the bulk of the state enterprise sectors. This proved in all cases to be a difficult, lengthy and frequently unsuccessful exercise. This result reflected several factors, including the relatively small formal private sectors, lack of fully functioning financial markets, corruption, the opposition of powerful, senior managers of state enterprises, lack of sufficient domestic private sector capital and the reluctance of foreign investors to enter the market. This suggests that the initial reform should be step-wise. It can focus, initially, on the restructuring of state enterprises, with a more considered privatization program being adopted progressively in the medium-term, as government and regulatory capacities develop, and growing investor confidence means that private investment in the infrastructure and other sectors dominated by state enterprises becomes more attractive.

Where infrastructure is dominated by state owned enterprises with monopoly positions, a key risk is that poorly planned privatizations would simply have created private sector monopolies, the effective regulation of which would have proved an extremely challenging task, given low capacities in this area. Systematic engagement with stakeholders through transparent, formal mechanisms can guard against "regulatory capture" by one or more stakeholder. Key data and adequate market-sounding and consultation needs to underpin decision-making.

Moreover, given the status of many state enterprises as public monopoly providers of key infrastructure services, significant attention should be paid to improving governance arrangements within these entities as part of the restructuring process. Improving governance, including adequate transparency and accountability in respect of these incumbent service providers can greatly facilitate the task faced by independent regulators that are typically established as private participation in infrastructure is established and expanded.

5. **The need to ensure that the design of regulatory bodies is cognizant of both the broader governance environment and key capacity constraints**—Both the overall degree of independence accorded to a regulator and the distribution of responsibilities between regulators and government

Ministries should be considered, in part, as a function of the governance environment. Where there are significant concerns about the quality of public governance generally, establishing a regulator with substantial independence, subject to appropriate accountability mechanisms can be an effective means of enhancing the credibility of regulation.

However, where capacities are low, there can be major challenges in establishing independent regulators with sufficient expertise and resources that can effectively perform their functions. In such contexts, considerations should be given the adoption of a single regulator with responsibilities that can be progressively extended across several infrastructure sectors as the reform process unfolds. This option can help to leverage limited regulatory expertise and ensure that the regulation of newly-reformed sectors is undertaken from the outside by an established and credible entity. It can also potentially reduce overall regulatory costs and increase the effectiveness of knowledge transfer where external expertise is brought into play to address key regulatory issues.

In addition, the lack of knowledge, experience and expertise of officials and regulators regarding the operation of markets, the determinants of economic growth and the role of high quality regulation in underpinning efficient markets was a major factor inhibiting reform in all three cases. This suggests that material on these issues should be included in the earliest training programs provided to senior and mid-level public sector officials in the post-conflict context.

NOTES

1. Available at http://regulationbodyofknowledge.org.
2. Investment patterns show private investment can occur immediately after conflict, followed by investments in the energy sector, whereas they occur much later in transport and the water sector (Schwartz, Hahn, and Bannon 2004).

REFERENCES

Bray, J. 2004. *MIGA's Experience in Conflict-Affected Countries: The Case of Bosnia and Herzegovina*. Social Development Papers. Conflict Prevention and Reconstruction Series, No. 13. Washington, DC: World Bank. http://documents.worldbank.org/curated/en/259151468768013033/MIGAs-experience-in-conflict-affected-countries-the-case-of-Bosnia-and-Herzegovina.

Chisari, O., A. Estache, and C. Romero. 1999. "Winners and Losers from the Privatization and Regulation of Utilities: Lessons from a General Equilibrium Model of Argentina." *World Bank Economic Review* 13 (2): 357–78.

Estache, A., and M. A. Rossi. 2005. "Do Regulation and Ownership Drive the Efficiency of Electricity Distribution? Evidence from Latin America." *Economics Letters* 86 (2): 253–57.

Jalilian, H., C. Kirkpatrick, and D. Parker. 2007. "The Impact of Regulation on Economic Growth in Developing Countries: A Cross-Country Analysis." *World Development* 35 (1): 87–103.

Schwartz, J., S. Hahn, and I. Bannon. 2004. *The Private Sector's Role in the Provision of Infrastructure in Post-Conflict Countries*. Trends and Policy Options Series, No. 1. Washington, DC: World Bank. http://documents.worldbank.org/curated/en/619941468141576377/The-private-sectors-role-in-the-provision-of-infrastructure-in-post-conflict-countries.

Zhang, Y., D. Parker, and C. Kirkpatrick. 2005. "Competition, Regulation and Privatisation of Electricity Generation in Developing Countries: Does the Sequencing of the Reforms Matter?" *Quarterly Review of Economics and Finance* 45 (2–3): 358–79.

Abbreviations

AFUR	African Forum for Utility Regulators
BEDU	Business Environment Delivery Unit (Kenya)
BRRU	Business Regulatory Reform Unit (Kenya)
EAPIRF	East Asia and Pacific Infrastructure Regulatory Forum
ERO	Energy Regulatory Office (Kosovo)
ESCA	Essential Services Commission Act (Australia)
EWSA	Energy, Water and Sanitation Authority (Rwanda)
GNEWSRC	Georgian National Energy and Water Supply Regulatory Commission
IA	impact assessment
IFC	International Finance Corporation
KPPU	Commission for the Supervision of Business Competition (Indonesia)
LENG	Law on Electricity and Natural Gas (Georgia)
MCC	Ministerial Coordination Committee
MD	managing director
NERC	Nepal Electricity Regulatory Commission
OECD	Organisation for Economic Co-operation and Development
PAC	Project Advisory Committee
PPIAF	Public-Private Infrastructure Advisory Facility
PSR	Payment Systems Regulator (United Kingdom)
PUC	Public Utilities Commission (Latvia)
RDB	Rwanda Development Board
RECO	Rwanda Energy Corporation
RIA	Regulatory Impact Assessments
RSC	Reform Steering Committee
RU	Reform Unit
RURA	Rwanda Utilities Regulatory Authority
RWASCO	Rwanda Water and Sewerage Corporation

A Introduction

The Importance of Ensuring Good Governance of Regulators

INTRODUCTION: THE PURPOSE OF THE MANUAL

This manual provides advice aimed at supporting improvements in the quality of infrastructure regulation in countries exiting situations of fragility. Improving the quality of the regulatory systems governing infrastructure will support both increased investment and better performance, thus enhancing overall economic development. This handbook focuses on how to improve the governance of regulatory agencies, since good governance helps to ensure that high-quality regulatory decisions are made systematically.

Context

Countries exiting situations of fragility face large numbers of urgent priorities and almost invariably suffer from substantial infrastructure deficits. Typically, little infrastructure investment occurs during the fragile and conflict affected period, while existing installations are often damaged or destroyed due to conflict. Immediately after the conflict, especially in poor, rural or peri-urban areas, small-scale providers often emerge to respond to pent-up demand for infrastructure services. While the services they offer, are often expensive and of uncertain quality, they fill a gap because private investment in infrastructure is limited at such times (Schwartz, Hahn and Bannon 2004).

Building or rebuilding infrastructure on a larger scale that provides high quality services to greater numbers of people at a more affordable rate, requires that countries exiting fragility raise capital to finance the projects; yet they have limited ability to do so. As a result, there is a strong need for private investment. The limited presence of local investors and capital suggests that much of this funding needs to come from foreign sources. Attracting this investment requires that governments ensure an investment environment sufficiently appealing to attract private and foreign investors, who require returns on their capital commensurate with the risks—invariably high in fragile environments. Indeed, research points to a significant correlation between the risk rating of conflict-affected countries and their success in attracting investment in private infrastructure projects (Schwartz, Hahn and Bannon 2004).

Building a favorable investment environment entails a wide range of factors, with some of the most basic including secure property rights, the enforceability of contracts by an impartial legal system and the free movement of capital. The quality of the regulatory system is also widely recognized as a fundamental element in this equation: researchers have found repeatedly that limited regulatory capacity has an adverse impact on economic growth and, in turn, on a range of social issues (see, for example, Chisari, Estache, and Romero 1999; Estache and Rossi 2005; Jalilian, Kirkpatrick, and Parker 2007; Zhang, Parker, and Kirkpatrick 2005). Thus, while fragile states face an immediate need to focus on reconstruction in post-conflict situations, it is just as important for them to address the medium- and long-term objectives of creating an institutional, legal and regulatory environment to attract private investment (Bray 2004). In the absence of proper regulation, countries become less attractive places to work, do business and live in. Appendix B summarizes the literature on the links between regulatory capacity and economic performance, as well as on the more limited, but rapidly growing, research on the connections between regulatory governance (including the governance of regulators) and economic outcomes.

A wide body of literature devoted to infrastructure regulation exists and has helped guide the development of this manual. For example, the reader is strongly encouraged to examine the World Bank's *Body of Knowledge on Infrastructure Regulation*.[1] This provides an excellent summary of most of the literature, as well as links to key texts and documents.

Defining the governance of regulators

The term "governance" refers to the rules applied in the establishment and operation of organizations. Governance is concerned with the processes whereby organizations make and implement decisions, including how these can be challenged or appealed. Working to ensure good governance is a way of making certain that an organization has a clear set of objectives and functions, and that it acts consistently in their pursuit. In other words, ensuring good governance is equivalent to pursuing good outcomes.

The concept of governance can be applied to a wide range of organizations and situations, both public and private. Public governance is the application of governance principles to the operation of government. Regulatory governance constitutes a specific area of public governance and involves the application of governance principles to the exercise of regulatory powers by governments. Regulatory governance addresses all stages of the regulatory cycle: problem identification and analysis; regulatory development; implementation and enforcement; review and evaluation; and, finally, reform.

The governance of regulators is one element within the regulatory governance concept. It refers to the processes used to set up regulatory agencies and govern their operations. Governance of regulators' concerns regulatory implementation and enforcement.

Key elements include:

- ensuring that regulators have sufficient independence from government to carry out their authorized functions, and that that regulatory decisions are consistent and impartial;
- making certain that the operations of regulators are based on clear legislation which explicitly identifies their objectives, powers, responsibilities and functions;

- ensuring that regulators have sufficient funds to carry out their functions and that these funds are provided in a way that does not compromise their independence or accountability; and
- ensuring that the regulator is subject to adequate accountability mechanisms, including reporting requirements and independent appeals processes against regulatory decisions.

Governance has both external and internal dimensions. The former aspect relates to an organization's interaction with its external stakeholders, while the latter refers to the way in which the organization itself is structured and managed. In relation to regulators, the external dimensions of governance include the roles and relationships and the distribution of powers and responsibilities between the legislature, the minister responsible, the ministry, the judiciary, the regulator and the regulated. Internal governance dimensions include the regulator's organizational structures, standards of behavior, compliance and accountability measures, oversight of business processes, financial reporting and performance management.

The ten principles of good governance for regulators, listed on page 7 onwards, address both dimensions of governance. They are drawn from a variety of sources and reflect the state of knowledge in the application of general governance principles to the specific context of regulators, with particular reference to infrastructure. The principles are applicable in a wide range of country contexts. However, Part B highlights key considerations that arise as regards countries exiting fragility.

Improving regulatory governance

The linkage between improved regulatory capacities and better economic performance is well established. According to the World Bank:

> Good regulatory practices can determine the prospects for policy success or failure. Studies show strong correlations between regulatory quality and economic growth, better governance quality and higher incomes per capita.
> (World Bank 2015)

This means that all countries have an incentive to improve the quality of their regulatory systems across all major policy areas. Improving regulatory governance constitutes a systematic means of improving regulatory quality and has become the preferred approach in a wide range in many countries.

By systematically enhancing regulatory practices over time, improved regulatory governance strengthens the legitimacy and credibility of regulators and the regulation they administer, and helps to build trust among those being regulated. Within an established national policy, well-designed systems of regulatory governance can:

- **improve the ongoing review and assessment of regulatory processes and practices**, yielding improved regulatory quality over time;
- **improve regulatory practice**, using well-targeted review and assessment processes to help make management more consistent and predictable;
- **promote greater innovation in organizational structures, processes and practices**, encouraging regulators to work more strategically by promoting more systematic approaches to day-to-day operations;
- **encourage politicians and senior executives to grant more discretion to regulators** to apply regulation more flexibly, as better regulatory governance systems lead to enhanced accountability and transparency in operations; and

- **encourage more effective cooperation between regulators and those being regulated**, with more transparent, consistent and predictable regulatory practice leading to greater trust and more positive relationships.

However, achieving and sustaining such improvements is a complex and multifaceted task, especially as most post-fragile states have limited regulatory capacity. Regulatory institutions in such countries are often only a few years old, still gaining experience and attempting to build their management capacity (Eberhard 2006). In addition, regulatory frameworks and institutions established in developing countries are often based on prescriptions and models drawn from more developed nations. These may not translate readily into less-developed or fragile contexts (see Laffont 2005). Strategies for developing regulatory governance in fragile states must take account of key contextual differences. They must also acknowledge the fact that in an fragile context, governance and institutional development tend to progress intermittently, given scarce human and financial resources and varying levels of political support.

This manual takes these factors into account and seeks to tailor its advice to the post-fragile context as far as possible. It draws on a consistent, well-founded set of principles and shows how they can be applied in both the *evaluation* of existing regulatory governance systems and the *implementation* of programs aimed at reforming those systems.

Importantly, while the principles discussed in the manual can apply to a range of situations, it is recognized that different contexts require diverse approaches regarding, for example, priorities, pace and timing. The following discussion recognizes the importance of socio-economic and political contexts in determining how the principles should be applied and tailors the advice provided specifically towards post-fragile contexts. That said, it is important to acknowledge that there are substantial differences even among post-fragile countries. Thus, the advice provided must be assessed carefully in the light of where it is to be adopted, and modified accordingly.

The organization of the manual

The remainder of this manual is divided into two main parts:

- Part B identifies and discusses the application of ten principles forming the basis of a high-quality system of governance for infrastructure regulators. It is intended to help readers to determine key areas of weakness in current governance arrangements and priorities for reform.
- Part C focuses on designing and implementing a program of reform for existing governance systems and assessing capacities for achieving such reform. It also provides advice on using the ten principles to diagnose the strengths and weaknesses of existing governance arrangements, and set priorities for reform, as well as providing a governance template for establishing new regulatory agencies where required.[2]

A FRAMEWORK FOR THE MANUAL—TEN PRINCIPLES FOR THE GOVERNANCE OF REGULATORS

The view that systems of governance should be based on a set of clearly specified principles is not new: Principles exist for a wide range of governance contexts, like corporate governance, community governance, and environmental governance. In some cases, like the AS 8000 Australian Standard Good Governance Principles, countries develop national standards for good governance intended to be generally applicable. However, the development of underlying principles for *regulatory* governance is more recent, emerging gradually from several decades of experience with regulatory reform, in both World Bank client countries and OECD nations.

While a country's context will drive the types of regulatory practices, systems and agencies developed, as well as determine how they evolve in response to economic, social and political changes, a consistent set of principles should underpin them. These principles should be at the basis of a national policy for regulatory governance that aims to ensure *systematically* that the regulator's decisions are transparent, objective, impartial, and serve the public interest.

Ten principles for the governance of regulators

The following briefly introduces the ten principles that form the basis of this manual. While the principles draw on a range of sources, they rely particularly on previous work undertaken by Brown et al. (2006) and the OECD (2014). Part B provides more detail regarding the meaning of the principles, their importance and their implementation in the post-fragile context. The ten principles are:

1. **Mandate Clarity**. The regulator's purpose and regulatory objectives should be clearly defined and communicated to the regulator, the regulated, and the general public.

2. **Requisite powers**. The regulatory agency should have the authority to make final decisions within its statutory domain without having to obtain approval from any other government body. That authority varies with the regulator's objectives and functions, but typically includes the power to:
   - set tariffs;
   - establish market, technical and service quality rules;
   - address market power and market design problems;
   - investigate and adjudicate consumer complaints;
   - provide dispute resolution mechanisms for regulated entities;
   - monitor and enforce compliance with its decisions;
   - apply remedies—including sanctions—when necessary.

3. **Independence**. There should be a strong presumption in favor of establishing an independent body or bodies to regulate infrastructure. Where lack of qualified and experienced staff makes this impossible, establishing a regulator within a ministry as an "arm's-length"[3] body may be an appropriate interim solution. In this case, administrative and financial arrangements should maximize the independence of the regulator. It should also be clear that this will be a temporary arrangement.

4. **Decision-making and governing body**. Governance arrangements for regulators should promote efficiency, effectiveness and integrity. Independent regulators most often have governing bodies with several members. This reflects the fact that a pluralistic structure is considered better able to make high-quality decisions because collegiality and joint responsibility support independence and integrity.

5. **Funding**. Regulators require adequate funding to carry out their duties effectively, and funding arrangements should avoid giving rise to conflicts

of interest or represent inappropriate incentives. Regulators should receive sufficient funding to do their jobs, but no more.

6. **Integrity**. Like all public bodies, regulatory agencies must demonstrate high standards of integrity. They must hold all personnel to high standards of conduct and avoid any suggestion that impropriety or illegal behavior is tolerated. Regulatory integrity is essential to achieve decision-making which is objective, impartial, consistent, and avoids bias and improper influence. This is a major challenge for the infrastructure sector, where major procurement contracts and the revenue-raising processes involved provide rich opportunities for corruption. Hence the need for a system of rules or a code of conduct to prevent improper conduct and maintain integrity among regulatory decision-makers.

7. **Predictability**. Predictability implies that stakeholders can forecast, with a high degree of confidence, what decision a regulator is likely to take in given circumstances. Predictability is achieved by establishing and publishing clear decision-making rules and ensuring that the regulator follows them. This enables individuals and organizations to judge what behavior is acceptable and what is not so as to make certain they are acting within the law. It also allows them to determine whether the actions they are contemplating are permitted by the regulatory structure, increasing certainty regarding the investment and operating environments.

8. **Engagement**. Regulators should engage systematically with stakeholders through transparent, formal mechanisms such as consultations in order to guard against "regulatory capture" by one or more stakeholder. At the same time, such mechanisms should ensure that the regulator has the opportunity to obtain key data and opinions to underpin decision-making.

9. **Accountability and transparency**. Regulators should be accountable to the government and parliament, the regulated and the general public for their decisions and use of resources. This implies that their actions have a high level of transparency.

10. **Performance evaluation**. Regulators should measure their outputs so that they can update regulatory actions and internal functioning to improve or maintain efficiency. Performance data should be available to anyone to whom the regulator is accountable, including the regulated and the general public.

In addition, when the principles are to be applied as part of a review of regulation, it should be noted that the extent to which existing regulation corresponds to the principles will vary from country to country, as can be seen in tables ES.2 and ES.3 in the Executive Summary. The tables briefly summarizes the extent to which each of the ten principles is addressed in regulation establishing the energy regulatory agency in five different countries.

NOTES

1. Available at http://regulationbodyofknowledge.org.
2. As noted above, readers should also refer to http://regulationbodyofknowledge.org for further material on improving infrastructure regulation. The material on the site provides a wealth of resources for reformers in this field, including:
   - ideas that will assist in the launching or revitalizing of regulatory systems in fragile or conflict-affected states;
   - a number of key reform strategies;

- a self-assessment tool for evaluating a variety of challenging situations;
- a variety of case studies; and
- a set of Frequently Asked Questions and answers for officials in fragile states.

This material can and should be used in conjunction with this manual to help decision-makers evaluate their current situation, set priorities for reform and plan implementation strategies to improve the regulatory environment and increase the attractiveness of investment in infrastructure.

3. According to a World Bank definition, arm's-length bodies are commonly removed from the control of politicians and outside the hierarchical control of traditional vertically-integrated line ministries and departments (see Manning and Shepherd 2009).

REFERENCES

Bray, J. 2004. *MIGA's Experience in Conflict-Affected Countries: The Case of Bosnia and Herzegovina.* Social Development Papers. Conflict Prevention and Reconstruction Series, No. 13. Washington, DC: World Bank. http://documents.worldbank.org/curated /en/259151468768013033/MIGAs-experience-in-conflict-affected-countries-the-case -of-Bosnia-and-Herzegovina.

Brown, A. C., J. Stern, B. Tenenbaum, and D. Gencer. 2006. *Handbook for Evaluating Infrastructure Regulatory Systems.* Washington, DC: World Bank. http://documents.worldbank.org/curated /en/428111468177849284/pdf/364990Handbook101OFFICIAL0USE0ONLY1.pdf.

Chisari, O., A. Estache, and C. Romero. 1999. "Winners and Losers from the Privatization and Regulation of Utilities: Lessons from a General Equilibrium Model of Argentina." *World Bank Economic Review* 13 (2): 357–78.

Eberhard, A. 2006. "Infrastructure Regulation in Developing Countries: An Exploration of Hybrid and Transitional Models." Paper prepared for the 3rd AFUR (African Forum of Utility Regulators) Annual Conference, Windhoek, March 15–16.

Estache, A., and M. A. Rossi. 2005. "Do Regulation and Ownership Drive the Efficiency of Electricity Distribution? Evidence from Latin America." *Economics Letters* 86 (2): 253–57.

Jalilian, H., C. Kirkpatrick, and D. Parker. 2007. "The Impact of Regulation on Economic Growth in Developing Countries: A Cross-Country Analysis." *World Development* 35 (1): 87–103.

Laffont, J. J. 2005. *Regulation and Development.* Cambridge: Cambridge University Press.

Manning, N., and G. Shepherd. 2009. "Arms Length Bodies". Global Expert Team (GET) Brief. World Bank, Washington, DC. http://documents.worldbank.org/curated/en /804021468163449274/pdf/534640BRI0GET01n0title010GET0Briefs.pdf.

OECD (Organisation for Economic Co-operation and Development). 2014. *The Governance of Regulators.* OECD Best Practice Principles for Regulatory Policy. Paris: OECD Publishing. http://dx.doi.org/10.1787/9789264209015-en.

Schwartz, J., S. Hahn, and I. Bannon. 2004. *The Private Sector's Role in the Provision of Infrastructure in Post-Conflict Countries.* Trends and Policy Options Series, No. 1. Washington, DC: World Bank. http://documents.worldbank.org/curated/en/619941468141576377/The -private-sectors-role-in-the-provision-of-infrastructure-in-post-conflict-countries.

World Bank. 2015. "Regulatory Policy and Management". June 18. http://www.worldbank.org /en/topic/governance/brief/regulatory-policy-and-management-incubator-global -solutions-groups.

Zhang, Y., D. Parker, and C. Kirkpatrick. 2005. "Competition, Regulation and Privatisation of Electricity Generation in Developing Countries: Does the Sequencing of the Reforms Matter?" *Quarterly Review of Economics and Finance* 45 (2–3): 358–79.

B Principles for the Governance of Regulators

GOALS OF THE SECTION

- To identify and briefly describe the key principles that need to be embodied in a sound governance structure for an infrastructure regulator;[1]
- to explain how each principle contributes to a quality system of governance;
- to discuss a range of issues related to ensuring the principles are addressed in fragile contexts; using examples drawn from ex-fragile countries;
- to provide practical advice on how to implement needed reforms in practice.

NOTE ON THE PRINCIPLES

In situations where a country is developing legislation for regulatory arrangements designed to support a new, competitive structure in a key infrastructure sector, all principles should be addressed. Importantly too, the principles should be used as the frame of reference for subsequent reviews assessing the progress of the reforms. Finally, they can be helpful when *ad hoc* review and reform activity is conducted in response to specific problems. In this context, it is feasible to address only a subset of the principles.

Many examples contained in Part B illustrate that, while the principles themselves are applicable in many country contexts, the specific ways in which they are implemented may differ significantly. Implementation strategies must consider the country situation in all cases. Part C considers this point further, taking a broader approach to reform implementation issues and providing additional strategic guidance.

IMPLEMENTING THE PRINCIPLES OVER TIME

While new legislation for regulatory arrangements should address all principles, the relative importance of the principles can vary both as a function of the initial circumstances of the fragile state in question and as a state gradually moves out of fragility. The translation of principles into specific rules and responsibilities will also need to evolve over time, making periodic progress review and reform of laws and policies a key requirement.

In general, mandate clarity, requisite powers and adequate funding, together with a well-designed governing body with appropriate decision procedures, are particularly important in guiding initial moves out of the fragile situation. By contrast, independence and engagement, while always important, grows in relative importance as both the regulatory agency and the sector(s) for which it is responsible develop in scale and sophistication over time. The principles of predictability and performance evaluation can only be addressed substantively once regulators have become established and experience and expertise have developed. However, they then become fundamental to maintaining reform momentum over the longer term.

By contrast, the principles of integrity, accountability and transparency are always of great importance as serious deficiencies in these areas are usually accompanied by corruption, regulatory capture, inefficiency and poor performance.

Governments may also need to set sectoral priorities in implementing the principles. The telecoms sector is often more readily developed in an early post-conflict situation, as its investment needs can be lesser than other infrastructure sectors and can be more readily recouped within shorter periods. Conversely, the long lead-times for investment in the electricity sector mean that putting the regulatory building blocks in place for the development of the sector at an early stage can also be a key priority. While synergies can be obtained from moving to reform several key sectors simultaneously, capacity constraints will often make this unrealistic in fragile contexts, making the selection of priority sectors a key task. Chapter 15 discusses reform strategy, including the staging of reform.

NOTE

1. As mentioned above, the principles draw on previous work undertaken by Brown et al. (2006) and the OECD (2014).

REFERENCES

Brown, A. C., J. Stern, B. Tenenbaum, and D. Gencer. 2006. *Handbook for Evaluating Infrastructure Regulatory Systems*. Washington, DC: World Bank. http://documents .worldbank.org/curated/en/428111468177849284/pdf/364990Handbook101OFFICIAL0U SE0ONLY1.pdf.

OECD (Organisation for Economic Co-operation and Development). 2014. *The Governance of Regulators*. OECD Best Practice Principles for Regulatory Policy. Paris: OECD Publishing. http://dx.doi.org/10.1787/9789264209015-en.

2

Mandate Clarity

ABSTRACT

Regulators should have a clearly defined mandate, with specific objectives and functions that are clearly linked to the government's policy objectives for the sector. They should also be able to coordinate their work with that of other entities in a positive, cooperative fashion.

KEY TAKEAWAYS

General takeaways

- A regulator's purpose and objectives should be clear if it is to do its job effectively.
- The regulator's supervising ministry and the entities it regulates should be transparent on its functions and role; this requires clear communication concerning the regulator's mandate.
- The regulatory goal of promoting competition often receives most pushback.
- A regulator's mandate can be evaluated over time and altered later as needed.

Takeaways specific to post-fragile contexts

- Assessing and determining mandate clarity should begin in the immediate post-fragile stage.
- Developing a mandate involves drafting legislation. In fragile contexts, capacity constraints can make this difficult.
- To work around capacity constraints, those determining a regulator's mandate could use key elements of legislation from similar jurisdictions and customize them.
- Particularly in fragile contexts, continuous assessment is needed to ensure that the regulator's mandate is feasible.

THE IMPORTANCE OF MANDATE CLARITY

Specifying a regulator's mandate involves identifying its purpose and objectives and setting out the functions it is required to undertake. These need to be clearly understood so that the regulator can set appropriate priorities and develop strategies to ensure their achievement. Clearly specifying the regulator's mandate is also a precondition for effective evaluation of its performance over time and, in a more general sense, for holding the regulator and its officials accountable for their actions. As box 2.1 indicates, a lack of clarity can lead to uncertainty as to the appropriate actions for the regulator to take and to delays in decision-making.

A regulator's mandate consists of its overall purpose or goal, its specific objectives or aims, and the functions it is required to undertake. These need to be clearly understood so that:

- The regulator can set appropriate priorities and develop strategies, plans and related activities to achieve them.
- The supervising ministry or department is aware of the regulator's priorities, strategies, plans and activities and how they fit into the government's broader policies.
- The regulated entities and the public are aware of the regulator's priorities, strategies, plans and major activities and how they may impact on their activities.
- Potential investors, domestic and international, have a clear and easily accessible understanding of the regulator's role regarding their previous or future investments in the sector.
- Regular and systematic evaluation can be undertaken of the regulator's performance in achieving its stated goals, objectives and aims.
- The agency can be held fully accountable for its actions by assessing its activities in relation to its explicit goals and objectives.

BOX 2.1

Unclear wording, mandate clarity, and the Rwanda Utilities Regulatory Authority

In 2011, Law No. 21/2011 governing Electricity in Rwanda was introduced, with four objectives identified: the liberalization and regulation of the electricity sector; the harmonious development of distribution of electric power for all of the population and for all economic and social development sectors; the creation of conditions enabling electric power investments; respect for the conditions of fair and loyal competition and for the rights of users and operators.

While the Law was framed to further the "harmonious development of distribution of electric power" it did not clarify what was meant by "harmonious development of distribution," or the criteria to be applied in assessing whether a decision or action was, or was likely to be, "harmonious." As a result, it was unclear what the Rwanda Utilities Regulatory Authority's (RURA) role should be in regard to achieving the objective.

Similarly, the requirement for "respect for the conditions of fair and loyal competition and for the rights of users and operators" does not indicate what is meant by "fair and loyal competition," or the criteria to be used in assessing whether the relevant "conditions" for achieving it are met. This shows how important it is to ensure that the regulator's objectives and functions are specified, using commonly understood phrases and concepts wherever possible. Any more specialized terms and concepts should be explained.

Discussions involved in clarifying the agency's mandate provide an opportunity for stakeholders to participate in the work of the agency in the early days of its operations. This helps promote understanding and a commitment to the agency's work. In addition, the development of clear, publicly available documents that describe the role of the regulator help to avoid:

- **Unnecessary duplication or overlap of functions between regulators and other bodies.** Resulting in unnecessary conflict and costs. In Georgia, for example, the supervising ministry had responsibility for attracting short-, medium-, and long-term investments in electricity, a role which overlapped with that of the National Investment Agency. There are sometimes good reasons for the existence of overlapping functions and objectives but, where they exist, it is important that the reasons for the overlap are made clear and ways found to coordinate the work of the agencies involved.
- **Possible non-compliance by those being regulated because of a lack of certainty and understanding of the legislation.** This could be the case for those interacting with Rwanda's utilities regulator, as described in box 2.1.
- **Compliance and enforcement difficulties caused by a lack of clarity as to the regulator's authority and responsibility.** The Georgian National Energy and Water Supply Regulatory Commission (GNEWSRC), for example, has authority to grant permits and licenses for the siting of electricity generation facilities. However, the Georgian Law on Electricity and Natural Gas specifies that the supervising ministry, not the National Energy and Water Supply Regulatory Commission, has authority for granting permits for facilities that are not to be connected to the transmission grid. This could result in electricity enterprises not connected to the power grid facing different conditions than those that were part of the grid, and falling under the authority of the Regulatory Commission. Such conflicts can both create tension between the Ministry and the Commission and lead to strategic behavior by regulated entities seeking to evade the conditions for permits set by either body.
- **Stakeholder confusion as to compliance obligations.** This could occur in the above example of split responsibilities for the issue of permits in Georgia.
- **Delays, uncertainty and increased costs.** These may arise from the need to obtain authoritative interpretations of the meaning of ambiguous terms and phrases.

As box 2.1 indicates, a lack of clarity leads to uncertainty on the regulator's part about what action to take, resulting in delays in decision-making while clarification is sought. Similarly, a clear statement of the regulator's objectives and the extent of its authority can help determine the legality of the regulator's actions.

MANDATE CLARITY AND THE GOAL OF COMPETITION

Responsibility for promoting competition is an area in which the question of mandate clarity frequently arises. In almost all developing countries, infrastructure sectors are dominated by government monopoly suppliers. Thus, a key objective in reforming the regulatory system governing those sectors is to establish effective competition as extensively as possible. Newly appointed sector regulators are frequently given the explicit objective of encouraging and, if necessary, regulating competition.

At the same time, broader economic reforms often entail establishing a specialist competition authority, with a remit to address competition issues across the economy. This can give rise to confusion as to the relative responsibilities in this area, particularly where the specific role of the sectoral regulator is not clearly identified. Box 2.2 provides an example.

To avert confusion, it is important that legislation governing infrastructure regulators provide specific guidance on the nature and extent of their responsibilities in promoting competition, where these are allocated. Consideration should also be given to the appropriate assignment of functions as between infrastructure regulators and competition authorities. As noted, competition issues should generally be the responsibility of the competition authority rather than industry regulators. However, they are not likely to exist in fragile contexts.[1] In such situations, it may be therefore appropriate for sectoral regulators to wield these responsibilities. But clear mechanisms for consultation and cooperation with any competition authority should be established.

Regulators should promote an understanding of their mandate by making its functions clear to stakeholders. Mention should also be made of the principles adopted for decision-making and any guidelines developed on what regulated entities should expect, including their responsibilities to the regulator and the consequences of misbehavior.

Legislation establishing the regulator should, at the very least, specify the following:

- a clear, written purpose and a set of objectives facilitating their achievement;
- a set of specific functions clearly linked to the statement of purpose and objectives;
- prescribed mechanisms for coordinating its work with other relevant bodies to achieve the desired regulatory outcomes;

BOX 2.2

Promoting competition in Madagascar's infrastructure sectors

Legislation governing the regulatory agencies responsible for electricity and telecommunications (ORE and ARTEC, respectively[a]) in Madagascar made them responsible for promoting competition. However, the precise role these regulators would play in fostering competition and the priority that should be given to that role, was not detailed in the relevant legislation.

In the post-fragile period, general competition law was rudimentary and no separate competition authority existed. In 2005, the government formally passed legislation to establish such an authority, but the implementing decree giving practical effect to the regulation was not adopted until 10 years later. Hence,

there was little expert guidance available on the specific responsibilities of the industry regulators regarding competition and it was not viewed as a priority in their work.

When a competition authority finally emerged in 2015 there was no clear specification—either legislative or administrative—as to the respective roles of the competition authority and existing industry regulators in addressing competition issues. In addition, all three regulatory agencies—that is, power, telecommunications and competition—were poorly funded and lacked expert staff, so that competition continued to receive limited attention, effectively favoring the continued dominance of government-owned enterprises.

a. Office de Regulation de l'Electricité (ORE) and Autorité de Régulation des Technologies de Communication (ARTEC).

- clear and comprehensive statements of responsibilities, powers and duties that distinguish it from other government bodies and agencies that also wield authority in the sector.

Mandate clarity is particularly important for regulating bodies that have responsibilities for several infrastructure sectors, such as electricity, gas and water, often known as "multisector regulators." In such cases, it is vital that relevant legislation sets out as precisely as possible the varying objectives and functions of the regulator for each sector. While a single law will often address these issues, each sector should be covered in a separate section.

Mandate clarity is also important in federal states and those with several levels of government, where separate regulatory agencies may exist at each level. In such cases, where coordination between separate agencies is a priority, it is important that legislation explicitly empowers the agencies to cooperate in the achievement of their objectives. Box 2.3 provides an example of this kind of legislation in Mexico.

ASSESSING MANDATE CLARITY IN THE POST-FRAGILE CONTEXT

Assessing mandate clarity for regulators should begin in the immediate post-conflict stage, during initial policy development, and continue when the process of legislative drafting begins. Policymakers and drafters should aim to ensure that the draft legislation accurately reflects the original intent of the policy as well as identify and address any ambiguities arising from the development of detailed statements of goals, objectives and functions. This will provide an important and necessary basis for:

1. ensuring that the new or amended legislation assigns requisite powers to the agency (for further details see chapter 3);
2. the process of "corruption proofing," (for further detail see chapter 3);

BOX 2.3

Coordination mechanisms for the Mexican Federal Institute of Telecommunications

1. The Mexican Federal Institute of Telecommunications (IFT) will coordinate with the federal executive to ensure the installation of a shared public telecommunication network that promotes effective access by the population to broadband communication and telecommunications services.
2. Congress will create an Advisory Council of the IFT, which will be called on to act as an advisory body.
3. The IFT must notify the federal executive before proceeding with the revocation of concession titles in order for it to obtain, where appropriate, the powers necessary to ensure continuity of service.

4. The IFT may receive non-binding opinions from:
   - The Ministry of Communications and Transport (SCT) when granting, revoking or authorizing concessions or changes in the control, ownership or operation of companies related to such concessions.
   - The Ministry of Finance and Public Credit (SHCP) for fixing the fees or dues for the granting of concessions and the authorization of related services.

Source: OECD 2014, 39.

BOX 2.4

Checklist of questions and issues for use in reviews of mandate clarity

1. What are the goals and objectives of the legislation and are they clearly defined?
2. Are there any potential conflicts between the objectives? If so, is guidance provided to the regulator on how to manage these conflicts when making regulatory decisions?
3. Does the legislation clearly specify the regulator's functions? Are these clearly related to achieving the identified objectives of the legislation?
4. Are the goals, objectives and functions of the regulator clearly specified and publicly available? If not, why not?
5. Does the legislation enable the minister to provide direction on priority setting when managing conflicting objectives? Is this power appropriately constrained? Is its transparency required in its use?
6. Are the respective roles of the minister, ministry and regulator in policy and legislative development clearly defined and supported by processes to ensure their effective collaboration? If not, why not, and what changes should be introduced?
7. Are there overlaps or gaps in responsibilities between regulators, or between the roles of regulators, ministries and ministers? If so, what changes are necessary?
8. Does the legislation enable the regulator to cooperate with other bodies with similar objectives? If not, what changes are necessary?

3. the process of regulation impact assessment, where this is a requirement, as is increasingly the case;
4. the process of environmental impact assessment.

However, qualified and experienced legislative drafters are often in short supply in fragile states, public consultations are frequently limited and there is little informed public debate. Weaknesses can therefore persist after the passing of the legislation, requiring later amendment and further clarification (see Nzanze [2012] for a consideration of the impact on legal drafting of Rwanda's fragile experience). This issue is acute where legislation must be developed in two or more official languages. In such situations, using key elements of similar legislation sourced from other, relevant jurisdictions can be a useful mechanism. It is important, however, to assess whether any such templates are consistent with local circumstances and needs.

Even in the best-resourced policy development and drafting contexts, unanticipated problems can arise once new legislation has taken effect. In such cases, it is important to ensure that the practical experience of the new, or reconfigured regulatory agency is assessed, and any problem areas addressed. The views of stakeholders should be weighed in this context, as should feedback from the regulatory agency. Where substantial issues are identified, a more formal assessment may be required. Box 2.4 provides a checklist of the types of questions and issues that should be addressed in such a context.

NOTE

1. Among the states on the 2018 *Harmonized List of Fragile Situations* (http://pubdocs .worldbank.org/en/189701503418416651/FY18FCSLIST-Final-July-2017.pdf), only around 20 percent have competition authorities in place.

REFERENCES

Nzanze, V. 2012. "Challenges of Drafting Laws in One Language and Translating Them: Rwanda's Experience." *The Loophole, Journal of the Commonwealth Association of Legislative Counsel* 1: 42–53.

OECD (Organisation for Economic Co-operation and Development). 2014. *The Governance of Regulators.* OECD Best Practice Principles for Regulatory Policy. Paris: OECD Publishing. http://dx.doi.org/10.1787/9789264209015-en.

3

Requisite Powers

ABSTRACT

The term "requisite power" implies that the regulator has the legal authority necessary to undertake the functions and responsibilities assigned to it. If it does not have adequate legislated powers, the regulator is unlikely to be able to achieve the objectives set in the legislation as it will be constrained in its ability carry out key functions, for example, gathering information, ruling on key issues and enforcing compliance with its decisions.

KEY TAKEAWAYS

General takeaways

- Regulators should have power to:
  - set tariffs at reasonable levels;
  - establish, modify and monitor market, technical and service quality rules and policies that are within its authority;
  - address market power and design problems (if the agency has a pro-competitive role);
  - carry out routine functions;
  - investigate, adjudicate, or mediate consumer complaints;
  - provide dispute resolution mechanisms;
  - compel communication of information;
  - monitor and enforce decisions;
  - resolve problems with appropriate remedies.
- Regulator powers should be assessed periodically against the objectives set out in legislation.

Takeaways specific to post-fragile contexts

- Granting powers to an independent regulator may face resistance. Nonetheless, ensuring that a regulator has adequate powers, and making sure those are clearly communicated and understood by relevant stakeholders, is very important to prevent outside interference.
- One way to ensure that a regulating body is strong enough to exercise its powers without outside influence is to rapidly shore up its capacity. In the fragile context, this could entail crowding in donor support.
- Having a supportive enabling environment that includes strong rule of law is also helpful in enabling the regulator to exercise its powers correctly. Although this is probably difficult to achieve in a post-fragile context, it is important that any proposal for new or modified legislation or regulation is carefully assessed to ensure that the regulator has all the legal authority required.

WHAT ARE THE POWERS A REGULATOR SHOULD POSSESS?

Fundamentally, the regulatory agency should have authority to make final decisions within its statutory domain without having to obtain prior approval from any other government agency. While powers required by a regulatory agency responsible for infrastructure will vary, depending upon the objectives and functions for which it is responsible, typically they should include:

- setting tariffs at reasonable levels for regulated entities for the benefit of consumers and regulated bodies;
- establishing, modifying, and monitoring any market, technical and service quality rules and policies within its legal authority necessary for carrying out its functions and consistent with the policies and principles articulated in other, related laws;
- addressing market power and market design problems adequately, where the agency has a pro-competitive role;
- carrying out routine administrative functions;
- investigating, as well as adjudicating or mediating, consumer complaints;
- providing dispute resolution facilities for regulated entities;
- compelling the provision of information;
- monitoring and enforcing its decisions;
- resolving problems with appropriate remedies, including penalties.

ASSESSING THE ADEQUACY OF A REGULATOR'S POWERS

Assessing issues related to requisite powers entails identifying the objectives and functions assigned to the agency in the legislation and examining the agency's powers in the light of these. As with mandate clarity, the process of assessing the adequacy of the regulator's powers should begin early on in the development of the regulatory reform policy and continue throughout the legislative drafting process. Focus should be placed on ensuring that the key objectives identified, in terms of the adequacy of the regulator's powers, are appropriately addressed in the law.

Once the new regulatory arrangement has existed long enough for there to be experience to review, policymakers and governments should also conduct *ex-post* reviews to determine the adequacy of the powers provided. Where the newly established regulatory system functions well, this will be simple. Where key regulatory objectives are not being achieved for want of requisite powers, a more thorough review is required. Box 3.1 presents a case where wider powers for a regulator would make the system function more efficiently.

Where assessments of the powers of existing regulators are being conducted, these should include full consultation with relevant officials in the regulatory agency concerned and a careful scrutiny of legal cases involving the agency and the use of its powers, initially guided by the type of questions listed in box 3.2.

REQUISITE POWERS IN THE POST-FRAGILE CONTEXT

In the fragile or immediate post-fragile context, where governments have gone through a period of conflict and their authority is uncertain, a proposed decision to grant substantial powers to an independent regulatory agency is often met with resistance. This may come from ministers, who are often reluctant to give up any significant authority, or departments, who are reluctant to lose control of activities to a new agency, especially where this means the loss of rewarding jobs and promotion possibilities.

However, ensuring the adequacy of these powers is particularly important in the post-fragile context, as governments will often have strong incentives to make decisions that would be contrary to those which a robust, independent regulator is required to take. For example, it was noted in the Latvian example above that an independent regulator should have the power to set prices when the market is not yet fully competitive. Yet, price-setting is a particularly sensitive function in post-fragile contexts, where many customers may have limited ability to pay cost-reflective tariffs. In such situations, supervising ministries and governments are often reluctant to accept new tariffs or increase existing ones. For example, in both Kosovo and Madagascar, successive governments have used their influence to prevent or reduce planned tariff hikes.

Thus, it is particularly important that the powers of the regulatory agency in this area are very clear and can, as far as possible, be exercised without political interference. One way to help achieve this is by rapidly shoring up the capacity of public-sector entities and regulatory agencies in the immediate aftermath

---

BOX 3.1

A case of insufficient powers for the Latvian Public Utilities Commission?

Latvian companies are required to submit proposed tariffs for municipal waste disposal in landfills to the Latvian Public Utilities Commission (PUC), which approves or rejects them after performing an analysis and assessment of costs and profits. The PUC does not have amendment powers regarding tariff proposals, although it can propose a tariff review. A recent OECD review highlighted the resulting "back and forth" between the regulator and the operators and noted that it could be simplified and shortened if the regulator had the power to amend tariff applications.

Source: OECD 2016, 57.

BOX 3.2

A checklist for reviewing the adequacy of regulators' powers

To check whether a review is needed of the powers exercised by a regulator and determine the likely scope of such a review, several preliminary questions need to be asked, including:

1. What sources of information indicate a lack of adequate powers and how reliable are those sources?
2. What are the issues identified by the available sources of reliable information? How significant are they, particularly in terms of the potential to constrain business investment and/or efficient market operation?
3. How can the issue(s) identified be resolved? What are the views of key stakeholders, especially those who have been affected by the issues.
4. What changes are needed to resolve the issue? Is change needed to the law establishing the regulator? Are changes to other laws required? Are broader changes affecting the machinery of government, or changes to market rules likely to be required?

of a conflict. Where the government desires to protect vulnerable groups from the price increases needed to achieve cost-reflective tariffs, explicit subsidy arrangements should be put in place, rather than artificially limiting the ability of the regulator to set the right prices.

A further issue in the post-fragile context is that the market is frequently characterized by a dominant, state-owned enterprise reluctant to defer to the authority of an agency. It is vital that the latter's powers are sufficiently clear and substantial to enable it to compel compliance, since ensuring appropriate behavior by the dominant entity is fundamental to enabling the development of more competitive markets over time. This can be particularly important in terms of the entry of new competitors into downstream markets (e.g., in the telecoms sector), where dominant incumbents may seek to prevent network access by resellers. Building new or refining existing regulatory systems in the aftermath of a conflict with wide national consensus can help ensure that other parts of government and regulated entities know, understand and agree to the powers of the regulator.

Finally, it is important to note that having adequate powers is a necessary, but not sufficient, condition for regulatory effectiveness. If the rule of law is limited, as is often the case in a post-fragile context, then ensuring that the regulator has the necessary powers might not, in itself, be sufficient to result in high levels of compliance with its decisions. In other words, the effective presence of rule of law is a key factor in enabling powers to be exercised appropriately. Hence, it is important that any proposal for new or modified legislation or regulation be carefully assessed to ensure that the regulator has the full legal authority or "competence" necessary to undertake the desired functions and responsibilities. As noted in box 3.1, failure to provide an agency with requisite powers can result in delays in decision-making, increased costs and loss of credibility.

REFERENCE

OECD (Organisation for Economic Co-operation and Development). 2016. *Driving Performance at Latvia's Public Utilities Commission*. The Governance of Regulators. Paris: OECD Publishing. http://dx.doi.org/10.1787/9789264257962-en.

4

Independence

ABSTRACT

An independent regulator should be able to make decisions within the scope of its authority without interference from the government or individual ministers.

KEY TAKEAWAYS

General takeaways

- Regulators can exist in three broad organizational contexts:
  1. as part of the ministry
  2. at arm's length from the ministry
  3. as an independent body, established by law.
- For infrastructure regulation, it is important for regulatory decision-making to be independent of political processes. An independent regulator should be established.
- A regulator's independence should be guaranteed in legislation: specifically, legislation should grant a regulating body powers to make decisions on its own.
- Where ministries or governments can "direct" regulators, those directions must be clearly limited, policy-oriented and subject to transparency and accountability.
- While it is important for a regulator to achieve independence, it must also be held accountable for the independent decisions it makes.

Takeaways specific for post-fragile contexts

- While aiming for an entirely independent structure is recommended, in fragile contexts achieving an arm's-length arrangement is a good interim solution.
- It is common in fragile environments for governments to want to change the regulatory structure, if/when a regulator is perceived as not meeting expectations. Yet such rapid policy changes can impede a regulator's independence.

Concerns regarding a regulator's performance should be addressed through careful analysis and the subsequent implementation of targeted reforms focused on specific, identified problem areas (see Part C, *Implementing Reforms to Regulatory Systems and Governance*, for details).

- Transparency mechanisms (e.g., annual reports, making decisions public, as detailed in chapter 10) can help counter outside interference, quite common in fragile contexts, and preserve regulator independence.
- Regulatory capture, whereby the regulator is beholden to powerful stakeholder groups, is a risk in fragile contexts. Favoring a multisectoral regulatory model, which can enable the regulator to scale up to sufficient size more quickly, thus serving as a stronger counterweight to outside pressure, can help mitigate this risk. Ensuring a strong regulatory governance system with transparency, accountability, and probity rules as well as a strong performance evaluation system is also important.

INTRODUCTION

Infrastructure regulators generally require a substantial degree of independence to perform their functions effectively, though the degree of freedom that is appropriate may vary with circumstances and time. Achieving independence requires that a regulator can make decisions free of political interference by government or regulated entities. This chapter aims to examine the value of independence, how it can be gained and maintained, and its relationship to other issues.

A regulator generally exists in one of three forms:

1. as an integral part of a ministry;
2. as an arm's-length body, which is formally a part of a ministry but has a degree of independence resulting from administrative and/or financial arrangements; or
3. as an independent body, usually established by law.

The choice as to which form is most appropriate in a particular regulatory context depends on the relative importance attached to operational independence on the one hand, and to accountability and responsiveness to government, on the other.

Regulatory decision-making that is independent of the political process is likely to be appropriate where:

- It is considered important that the regulator should be seen as independent so that the public is confident its decisions are objective and impartial.
- It is important for government and non-government entities (SOEs, private businesses), to be regulated under the same framework to achieve "competitive neutrality"—that is, equal treatment of government and non-governmental entities.
- Regulatory decisions can substantially affect particular interests in a positive or negative fashion, making impartiality important.

These factors will almost invariably be present in infrastructure regulation. The first—that is, the need for the regulator to be seen as independent—is likely to be of particularly importance with states in, or emerging from, a fragile or conflict-affected situation since such contexts are typically characterized by low levels of trust in government.

That being the case, there should be a strong presumption in favor of establishing an independent regulator or regulators. However, this might not be practical in a fragile context, where there is an acute shortage of qualified and experienced staff. Thus, those leading the reform process could consider interim alternatives:

- **Start with an arm's-length arrangement**. It may be preferable to establish a regulator within a ministry as an arm's-length body. When choosing this option, it is essential not only to ensure that administrative and financial arrangements maximize the regulator's independence but also to make clear to the public that this is a temporary arrangement. An explicit commitment to establish a fully independent regulator within a set period can help to increase confidence in the government, particularly if the commitment is written into in legislation.
- **Work through an existing independent regulator**. Where an independent regulator already exists with responsibilities in another sector of the economy, expanding its remit to include a newly reformed sector can leverage existing expertise and experience and may help establish independent regulation in the short term. Empirical evidence shows that expanding the scope of an existing regulator is a common strategy in many countries (Jordana and Levi-Faur 2010), while multisectoral regulators are relatively common in the specific context of post-FSC countries. In Madagascar, for example, both electricity and water services are the responsibility of one regulatory agency, while in Georgia, both electricity and gas fall under one agency.

HOW IS INDEPENDENCE ESTABLISHED AND MAINTAINED?

While regulators cannot and should not be completely independent of government, an "independent" regulator must be able to make decisions without needing prior approval from ministers, other agencies, government officials or non-governmental actors and stakeholders. Such arrangements are necessary (but not sufficient) to ensure that the regulator is insulated from political pressure, thus favoring consistent decision-making in line with the regulator's objectives and priorities.

Regulators' ability to make autonomous decisions should be clearly limited to the specific areas of authority granted to them by government in legislation (these areas of authority or requisite powers are addressed in chapter 3). Moreover, they must remain subject to broad government policy. This may mean that there may be provisions enabling the minister or government to give direction to the regulator in certain circumstances. However, where ministers or government have such power, it must be:

- **Clearly limited.** Legislation should spell out specific circumstances in which direction can be given, the kind of direction allowed, and the extent of the power to direct.
- **Policy-oriented.** Power to give directions concerning regulatory decisions should be set out in broad terms, rather than in specific terms that would enable the minister to influence decision-making only in certain cases.

- **Subject to transparency and accountability requirements.** Directions given to the regulator by a minister or government should be published at the time and as part of the regulator's annual report.

The most effective means of establishing independence in decision-making is to set out in legislation the powers of the regulator, as well as the powers of the minister or government vis-à-vis the regulator. Since these matters are fundamental to the operation of the regulator, such provisions should be contained in primary legislation—that is, Acts of Parliament/Congress, rather than in decrees or subordinate regulations.

INDEPENDENCE VERSUS ACCOUNTABILITY

Independence and accountability must be finely balanced. The greater the independent regulator's room for action, the more substantial the accountability mechanisms should be.

Key mechanisms of this kind include:

- the requirement to give reasons for major decisions;
- provision for an independent process of appeal against the regulator's decisions;
- the requirement to publish annual reports containing enough information to judge how the regulator is exercising its functions;
- provisions for regular assessments of the regulator's performance by an independent assessor or body.

Chapter 10 addresses accountability issues in detail and chapter 11 examines performance evaluation.

In addition to these specific accountability tools, it must be ensured that the key regulatory principles, practices and procedures to be followed by the regulator are identified and specified in sufficient detail in legislation. This issue is discussed further in chapter 7, which deals with specific ways of ensuring the regulator's integrity. It may also arise during the process of corruption proofing.

INDEPENDENCE AND OTHER GOVERNANCE PRINCIPLES

In addition to being balanced by appropriate mechanisms, giving a regulator independent status involves addressing other key governance issues. Without adequate governance arrangements, for instance, there is a significant risk that giving the regulator a free hand could lead to undesirable outcomes.

It is essential that effective arrangements are in place in relation to:

- funding
- the decision-making and governing body
- integrity
- predictability
- performance evaluation.

The links between independence and these other governance principles are addressed in chapter 5 (Decision-Making and Governing Body), chapter 6 (Funding Regulatory Agencies), chapter 7 (Integrity), chapter 8 (Predictability), and chapter 11 (Performance Evaluation).

INDEPENDENCE ISSUES IN THE POST-FRAGILE CONTEXT

Policy stability

Policy stability is an important factor in developing and safeguarding effective independence in all contexts, but particularly for regulatory agencies in the fragile context. Where the performance of recently established regulators fails to meet expectations, there is often a tendency for governments to respond by making major changes to the regulatory structure, including abolishing and replacing existing agencies. However, such major policy realignments tend to come at substantial cost, including that of hindering the development of a robust, independent culture within the regulator. Such a culture, bolstered by a clear view of the regulating agency's role and functions and the development of a critical mass of expertise and experience, is essential in order to guarantee the body's effective independence.

This implies that concerns regarding the performance of regulators should be addressed through careful analysis of their legislative and policy environment, in terms of regulatory governance principles, and the subsequent implementation of targeted reforms that address identified problem areas. This issue of policy stability is discussed further in Part C.

Transparency mechanisms

Recently established regulators, particularly in post-conflict contexts, may be relatively poorly placed to push back against government attempts to undermine their independence. These could include a government pressuring for of particular decisions, often by reducing budget allocations, especially where a minister of finance has control over the funds (e.g., in Kosovo and Madagascar). Transparency mechanisms can help counter such attempts by involving other actors in defending independent decision-making, thus providing a "distributed" network of accountability safeguards. Such actors may include the press, parliament, other regulated entities, donor bodies and international organizations. However, transparency in regulatory processes, including decision-making, is essential to enable the effective involvement of these groups. Without access to relevant information they cannot determine if a government decision has been made in relation to a regulatory agency, or whether it is appropriate.

Avoiding regulatory capture

Ensuring that regulators are not "captured" by the regulated is a second major consideration in the maintenance of independence. Avoiding capture is particularly important in the post-fragile context, where trust in institutions is fragile and robust transparency and accountability mechanisms are absent.

BOX 4.1

Questions to guide a desk review to determine the appropriate institutional structure and mechanisms needed to ensure independence in a regulator in a post-fragile state

Determining institutional structure for independence:

1. Are the powers of the regulator set out in legislation? Are the powers of the minister in relation to the regulator set out in legislation? Is this material in primary legislation?
2. What is the government's commitment to independent regulation? Is it strong or weak? Similarly, what is the government's institutional capacity to oversee an independent regulatory function?

Ensuring independence over time:

1. Are there transparency and accountability mechanisms in place to help safeguard the regulator's independence? (e.g., are decisions public? Can outside stakeholders like the press track these decisions and comment on them?)
2. Are there transparency, probity and accountability rules governing the regulator? Is the regulator's performance reviewed through performance evaluations?

At a structural level, it is generally accepted that regulators with broad mandates spanning several industries are less likely to become captive than those which regulate a single industrial sector. This is a further element (in addition to leveraging limited expertise and experience, as noted in chapter 4, *Introduction*) favoring the multisectoral regulatory model.

However, while this basic structural characteristic will lessen the probability of capture significantly, the prevention of capture is a multifaceted task. Various elements of the regulatory governance system should work together to address and minimize the risks of capture, including:

- **Transparency rules.** These should require the regulator to publish information detailing the basis on which regulatory decisions have been taken, and their expected effects.
- **Probity rules.** Employees of the regulator should be prohibited from taking up positions in the regulated industry for a set period (e.g., 2 or 3 years).
- **Accountability rules.** The regulator should be required to include information on its performance in terms of set benchmarks in published annual reports.
- **Performance evaluation.** Regular performance evaluations of the regulator, conducted by independent bodies with adequate resourcing and using set benchmarks, can identify major problems and assess whether capture is a contributing factor. Box 4.1 provides a list of questions that can be included in a desk review of regulators in post fragile contexts.

REFERENCE

Jordana, J., and D. Levi-Faur. 2010. "Exploring Trends and Variations in Agency Scope." *Competition and Regulation in Network Industries* 11 (4): 342–60.

5

Decision-Making and Governing Body

ABSTRACT

Regulators require governance arrangements that ensure that they operate effectively, provide for high-quality decision-making, safeguard the agency's regulatory integrity and thereby deliver the regulatory objectives of its mandate.

KEY TAKEAWAYS

General takeaways

- When developing a regulator's decision-making body, or board, a key choice to make is whether it will be a single-, or multi-member body. Multi-member bodies are recommended: they are known for more robust decision-making.
- Two main variants of a multi-member board include the "governance board model" and the "commission model": each have their pros and cons.
- Distribution of decision-making powers between the regulator and political authority should be clearly stated in legislation.
- Members appointed to a regulatory decision-making body should serve the general public interest; the appointment process should help ensure this by being explicit, public, and fully transparent to those making decisions.
- When recruiting board members, the following factors should be considered: skills needed and availability of those skills on the market.
- Recruitment should guarantee enough decision-makers on board to ensure actions are expedited. Appointments should also be structured (or staggered) in such a way as to guarantee continuity and renewal in the decision-making body.

Takeaways specific to post-fragile contexts

- In a fragile context, the "commission model" for decision-making has advantages in that it may provide greater accountability for major

regulatory decisions. The direct, collegial accountability for major decisions that the commission model embodies is likely to provide greater confidence that capture will be avoided.
- Key considerations when structuring a decision-making body in a fragile environment include:
  - Ensuring the body has relevantly qualified staff but that qualifications are not prescribed in such detail as to limit the available pool of board members.
  - Documenting explicitly broader recruitment policies for board members.

CHOOSING THE DECISION-MAKING MODEL

Single member versus multi-member decision bodies

The decision-making model adopted for an independent regulator should reflect the nature and extent of its functions and responsibilities. The basic choice is between a single-member and a multi-member governing body. Most countries have multi-member ones. This is because the multi-member structure is considered more likely to take sound decisions.

Key benefits of the multi-member structure include:

- Collegiality and collective responsibility, making the regulator less vulnerable to capture. This helps maintain integrity.
- More robust decision-making processes, yielding higher-quality decisions, due to the presence of members with a range of backgrounds and skills. This is particularly important where discrete decisions by the regulator have major implications for stakeholders.
- Greater regard to principles and precedent, thereby supporting consistency and predictability in decisions due to collective decision-making. The maintenance of "corporate memory" over time is also a factor here.
- Improved ability to provide strategic guidance to the regulator CEO and staff and to support them in carrying out their functions.
- Greater guarantee of continuity over time, avoiding the risk that the regulator loses strategic focus or direction following the departure of a single decision-maker.

Many of these factors are likely to be important in the context of infrastructure regulators, including the need to avoid capture, to ensure decisions are predictable and consistent, and that continuity in key directions is maintained over time.

Governance boards versus commission boards

There are two main variants of the multi-member board model, known as the governance board model and the commission board model. The main differences are:

- **The governance board model** (such as Rwanda's, as described in box 5.1) sees responsibility for making key decisions as lying primarily with the CEO and senior officials of the regulatory agency, with the board's main function being to determine operational policy and provide strategic direction and oversight. This includes addressing governance standards and risk management.

- By contrast, **the commission model** (such as Georgia's, as described in box 5.1) has the members of the governing board (or commission) taking most substantive regulatory decisions, with the agency being responsible primarily for implementation and for day-to-day management of the regulatory system.

Choosing between these two models is not simple. Indeed, most regulatory boards exhibit some elements of both models. For example, while a regulatory commission will typically seek to make the most important decisions internally (often using sub-committees to increase effective decision-making), it will often need to delegate less fundamental decisions, or those that are time-critical, to the CEO or management committees. Conversely, a governance board may take on decision-making responsibility in respect of key strategic choices.

In the post-fragile context, the commission model, often but not always, has several important advantages over the governance board model, in particular with regards to accountability. The commission model's direct, collegiate accountability for major decisions is likely to instill greater confidence that capture will be avoided and that individual decisions may be subject to undue influence. By contrast, decision-making by the CEO under the regulatory board model, while subject to board oversight, may neither provide the same degree of institutional robustness nor prevent undue influence being exercised.

Second, given the commission model allows members more decision-making authority, it may attract candidates with the necessary expertise and experience more easily. This may be a particularly important consideration in low-capacity environments.

Conversely, the commission model is not without risks either. If there are only a small number of commissioners (as in Georgia), there may be a greater risk of undue influence being exercised as there are only the three commissioners to influence. This suggests the benefit of appointing a larger commission (for example, Kosovo's Law on the Energy Regulator provides that the Board of the Energy Regulatory Office [ERO] should have five members),[1] although capacity constraints may make this difficult to achieve.

Second, the method of appointment of board members, or commissioners, and their broader terms of engagement, are of key relevance. For example, where commissioners are nominated and appointed by the President or Prime Minister without any other checks or controls, they may be as susceptible to undue influence as a CEO. Recognizing this issue, some legislation provides for board members to be appointed by parliament, as in the case of Kosovo's ERO, while others specify that appointments be made by a minister or president but confirmed by parliament.

BOX 5.1

Differing governing structure models: Georgia and Rwanda

The 1997 Georgian Electricity Law established an independent National Electricity Regulatory Commission consisting of three commissioners appointed by the President for 6-year terms, with authority to regulate the sector. The commission members were to make all regulatory decisions, with staff being responsible for implementation. This exemplifies the **commission model**.

In contrast, the 2001 Rwandan law establishing an Agency for the Regulation of Certain Utilities put in place a seven-member Regulatory Board that was primarily responsible for oversight, strategic guidance and operational policy, with regulatory decision-making functions largely delegated to the Managing Director (MD) and senior staff. This is an example of the **governance board model**. (Note, however, that the President, not the Regulatory Board had the power to appoint the MD, reducing the Board's authority in relation to the President and placing the MD in a difficult position if the views of the President and the Regulatory Board differed.)

TABLE 5.1 **Regulatory commission versus governance board model—key characteristics**

	COMMISSION MODEL	GOVERNANCE BOARD MODEL
Accountability for Regulatory Decisions	Commission collectively accountable to minister and/or parliament	Indirect accountability, with CEO accountable to board in the first instance, then to the minister/parliament
Ability to Attract Quality Staff	Greater possibility of recruiting commissioners due to more substantial roles/responsibilities	Potentially more difficult to attract board members due to limited roles
Key Risks	Small commission size or poor appointment provisions may compromise independence	Lesser access to a wide range of high-level expertise to underpin quality decision-making

The model initially adopted in Georgia for its National Energy and Water Supply Regulatory Commission (GNEWSRC) combined appointment of commissioners by the president with a provision in the law that the state would assist commissioners to gain further employment once their terms were complete. This latter provision made commissioners susceptible to undue government influence for fear of losing the assistance of the state on expiry of their terms. Recognition of these issues led to subsequent changes that severely curtailed the Georgian President's power to nominate and appoint commissioners and increased the number of commissioners to five. Key characteristics of commission versus governance board models are summarized in table 5.1.

ALLOCATION OF DECISION-MAKING POWERS

Decision-making powers must be allocated carefully between the responsible political authority, the regulator's governing body and the CEO. The responsible political authority is typically an individual minister but may also be the cabinet or parliament. In allocating powers, the following should be considered:

- broad policy frameworks;
- key decisions under the enabling legislation;
- criteria for deciding more routine regulatory matters; and
- the implementation of higher-level decisions.

The distribution of powers between the political authority and the regulator should be clearly and unambiguously specified in legislation and the powers provided to the regulator should be consistent with the functions and responsibilities given to the agency—which should also be identified clearly in law, as discussed in chapter 3.

Specifying powers in legislation may be supplemented by formal correspondence between the two parties that explores the distribution of power in more detail and contributes to the development of a clear shared understanding of respective roles. One option is to develop a formal "framework agreement" between the minister and the agency to clarify key issues such as the corporate identity of the regulator and the extent to which it is bound by general government policies. Importantly, such materials should be made publicly available in the interests of transparency and accountability.

Where the regulator has a multi-member governing body (i.e., a governance board or a commission), the CEO should be accountable solely to this body, not to the supervising ministry. Hence, the CEO should be appointed by (or on the recommendation of) the governing body, helping to maintain both the accountability of the CEO and the independence of the regulator.

MEMBERSHIP OF THE GOVERNING BODY

The issue of accountability is also important in determining the membership of the governing body. It should be clearly established that members are appointed to serve the general interest. This requires independent, impartial decision-making, which in turn requires that members of the governing body are insulated from inappropriate pressure from ministers, industry, and other stakeholders.

This principle has important implications for the appointment process. Using appointment mechanisms in which members are nominated by specific stakeholders is obviously problematic –appointees risk seeing themselves as representing the interests of the stakeholders that nominated them, rather than that of the broader community.

This risk can be reduced if the legislation governing appointments clearly specifies that any appointees nominated by stakeholder groups are to serve as members of a collegiate governing body and not as representatives of the stakeholders who nominated them. However, nominations by stakeholders will still entail risks, to the extent that nominees feel themselves to be indebted to the nominating body. This may be important if the renewal of their terms of office depend on the stakeholder group.

But governments may favor the nomination of board or commission members by stakeholder groups to ensure that:

1. The views of these groups are adequately represented in decision-making.
2. Their specific expertise and knowledge is available to the regulator.

Both of these are potentially important considerations, but they can be addressed in different ways. One preferred approach is to establish a formal advisory group to provide specialist inputs to the governing body. In fragile contexts, the presence of such a group, while not a long-term solution, will also help address capacity constraints by bringing in external experts.

This approach is preferable because:

- It helps ensure transparency and accountability regarding the advice provided to the regulator by stakeholders.
- It creates a clear separation between technical advice (and representation of sectoral interests), on the one hand, and decision-making by the regulator, on the other.
- It avoids any uncertainty on the part of governing body members about the nature of their role.

For similar reasons, the appointment of ministerial representatives to the governing body should be avoided. Where a regulator is intended to act independently (as these principles indicate), the key concern is maintaining that independence and avoiding role conflict. Such conflicts can arise where the short-term political priorities of government—or even of the minister responsible—differ from the long-term orientations for the sector. In such a situation the ministerial representatives may tend to favor short-term solutions.

This principle also indicates that senior staff of the regulator should not generally be members of the governing body. That is because they are usually civil servants and thus accountable to the minister. At the very least, wherever senior staff of the regulator are members of the governing body, consideration should be given to according them non-voting status.

It is also important that the appointment of board members be predictable, in the sense that the criteria and processes for recruitment, selection and appointment be:

- explicit
- public
- fully and properly observed by those making the decisions.

This will help ensure that their decisions as to who will be appointed as board members comes as no surprise to interested parties and the public. There is always a degree of subjectivity involved in making such decisions, but a properly constituted process can reduce it to a minimum and produce more acceptable decisions.

RECRUITMENT AND REAPPOINTMENT

As indicated on page 31 a multi-member governing body can help ensure appointment of members with a range of skills and experience, thus supporting robust, high-quality decision-making. In weighing the appropriate size of the governing body, the following considerations should be taken into account and balanced against each other as necessary:

- **Skills Needed**. The governing body should be large enough to enable a sufficient breadth of skills and experience to be represented on it.
- **Availability of qualified staff on the market**. Capacity constraints should be recognized: the governing body should not be so large as to raise practical problems in filling the required positions.
- **Decision expediency**. The governing body should be large enough to ensure that a quorum of members to take significant decisions can be maintained, even if some members are absent from time to time. In Georgia, for example, only three commissioners were initially appointed to the Georgian National Energy and Water Supply Regulatory Commission. But it became extremely difficult for proceedings to be expedited if only two members attended a meeting and there was a disagreement between them. At the same time the body should not be so larger as to be unwieldy.

TERM OF APPOINTMENTS AND TERM LIMITS

Appointments should be structured to ensure both continuity and renewal of the governing body. This implies that appointments should be for fixed terms, and "staggered" so that the governing body board typically includes a mix of recent appointees and members with longer experience. One way of achieving this is to replace any members who resign with appointees who serve a full term, rather than simply filling the departing member's remaining term.

Appointees should have security of tenure, as this is important in safeguarding their independence. Consequently, it should only be possible to dismiss members in limited and very specific cases such as unresolved conflicts of interest, significant criminal behavior, failure to carry out their functions, and corruption. Termination should ideally only be based on findings from an independent investigative body. However, the requirement for a minister or the cabinet to explicitly state the grounds of termination, together with the right of appeal, also provides significant protection against political interference in the governing body.

Consistent with the need to ensure both continuity and renewal, there should be a clear limit on the number of terms members of the governing body can serve. However, the importance of continuity—that is, of the regulatory agency at all times having a quorum on its decision-making body—makes it desirable that board members remain in their positions until replacements are appointed. Such a provision can guard against decision-making bodies being blocked due to political disputes over new appointments (as happened in Kosovo).

Regulated entities must have confidence in the competence and impartiality of the regulator's governing body. To help ensure this, the criteria for appointing members of the governing body and the policy and processes to be followed in selecting and appointing members should be published and readily available, as well as being consistent with any wider rules or policies on appointments to public bodies. The appointment policy should address all of the following issues:

- Who is responsible for managing the appointment process;
- What are the key elements of the appointment process;
- Who makes the appointments;
- How is the Chair nominated and appointed;
- What is the role of the Minister, the Parliament and the Cabinet (if any); and
- How are conflicts of interest to be addressed.

Governing body appointment policies should include all relevant details.

SECTOR-SPECIFIC VERSUS MULTISECTORAL REGULATORS

All governments reforming the regulation of infrastructure (and, as part of this process, establishing independent regulators) must decide whether to set up separate regulators for each sector or whether to establish one or more multisectoral regulators instead.

Each of these options has trade-offs and the research literature yields no clear, generally applicable conclusion as to which model is preferable. Table 5.2 outlines some of the benefits of each.

As noted in chapter 4, some empirical research shows that there is a clear tendency to progressively broaden the remit of established regulators, suggesting that practical experience leads governments to favor leveraging the skills and reputations of established regulators by giving them responsibility for new sectors (Albon and Decker 2015; Jordana and Levi-Faur 2010). Box 5.2 summarizes

TABLE 5.2 **Benefits of multisector versus single-sector regulators**

BENEFITS	MULTISECTOR REGULATOR	SINGLE-SECTOR REGULATOR
Resource efficiency	• Potential to exploit economies of scale by establishing a small number of larger regulatory institutions	• May help ensure appropriate allocation of resources between sectors, avoiding that a multisectoral regulator will focus too closely on one sector while neglecting others
Regulatory expertise	• Better use of existing regulatory expertise— experienced regulators can apply skills to newly reformed sectors	• Can foster greater build-up of sector expertise over time
Approach	• Consistency across related sectors reducing likelihood of regulatory distortions • More strategic, able to take account of circumstances and dynamics in several sectors	• Legislation likely more appropriately tailored to the requirements and circumstances of individual sectors
Accountability	• Less potential for regulatory capture because likely to achieve critical mass more quickly, enabling a more robust, independent culture, and because it does not interact exclusively with one "client" sector	• Higher level of accountability on the regulator since it is responsible for the performance of one sector only

how India arrived at the decision to favor a multisector regulator approach. In practice, multisectoral regulators are often the long-term result of this dynamic, rather than a deliberate choice.

Choosing the regulatory model in post-fragile contexts

Several factors appear to favor the adoption of multisectoral regulators in post-fragile societies. A key consideration relates to the often pressing limits on available resources and expertise. Independent regulators in post-fragile countries are often extremely few and face uncertain budgetary environments. For example, Madagascar's ERO has around 25 staff in total, including both professional and support employees. Moreover, while it notionally receives direct payments from regulated entities totaling 1.2 percent of turnover to fund its activities, the ongoing financial difficulties of the incumbent electricity provider mean that much of this notional revenue is not received in practice.

In these circumstances, a multisectoral regulator is significantly more likely to reach a critical size enabling it to operate effectively and to benefit from economies of scale. The ability to leverage the skills of experienced regulators by applying them to newly reformed sectors is also likely to be important in the post-fragile context and, in particular, in relatively small countries. This latter point was highlighted in a review of the first decade of operation of Jamaica's multisectoral infrastructure regulator:

> The operation of the multisector model is not without its drawbacks but the experiences of the OUR[2] over the last decade or so, lend credence to the claim that it offers effective pragmatic solutions for small countries with limited financial resources, small technical skill pool and the risk of political intervention. Employing this model, Jamaica has been able to oversee full liberalization of its telecommunication sector, privatization of its electricity sector with some scope for fostering competition on the generation side and undertake greater scrutiny of its still state dominated water sector. At the same time, time it is demonstrable that the model delivers in terms of rationalizing costs and sharing limited resources. (Hewitt 2009)

Moreover, if the regulator relies on a wider range of revenue sources, uncertainty as to budgetary position may be minimized. In addition, concerns about regulatory capture is necessarily heightened in environments in which

BOX 5.2

View of the Indian Government

The Government of India reviewed international approaches to the regulation of infrastructure industries and assessed them in the light of India's context and objectives, with the Committee for Infrastructure publishing the resulting guidance document, *Approaches to the Regulation of Infrastructure*, in September 2008 (Government of India 2008). The paper concluded that a general preference in favor of multisectoral regulators should be adopted, stating:

Drawing from international experience from several countries, India should consider opting for multisectoral regulators such as for (a) communications; (b) electricity, fuels and gas, and (c) transport. This would eliminate proliferation of regulatory commissions, help build capacity and expertise, promote consistency of approach and save on costs. The central government would take a decision on a case-by-case basis about the institutional location of the multisectoral regulator. In the case of States, a single regulatory commission for all infrastructure sectors may be more productive and cost-effective as compared to sectoral regulators for each sector.

States should be encouraged to consider this approach and the scope of their existing electricity regulators could be extended to other sectors.

The document also highlighted the increasing importance of regulators being subject to consistent, good governance arrangements and nominated in full independence and autonomy. Directions to regulators, their functions, accountability, transparency, competition and appeals mechanisms are key mattes to be addressed by the governance framework:

Given the growing importance of regulation in several critical sectors of the economy, the governance relating to regulatory institutions has assumed an important role. It is, therefore, necessary to specify an agreed philosophy and overarching principles that would govern regulatory commissions across sectors. Consistent with an overarching regulatory framework for the orderly development of infrastructure services, the regulators could continue to function under sector-specific statutes that are administered by the respective Ministries.

Source: Government of India 2008.

institutions, including government bodies, are relatively weak and concerns about corruption widespread. Thus, the tendency for the multisectoral model to provide greater resistance to regulatory capture, noted above, is likely to be a particularly important factor.

All this suggest that the merits of adopting a multisectoral model should be weighed carefully in post-fragile contexts and, if a sector-specific model is preferred, that care should be taken to design governance and other supporting arrangements that minimize the issues identified above.

DECISION-MAKING BODIES IN POST-FRAGILE CONTEXTS

A major concern in post-fragile contexts is the tendency for high-level political appointments to be made in regulatory bodies. This undermines independence and is likely to yield appointees with lesser professional skills in some circumstances, thus compromising decision-making at the technical level.

To safeguard against this risk, key elements of the appointment process should be made explicit and public, so that wide scrutiny of these elements can exert pressure toward the maintenance of its integrity:

- **Relevant qualifications and other requirements should be established**. However, these should avoid undue prescriptiveness, which can exclude high-quality candidates and give rise to legal challenges. It is not, for example, necessary that all board members of a regulatory agency responsible for electricity have substantial qualifications or experience in working in the electricity sector (although some should), so long as they have other qualifications and substantial business experience.

- **Broader recruitment policies and processes should be documented explicitly**. This should include key details such as who is responsible for managing the process, who makes appointments (or who recommends candidates and who has final decision-making authority), who nominates or appoints the Chair and how conflicts of interest are to be addressed. An appointment process which involves appointments formally made by the executive branch but requiring ratification or approval by the legislature can improve the accountability of the process.

These policies and processes should, as far as possible, be consistent with generally applicable, public- sector appointment requirements. However, where broader public-sector reforms have not been undertaken, higher standards may need to be developed and adopted in key regulatory bodies.

A further issue related to the tendency for political appointments to be of particular concern in post-fragile countries is ensuring continuity in the operations of the governing body. Where rival groups seek to have their own candidates appointed to key positions, the outcome can often be a failure to make such appointments. This can be of particular concern where the commission model has been adopted, since the regulator may be unable to take key decisions for extended periods due to the lack of a quorum. This issue, and potential means of addressing it, are discussed further on page 34. Box 5.3 provides a set of questions that can guide a desk review of a regulator's decision-making body.

BOX 5.3

Questions for guiding a desk review of a regulator's decision-making body

With regards to staffing of the governing board:

1. How many sectors are covered by the regulator?
2. What skill sets are needed to make regulatory decisions? Are these skills detailed in the regulatory agency's founding legislation?
3. Are the appropriate skills available on the local market?
4. Is there sufficient budget to pay the salaries needed to attract well-qualified staff

With regards to decision-making continuity:

1. Does the regulator's founding legislation describe how the governing board will be appointed? Does such a process ensure continuity in decision-making ability—that is, a quorum to take decisions?
2. Are there clearly defined term limits for board members?

NOTES

1. See Article 5. https://mzhe-ks.net/repository/docs/law_no._05_l-084_on_the_energy _regulator_(1)eng.pdf.
2. Office of Utilities Regulation.

REFERENCES

Albon, R., and C. Decker. 2015. "International Insights for the Better Economic Regulation of Infrastructure." Australian Competition and Consumer Commission (ACCC)/Australian Energy Regulator (AER) Working Paper Series, Working Paper 10. https://www.accc.gov .au/system/files/International%20Insights%20for%20the%20Better%20Economic%20 Regulation%20of%20Infrastructure.pdf.

Government of India. 2008. *Approach to the Regulation of Infrastructure*. New Delhi: Secretariat for the Committee on Infrastructure, Planning Commission, Government of India. http:// planningcommission.gov.in/sectors/ppp_report/reports_guidelines/Approach%20to%20 Regulation%20of%20Infrastructure.pdf.

Hewitt, A. E. 2009. "Country Report: Jamaica." Paper presented to the UNCTAD (United Nations Conference on Trade and Development) Multi-Year Expert Meeting on Services, Development and Trade: The Regulatory and Institutional Dimension, Geneva, 17–19 March 2009. http:// unctad.org/sections/wcmu/docs/c1mem3p33_en.pdf.

Jordana, J., and D. Levi-Faur. 2010. "Exploring Trends and Variations in Agency Scope." *Competition and Regulation in Network Industries* 11 (4): 342–60.

6

Funding Regulatory Agencies

ABSTRACT

The two key considerations regarding the funding of regulators are adequacy and incentives. The regulator must have access to sufficient resources to allow it to carry out its assigned functions effectively, while funding must be supplied in ways that do not risk distorting the regulator's decisions.

KEY TAKEAWAYS

General takeaways

- Giving regulators access to appropriate levels and sources of funding supports good regulatory decisions by strengthening regulators' independence
- Ways to ensure proper funding for regulators include:
  1. imposing direct regulatory fees on industry participants (the economically efficient option);
  2. allocating funds to the regulator as part of the budget process;
  3. a combination of the two.
- A regulator's funding levels should be commensurate with its responsibilities and be subject to oversight.
- The risks of a regulator receiving too little or too much funding should be managed through effective legislation and transparent processes.

Takeaways specific to post-fragile contexts

- In a resource-constrained post-fragile environment, ensuring funding for a regulator is challenging as there will always be other pressing areas in need of financing. Using a multisector regulator can help by promoting economies of scale.
- Allocating funds as part of the budget process is typically adopted in the initial phases of setting up a regulator and would make sense in a post-fragile context.

But such an approach should be phased out over time, given that arrangements of this kind are more susceptible to political interference.

- To counter pressure to divert funds earmarked for the regulator to other government purposes:
  - Funding arrangements can be detailed in legislation.
  - Reserve accounts can be set up to absorb unexpected expenses.
  - Legislative rules can be set, for example, if regulatory expenses fall below level x, then reduce levies charged on industry participants.
  - Be transparent about funding uses.

INTRODUCTION

The infrastructure sector requires large capital investments, making an impartial, competent regulator that produces predictable and appropriate regulatory decisions a key element for investors. This, in turn, requires that regulators have sufficient operating independence to ensure their decisions are not affected by political considerations, as discussed in chapter 4. It is therefore extremely important that the regulatory agency has sufficient funds to provide for a well-administered regulatory system. It is also essential that regulators have adequate access to, and control over, these funds, so that control of their supply cannot be used by other parts of government to influence regulatory decisions, as has happened, for example, in both Madagascar and Kosovo.

Access to appropriate levels and sources of funding supports good regulatory decisions by underpinning the independence of the regulator and thus supporting its ability to make impartial and high-quality decisions. In addition, it is important that the agency's funding arrangements—that is, the sources, management and uses of its funds—be fully transparent. This will enhance confidence that the regulator is fair, efficient and effective. Where, for example, an agency's budgeted funds are held in an account controlled by a ministry of finance, especially where it is not subject to detailed and effective parliamentary scrutiny, there is the potential for the agency to be "starved" of funds and unable to discharge its duties in an appropriate and efficient fashion.

FUNDING METHODS

The fundamental choice in the funding of infrastructure regulators is between funding via:

- the imposition of direct regulatory fees on industry participants;
- the budget process;
- some combination of the two.

There may also sometimes be a case for charging additional fees for specific services. The merits of each of these sources are discussed below.

Imposing regulatory costs on the regulated enterprises

The most common means of funding industry regulation is to impose fees on the regulated industry. This "internalizes" regulatory costs within the regulated sector, effectively ensuring that the producers' and consumers' decisions reflect the full cost of producing industry outputs—including the cost of regulation. Such an approach is *economically efficient* because of this internalization of regulatory costs to the industry. It is also equitable, because the industry and its consumers pay the costs of its regulation, rather than this being subsidized by taxpayers through the budget process.

These characteristics imply that there should be a presumption in favor of funding via industry fees and it is our preferred option. However, this model effectively assumes that there is:

- a tradition or culture of full payment for the provision of electricity or other forms of energy by consumers;
- a continuing capacity to pay; and
- that the enterprises have efficient financial systems, ensuring high levels of payment.

Where these conditions are met, industry fees constitute a reliable and relatively easy to administer means of funding. It can also easily be made transparent, assuming that the regulated entities agree (which should always be the case), or that the government requires them to do so. It is also consistent with the aim of regulatory independence as it frees, at least in theory, the regulator from dependence on the government as a source of funds.

However, some states in situations of fragility do not have a culture of payment for infrastructure services, with state agencies, for example, frequently failing to pay electricity charges (e.g., several of the ex-Soviet states in the early years after independence, such as Georgia [World Bank 2008]). Similarly, as is often the case in fragile states, where the economy is in a state of rapid decline, low-income consumers lack the capacity to pay commercial rates without state subsidies. Also, state-owned utility enterprises, often dominant in, for example, the electricity sector, frequently lack efficient payment and collection systems. The result is increasing indebtedness, making them heavily dependent upon state subsidies and reducing their independence from government. In such situations, imposing the cost of regulation on the regulated enterprises, at least in the short term, may simply increase the size of the government subsidies via the budget—as happened in the electricity sector in Madagascar, limiting the government's ability to fund other projects.

Even in these challenging circumstances, funding via regulatory fees sends a signal to the market that the costs of regulation form part of the cost-base of the industry and that government, ideally, will increasingly use regulatory fees as the major source of funding, as the financial performance of regulated entities improves.

Where regulatory fees are adopted to fund regulatory costs, they should be applied consistently to all industry participants, whether publicly or privately owned. While various factors can be significant, the cost of regulating an entity is likely to be broadly proportionate to the size of its operations. Thus, fees are typically set on a volumetric basis (e.g., kWhs for electricity). This process is in theory relatively simple, although the actual collection of revenues can be a serious issue, as noted above. In addition, in post-fragile countries where the rule of law is exercised in only a limited fashion, it can be difficult to enforce payment from large, often government-owned, enterprises. In Zambia, for example, ZESCO, the state-owned, vertically integrated generation and transmission enterprise, refused for several years to pay its assessment to the Energy Regulation Board (ERB, established in 1995), for a variety of financial and political reasons (Brown 2008, 15).

The costs of regulation can also be applied on the basis of "cost causation," where regulatory costs are imposed on those who bring them about, sending very clear price signals to regulated entities. However, the major problems here are that:

- the transaction and accounting costs are high relative to alternative models, with each enterprise needing to possess sophisticated financial systems and highly qualified staff to operate them, a situation not usually found in fragile states; and
- each enterprise has to be separately billed, in full detail. Moreover, it is likely to result in disputes about the costs they are being asked to pay, given that they are sent detailed invoices.

All this means that this approach is typically restricted to specific, high-cost regulatory activities that are usually undertaken only infrequently—such as assessing applications for the grant or renewal of licenses. Thus, in practice, these "cost-based fees" are usually combined with a volume-based levy, which covers a wider range of regulatory costs that cannot easily be measured for individual regulated entities.

In a post-fragile context, where sophisticated accounting systems and highly qualified staff are in short supply, funding on the basis of cost causation is not likely to be successful and volumetric approaches generally provide a more feasible option.

Funding by an appropriation from general tax revenues in the budget process

The second most common way of funding the cost of regulation is by an appropriation from general tax revenues in the normal budget process. This approach is very likely to be adopted in an initial, regulatory reform period, when there is likely to be limited opportunity to levy fees on regulated entities. However, this course of funding raises a number of issues in terms of the incentives to the regulator and its ability to carry out its functions credibly and impartially:

- It enables political interference, as governments may seek to change or restrict the funding according to the regulator's behavior, as noted above.
- Even where there is no political interference in the budget process *per se*, broader fiscal concerns mean that budget funding can result in less reliable revenue flows for the agency. Recently created regulators may be particularly vulnerable to government cost-cutting due to the lack of well-established networks and lobbying avenues. Diminished revenue restricts them in operating effectively and fully discharge their statutory duties.
- While a government and parliament can agree to an appropriation for an agency, there is usually a set of rules that govern when and how the agency can actually receive and use the funds.

One means of addressing many of the above concerns is to establish multi-year funding arrangements—for example, legislating that the agency's budget is established for a three-year period—thus protecting agencies from budget cuts motivated by, for example, short-term political reactions to unpopular decisions such as raising tariffs (Kelley and Tenenbaum 2004).

Funding by fee for service

The third and least-common general method is to charge specific fees for the services provided. This is invariably a supplementary funding source, used to ensure cost recovery for individual, regulated entities as regards particularly resource-intensive regulatory actions. It does send accurate price signals to the market but, again, has high transaction costs and can lead to less revenue stability and reliability, as revenue will fluctuate in line with demand for the services provided. However, fees can be a useful mechanism for providing additional funds for agencies when required for specific purposes, as in Rwanda (see box 6.1).

FUNDING OVERSIGHT

As a public body, a regulatory agency has an obligation to be efficient, effective and accountable in using the funds entrusted to it, whatever the means and sources of funding. In turn, the government and, often, parliament, have the right to review the funding of the agency.

Auditing considerations

The ordinary fiscal controls, auditing policies and practices, and budgetary controls of the government should apply to a regulatory agency. However, where a government lacks an effective auditing capacity, as demonstrated in box 6.2, it can be better for the boards of regulatory agencies to appoint their own auditors from the private sector, subject to approval by the Government or parliament, or both.

BOX 6.1

Sources of finance for the Rwanda Utilities Regulatory Agency

It is common for regulatory agencies to be authorized to use several means of financing. Article 35 of Rwandan Law No. 39/2001 OF 13/09/2001 establishing an Agency for the Regulation of Certain Public Utilities, specifies that the new Rwanda Utilities Regulatory Agency can fund its expenses from a number of sources, making it self-financing, but not profit-making, although the bulk of its revenue comes from annual fees levied on each utility it regulates (item 5).

The actual mix of means selected is left to RURA's discretion, from the following sources:

1. fees levied for the application for, and grant of, licenses, approvals, permits, contracts, concessions and allocations to each utility operator;

2. grants, donations and legacies;
3. fees for services rendered to each utility by the regulatory agency;
4. loans;
5. annual fees based on a percentage of turnover from the activities of each public utility: that percentage is set by a decree of the minister determined by the President of the Republic; and
6. fines imposed by the Regulatory Board.

In practice, the funds received from annual fees increased progressively over time, to become the dominant source of funding. Fees levied on licenses, approvals, permits, contracts, concessions and allocation also increased.

BOX 6.2

Limited government audit capacity in Madagascar

In Madagascar, for example, the Court of Auditors, which is the supreme audit institution, suffers from a shortage of magistrates, auditors and financial resources. Although the situation is improving, the consideration of annual Appropriations Bills and external audit reports is not systematic and falls far behind schedule. The monitoring arrangements regarding its audit recommendations are not formalized and external audit covers only a limited portion of the Court's field of control. It audits only half of total expenditure. As accounts and the draft Appropriations Bill Report are frequently submitted late for judgment, the Court has several times exceeded statutory timeframes in fulfilling its obligations of verifying financial statements. As of June 2014, for example, draft Appropriations Bills for fiscal years (FY) 2008, 2009, 2010, 2011, 2012 had not been passed by the National Assembly.

Source: African Development Bank Group 2014.

In a situation like Madagascar's, the appointment of a reputable auditor from the private sector would help ensure audits are completed in a timely and effective manner. It may also help limit any untoward pressure by a government auditing body too sympathetic to government wishes, thus providing some protection against corruption.

Determining funding levels

In general, the overall spending authority of an agency should be subject to government approval. This is especially the case if all, or the bulk of its funds are provided on a cost-recovery basis, with the consequent danger that the agency could overestimate its needs, imposing an unreasonable burden on the enterprises charged and, eventually, the consumer.

Hence, there needs to be arm's length oversight of the process to reduce the risk of unreasonable regulatory fees being charged, within the context of the policy objectives and fees guidance set by government, ideally in the statute establishing the agency. In Portugal, for example, initially the budget of the energy regulatory agency, ERSE, was prepared by the agency's Board of Directors then submitted to a Consultative Council, an internal body of the agency composed of representatives from consumers, electricity enterprises and three ministries. The Council was empowered to reject the budget, although it never did so.

There is *no* standard formula for determining an adequate level of funding for a regulatory agency. Adequate funding will depend upon:

- Number of:
  - functions and associated tasks undertaken
  - enterprises regulated
  - customers the enterprises serve
  - licenses awarded.
- frequency of tariff proceedings;
- complexity of the sector the agency is responsible for;
- extent to which the details of its funding sources and processes have been specified in the law or decree establishing the agency.[1]

Some governments, such as Georgia's, have chosen to provide regulatory agencies with a high degree of discretion in relation to their levels of funding, while others exercise tighter controls, as can be seen in box 6.3. But whatever the means, level and sources of funding, the agency's annual report and accounts should make clear who pays for the regulator's operations, how much and why, including government subsidies. This helps to improve the agency's credibility.

Managing risks to regulator funds

In the case of budget-sourced funding, the risk of politically motivated budget reductions is ever-present. Often, determining the regulator's budget is either enshrined in law or is part of a "safeguard" process whereby the regulator presents a budget based on an assessment of its funding requirements for government approval. In the latter case, the fact that the regulator initiates the process by specifying the amount it believes necessary to perform its obligations provides some degree of safeguard against politically motivated attempts to constrain its activities. The risk of reduced funding can, however, be mitigated in two main ways: effective legislation and transparent processes.

Effective legislation can help insulate against risk of funding uncertainty

- by specifying that the agency be provided with a minimum level of funding, for example, a dollar amount per connected customer, or per kWh sold;
- by ensuring—in cases where government approves budgets proposed by the regulatory agency—that if the proposed budget has not been authorized by a specified date, then funding should be set at the level of the previous year's budget;
- by including statutes that the agency should have its own specific resources, over which only the regulator's governing body has control.

BOX 6.3

Controls on levels of funding by regulatory agencies: Georgia, Rwanda, and Latvia

Governments vary in the level of control they exercise over the funding levels set by regulatory agencies and the ways they calculate those levels. Examples from Georgia, Rwanda, and Latvia demonstrate this, and as shown in the Latvian case, how funding is allocated to the regulator can lead to conflicts of interest.

Georgia. The 1999 Law of Georgia on Electricity and Natural Gas, for example, gave the Georgian National Energy and Water Supply Regulatory Commission a high degree of discretion in setting its so-called "regulatory fee." Article 19 of the law indicates only that it should be based on "the [energy] load forecasts for the following year received from licensees, importers and suppliers," without giving further details.

Rwanda. Law No. 09/2013 establishing the Rwanda Utilities Regulatory Authority (RURA), in Article 36:3, goes a little further than Georgia, specifying that, in part, RURA's funding will come from an annual regulatory fee based on a percentage of the turnover (as opposed to load forecasts in Georgia) of each regulated service. But beyond saying that the fee should not exceed one percent of turnover the statute does not specify the actual level of the fee.

Latvia. The regulatory fee for the bulk of the funding for the operations of the Latvian Public Utilities Commission (PUC) is set by the cabinet. This raises some concern since state-owned enterprises in Latvia are important actors in the sectors overseen by the PUC. The *ceiling* of the regulatory fee is set in law, but the actual level is decided by the cabinet, which includes several ministries that are shareholders of the public utilities regulated by the PUC. This creates a potential conflict of interest and can serve to bring political pressure on the regulator.

Source: OECD 2016, 21.

Transparent processes can ensure enough pressure in the system to adequately fund the regulator

- Where the regulator's funding is not enshrined in law and a regulatory agency proposes a budget for government approval (usually via the Ministry of Finance or, in some cases, parliament), a more transparent process can help create external pressure on both government and regulator. Government will need to justify any reduction in funding vis-à-vis the proposed budget and the regulator will have to explain any proposed increases. Transparency can be achieved by making both budget proposals and the government responses public.

Dealing with unanticipated expenses

All regulatory agencies face the prospect of carrying out activities that were unanticipated in the budget, including complex and difficult license applications, special, "one-off," investigations, and major and unanticipated court actions. Sometimes funding these will be difficult or impossible within the standard budget allocation, yet they can be vital regulatory tasks as, for example, when the regulator's credibility requires it to start legal proceedings to enforce it decisions or to counter inappropriate conduct by regulated entities.

Three key options exist for funding such activities:

1. **Ad hoc requests to the portfolio minister.** Where the regulator applies to the minister responsible for additional funding for a specific purpose.
2. **Funding reserve**. Where the legislation governing the regulator authorizes the accumulation of a funding reserve, within stated limits, either via unspent levies, monetary sanctions, or some combination of the two, to cover unanticipated costs.
3. **Legislative power to raise loans**. Where legislation authorizes the regulator to raise loans from the non-government sector in identified circumstances, with loan expenses being covered by an increase in future fees levied on its sector of competence.

The first option, a funding request to the minister is the least-preferred option. In the case of major litigation, for example, if an independent regulator has to seek ministerial and government approval for funds, it runs the risk of unwanted political interference and of reducing its credibility. On the other hand, it faces the same risks if it chooses *not* to take or to defend a costly legal action, opening itself to accusations that it took the decision under political pressure.

The second option, a funding reserve, is only feasible where funds from unspent levies, monetary sanctions or a combination of the two are likely to be sufficient to cover large, unexpected costs such as major litigation. Where a government is not providing sufficient funds to cover a regulator's normal activities, then building up a sufficiently large reserve is unlikely.

Hence, the third option, raising loan funds is the preferred option, with the statute specifying how the agency can secure the necessary funds, authorizing it, for example, to take out loans from the non-government, financial sector.

The processes of setting fee levels, gaining funding approval and controlling and reviewing finances should be clear, understandable and accessible to all stakeholders and the general public, including by parliamentary scrutiny. Such transparency can reduce the risks to the regulator's political and administrative independence from both government and major interest-group lobbying (Kelley and Tenenbaum 2004). It can also improve the efficiency of regulatory operations by providing the information necessary to hold the regulator to account for its activities and expenditures and making any attempt to exercise undue influence more visible (Hüpkes, Quintyn, and Taylor 2006).

INCENTIVE ISSUES IN RELATION TO FUNDING

Imposing regulatory fees or levies can help make regulatory agencies accountable for their budget. If the government increases the fees charged to industry to fund its regulation, it should be able to demonstrate that such increases are justified and necessary and that the regulator is operating efficiently. If fees are significantly higher than in comparable industries or countries, this potentially provides a signal that this is not the case.

However, revenue from industry fees is typically collected by the Ministry of Finance, with the regulator being funded through a separate budget allocation. While this process of central collection of fees is a very widespread accountability mechanism within government, it has the potential to create perverse incentives in relation to the funding of regulators and to break the link between the size of the levies charged and the expenditures of the regulator. This both substantially reduces the accountability of the regulator for its use of resources and means that the regulator does not benefit from the secure and predictable funding that a regulatory fee is intended to provide. This issue is likely to be particularly acute in post-fragile environments, as discussed in the next section.

Another common issue in relation to the funding of regulators is their lack of access to, and control over, their budgets. Control over the spending of the allocated budget is a major aspect of the independence enjoyed by a regulator in practice. This requires that it have a separate account, into which its budget is paid and over which it has control, subject only to the specific limits on its financial powers set out in authorizing legislation.

FUNDING AND FRAGILE STATES

While funding is a constraint on all government actions, it is felt even more sharply in post-fragile states with very limited financial and human resources. Thus, the funding of a regulatory agency is a significant challenge in the post-fragile context. This issue is likely to be particularly acute in small countries unable to benefit from the economies of scale available in countries with larger populations, where the relatively fixed costs of regulation as spread over a larger base (Domah, Pollitt, and Stern 2002). As discussed in chapter 4, the use of a multisectoral regulatory model may help reduce funding pressure by using scarce resources to regulate several sectors.

A significant issue identified in some post-fragile contexts is that industry levies designed to constitute a stable funding base for a sectoral regulator can instead be diverted to general government revenue. This can occur if the relevant legislation does not explicitly link the revenue raised via industry levies to the budget allocated to the regulator. This can mean that substantial industry levies are imposed, which are paid directly into consolidated revenue, while the budget approved for the regulator is substantially smaller—and often inadequate to enable it to fulfill its tasks. Where governments face major problems in raising budget revenue—as is very commonly the case in post-fragile

Failure to hypothecate industry levies to fund the regulator's operations

In Kosovo, the Law on the Electricity Regulator authorizes an industry levy of up to 2 percent of turnover to provide funding for the Energy Regulatory Office (ERO). The actual levy is determined by the ERO board and is currently set a much lower rate of 0.56 percent. However, the budget provided to ERO has historically been substantially smaller than the revenue derived from the levy, with the remaining funds used for general government purposes. While ERO currently faces substantial budget pressures, it has nonetheless indicated a desire to reduce the levy rate from its current level, as it believes that it could be adequately funded if it received the full proceeds of a levy set at a lower rate. A similar dynamic has operated in the telecoms sector, where the industry regulator, ARKEP, has collected around €5 million annually in industry levies in recent years, but has had annual budgets averaging around €1 million over the same period.

In Madagascar, the 1998 Law on Electricity provides that the rate of the industry levy is determined jointly by the Ministers of Finance and Energy, rather than by the Energy Regulator (ORE), while the funds from the levy are also deposited into the consolidated fund. This means that, while the ORE budget is notionally subject only to the approval of its Council, in practice the ORE must ask the Ministry of Finance to provide funding to cover the approved budget. As in Kosovo, the practical reality in recent years is that the budget funding received by ORE has been only a small part of the revenue from industry fees.

contexts—there is a clear incentive for this approach. Box 6.4 provides some examples.

One means of limiting the size of this potential issue is to include a ceiling or ceilings on the size of the regulatory fees that can be imposed in the legislation establishing the regulator and setting out its functions. This is a commonly adopted approach, with the ceiling usually specified as a percentage of industry turnover. However, as shown in table 6.1, the specific percentage ceiling set in legislation varies widely. The ceilings identified in the table vary from 0.3 percent to 2.0 percent of turnover.

As noted above, the scope of the responsibilities and powers of the regulator is one determinant of the size of its budgetary requirement and is therefore a factor in explaining the difference in the fee ceilings. However, it is likely that governments' desire to use regulatory fees as a source of general revenue may be another. This appears be a significant factor in Madagascar, for example, where the fee ceiling is set at 2 percent, but there is no requirement for the revenue generated to be directed to its budget.

The use of regulatory fees to generate general revenue for the budget risks undermining the credibility of the regulatory system, particularly if the regulator is left too poorly resourced to provide high-quality regulatory services to regulated entities despite the payment of unusually large fees. Thus, it is important to ensure that adequate disciplines on the amount of fee revenue raised exist.

One means of counteracting the incentive for governments to divert fee revenue to the budget is for the legislation establishing the regulator to state clearly that funds received from any industry levy can only be used for the regulation of the industry. Such an approach can still be compatible with central approval of the regulator's budget. For example, any revenue which exceeds the budget

TABLE 6.1 **Legislated ceilings on regulatory fees**

COUNTRY	SECTOR/ACT	FEE CEILING	COMMENT
Rwanda	Law on the Electricity Regulator	1% of turnover	Actual fee set by Regulatory Board
Nepal	Telecoms Act 1997	None	Several fee sources established in law
Nepal	Nepal Electricity Regulatory Commission Act 2017	1% of turnover	No specified process for determining actual fee
Madagascar	Law on Institutional Reform of the Telecoms Sector [2005-023], Decree 2016-213	2% of turnover (licensed operators) 1.5% of turnover ("free plan" enterprises)	No requirement for fee revenue to be directed to regulator's budget
Madagascar	Electricity sector	None	Law 1998-032 authorises turnover-based fees. Decree 2001-803 authorises the fee to be set by joint order of Ministers for Finance and Electricity
Kosovo	Law on the Electricity Regulator	2% of turnover	Actual fee set by the regulatory board
Kosovo	Law on Electronic Communications 2012	0.5% of turnover	Actual fee established by the regulator via regulation
Georgia	Law on Electricity and Natural Gas 1999	0.3% of turnover	No specified process for regulator to determine actual fee

approved for the regulator could be required to go into a separate reserve fund, from which the regulator's board could draw, with Ministry of Finance approval, to meet unanticipated expenses (such as major legal actions). This approach provides a high degree of transparency on the use of the funds and creates incentives for industry levies to be limited to the amount required to fund regulatory costs.

An alternative approach is for the legislation governing the regulator to specify that if regulatory expenditure falls significantly below the level of revenues raised by industry levies, the levy amount must be reduced accordingly the following year. This approach has the additional benefit of directly ensuring that industry levies can only be used to defray the costs of regulating the industry. Both of these approaches have the benefit of eliminating the incentive for governments to starve the regulator of funds in order to increase the revenue it has available for other purposes.

A "lighter-handed" alternative is to provide for a high degree of transparency as to the uses made of the funds from the industry levy. For example, the regulator could be required to include information in its annual report on the revenue generated by the industry levy and its uses—including the proportion actually spent on industry regulation. This approach also provides a degree of incentive to limit industry levies to the amount needed to cover regulatory costs.

REVENUE FROM FINES AND PENALTIES

Regulators must have the ability to levy significant fines and other monetary penalties to ensure that their decisions are complied with and the conduct of market players conforms with legislative and other requirements. The revenue from such penalties can potentially be significant, raising the issue of whether the regulator should be able to retain this revenue as a partial funding source, or whether it should be required to remit the revenue to the Ministry of Finance.

Retention of the revenue from fines can potentially reduce the size of the fees that regulated companies must pay if the regulator is operating on a full cost recovery basis and has the advantage of helping ensure a larger proportion of the regulator's budget comes from companies whose non-compliance with the rules gives rise to significant regulatory activities and costs. However, allowing the regulator to retain fine revenues also has several disadvantages.

In particular, if the regulator is responsible for determining the size of the penalties levied, the ability to retain the revenue collected gives rise to a clear conflict of interest. In such circumstances, the existence of a credible appeals mechanism independent of the regulator becomes particularly important. In situations in which enforcement and the determination of penalties are responsibilities of the courts or administrative tribunals, it is usual practice that the resulting revenues are remitted to the central budget.

A second concern is that the amount of revenue derived from fines and other monetary penalties is likely to vary widely from year to year. Thus, reliance on this revenue as a significant source of funding for the regulator's budget is likely to give rise to significant uncertainty regarding the amount of funding available. This issue may potentially be addressed if fine revenues are hypothecated to the funding of a contingent liability—notably the need to fund legal actions.

A third concern is that retention of fine or penalty revenues can distort regulatory effort, both between and within regulators, reducing their focus on addressing the most important harms. The areas where imposing fines is easiest are likely to gain more resources, even if they are not those which are fundamental to ensuring that underlying regulatory objectives are being achieved. Areas where offenders have limited assets, or it is hard to establish an offence, may not receive sufficient regulatory effort. The incentive to maximize penalty revenue could also reduce the regulator's focus on encouraging compliance in favor of an excessive emphasis on enforcement.

Given these factors, it is generally preferable for the revenue from fines and other monetary penalties to be paid into the general budget, rather than used to fund the activities of the regulator. Where there is a desire to retain penalty revenue, the above incentive issues should be addressed. One model which does achieve this outcome has been adopted by the Payment Systems Regulator in the United Kingdom and is set out in box 6.5.

DIAGNOSING FUNDING ISSUES IN RELATION TO REGULATORY AGENCIES

In general, a review of the funding of regulatory agencies tends to be politically sensitive, involving key governmental and non-governmental actors, as well as media attention, even where the issue might seem to be minor and technical. This sensitivity, combined with the typical fragile context of serious resource limitations and political instability, makes

---

BOX 6.5

The United Kingdom's Payment Systems Regulator: Financial penalty scheme

The Payment Systems Regulator (PSR) is authorized to impose penalties for non-compliance. These must, in general, be remitted to the Treasury. However, the PSR is able to deduct amounts to recoup its enforcement costs before remitting the remainder of the penalty revenue. The governing legislation requires the retained revenue to be used for the benefit of those regulated under the scheme, but does not allow the entity sanctioned to benefit from it. Consequently, the revenue is used to reduce the fees that would otherwise be payable by compliant regulated entities in the following year. As the size of the PSR's budget is set independently of the penalty revenue it collects, the regulator has no direct organizational incentive to maximize penalty revenue.

Source: Payment Systems Regulator 2017.

BOX 6.6

Questions for guiding a desk review of regulator funding

1. What sources of information indicate that funding is an issue and how reliable are the sources?

2. What are the specific issues identified by the available sources of reliable information and do they represent a major issue or constraint for business and investment?

3. If it is a major issue or constraint, what are the government's priorities in relation to the funding of regulatory agencies compared to other issues faced by the infrastructure sectors?

4. How can the issue be resolved? This should involve consultation with key stakeholders, especially those who have been affected by the lack of clarity, but only after clearance has been gained at senior levels for such a consultation, given its sensitivity.

5. Develop a preliminary action plan for resolving the funding issue that is appropriate to the country's needs and context.

6. Support the action plan with strong arguments, such as those related to efficiency, effectiveness, communication, transparency and coordination.

7. If the action plan is endorsed, a communications strategy should be developed to ensure that all those inside and outside government likely to be affected by the reforms are informed of the changes in good time. This should include the media, as well as more institutional means of communication, such as speeches by officials and ministers, publication in the Government Gazette and annual reports.

it vital to identify and assess the need for a review of legislation, however small. It will also tend to involve senior staff from within the agency and, often, senior staff from within the supervising ministry, who should be informed of the potential issue as soon as possible. It also means that even greater attention should be paid to ensuring that a preliminary desk review be undertaken as thoroughly as possible. The typical questions to address in such a desk review are indicated in box 6.6.

Where desk review reveals that a more detailed and lengthy review is necessary, appendix D contains an example of the types of questions that could be addressed.

NOTE

1. A useful guide to the factors that should be taken into consideration in using a cost-recovery basis for funding agencies is OECD 1998.

REFERENCES

African Development Bank Group. 2014. *Madagascar*. Combined Report on the 2014–16 Interim Country Strategy Paper and the Country Portfolio Performance Review. Abidjan: African Development Bank. https://www.afdb.org/en/documents/document/madagascar -combined-report-on-the-2014-2016-interim-country-strategy-paper-i-csp -and-the-country-portfolio-performance-review-cppr-11-2014-50396/.

Brown, A. C. 2008. *The Funding of Independent Regulatory Agencies. A Special Report to the Public Utilities Commission of Anguilla*. Harvard Electricity Policy Group, John F. Kennedy School of Government, Harvard University, Cambridge. http://citeseerx.ist.psu.edu /viewdoc/download?doi=10.1.1.696.7010&rep=rep1&type=pdf.

Domah, P., M. G. Pollitt, and J. Stern. 2002. "Modelling the Costs of Energy Regulation: Evidence of Human Resource Constraints in Developing Countries." Working Paper WP 0229, Department of Applied Economics, University of Cambridge, Cambridge.

Hüpkes, E., M. Quintyn, and M. W. Taylor. 2006. *Accountability Arrangements for Financial Sector Regulators*. Economic Issues 39. Washington, DC: International Monetary Fund.

Kelley, E., and B. Tenenbaum. 2004. "Funding of Energy Regulatory Commissions." Energy and Mining Sector Board Working Notes 30525, World Bank, Washington, DC.

Payment Systems Regulator. 2017. *The Payment Systems Regulator's Financial Penalty Scheme.* https://www.psr.org.uk/sites/default/files/media/PDF/Financial-Penalty-Scheme_0.pdf.

OECD (Organisation for Economic Co-operation and Development). 1998. "User Charging for Government Services." Occasional Papers No. 22, OECD, Paris.

———. 2016. *Driving Performance at Latvia's Public Utilities Commission*. The Governance of Regulators. Paris: OECD Publishing. http://dx.doi.org/10.1787/9789264257962-en.

World Bank. 2008. *Georgia – Judicial Reform Project; Third Structural Adjustment Credit Project; Reform Support Credit Project*. Project Performance Assessment Report 46832, Washington, DC. http://documents.worldbank.org/curated/en/257411468032037102/Georgia-Judicial -Reform-Project-Third-Structural-Adjustment-Credit-Project-Reform-Support -Credit-Project.

7

Integrity

ABSTRACT

As with all public governance, regulatory agencies must demonstrate high standards of integrity. They must hold all personnel to high standards of conduct and avoid any suggestion that impropriety or illegal behavior can be tolerated. Regulatory integrity is essential to achieve decision-making which is objective, impartial, consistent, and avoids bias and improper influence. Safeguarding integrity is an ongoing challenge with the growing interconnectedness of government and the private sector, as well as public-private partnerships, increasingly large public expenditures, and the opportunities for corruption provided by the major procurement contracts and processes that are a feature of infrastructure sector.

KEY TAKEAWAYS

General takeaways

- A regulator that performs duties with integrity does so honestly and in the public interest.
- To protect integrity, a system of rules and a code of behavior are needed—for example, regulatory staff should abide by a code of conduct, which includes at the very least:
  - prohibition against: bribes; all forms of conflict of interest; any form of preferential treatment; and use of insider information for personal gain;
  - reasonable disclosure of personal financial interests;
  - clear specification of policy on external and post-separation employment.
- Regulators can develop their own code of conduct or abide by a government-wide code. When abiding by a government code, this should be clearly stated in regulatory policy.
- Establishing rules and codes of conduct need to exist alongside a "culture of integrity," where the manager and supervisors set the tone and employees have mechanisms to seek advice or report concerns.

- Integrity is affected by several other principles important for regulatory governance, including:
  - Mandate clarity: policy statement establishing a regulator should mention that it will perform its duties with integrity.
  - Independence can help reduce risks to a regulator's integrity—either at the institutional or organizational level.
  - Accountability and transparency are necessary to assess a regulator's integrity.
  - Funding: a system of checks and balances on funding can reduce the risk of "featherbedding" regulator budgets and of funds being misappropriated.

Takeaways specific to post-fragile contexts

- Establishing a culture of integrity may be more challenging in post-fragile environments, though given the often weak institutional situation there, it is important to try to develop one.
- In post-fragile contexts, government-wide integrity systems are likely underdeveloped. It is thus extremely important for the regulator to have its own, sufficiently robust code of conduct.

INTRODUCTION

Public officials should perform their duties with integrity—that is, discharge their duties honestly and in the public interest. One of the aims of regulatory governance is to help ensure that integrity is achieved and sustained systematically, with the governance mechanisms working together to both promote integrity and to protect the regulator from external actors seeking to have it favor private interests.

This chapter outlines the need for a system of rules, or code of conduct, to help govern the behavior of decision-makers in the regulatory agency, and to help prevent improper practices and maintain integrity. This is particularly important where corruption is deeply embedded and has become the norm. The chapter also briefly examines the relationship between integrity and the other principles for good regulatory governance, role clarity, requisite powers, independence, funding, decision-making and the governing body, predictability, engagement, accountability, transparency, and performance evaluation.

A FOCUS ON RULES—A CODE OF BEHAVIOR

Regulatory agencies must be seen to have or to be developing a culture of integrity, with all personnel held to high standards of conduct. They should be required to abide by an explicit, published set of ethical standards, or code (ideally, set out in law for all government employees, including those in regulatory agencies), with such standards binding and rigorously enforced. Where such a code does not exist, the board of the regulatory agency should require that one be developed.

The code should identify:

A competent and independent office or unit empowered to investigate and report on alleged breaches, for example, for cases of major corruption. This is generally the Auditor-General's office or the equivalent, if it has the capacity and expertise for such work. Alternatively, the board of the regulator should ensure that an independent unit is established within the agency and that its operations are fully transparent and its decisions made publicly available.

A competent mechanism for systematic disclosure of the financial interests of members of the regulator's governing body. The law establishing a regulatory agency should reference the standards code, where one exists, and the fact that members of the board or commission and the staff of the agency are subject to those standards and to investigation by the independent body, including a required declaration of interests (see box 7.1) by board members.

While the list of standards included in the code can vary (box 7.2 provides one example), it is important that the core minimum include:

- prohibition against the making and acceptance of bribes, gifts and gratuities of any kind;
- prohibition of all forms of conflict of interest;
- prohibition against any form of preferential treatment;
- reasonable disclosure of financial interests;
- prohibition of use of inside information for personal gain;
- a clear specification of policy on outside and post-separation employment;
- a clear specification of what constitutes a reasonable use of information and communications technology and other regulatory agency resources.

BOX 7.1

What is a declaration of interest?

A declaration of interest is an official statement by a board member that indicates his or her association with an outside person, organization or activity, in those cases where the board member might not be completely fair and independent when taking a decision affecting them.

BOX 7.2

The Mexican Ethics Code and rules of integrity

The Mexican Ethics Code is built on the constitutionally defined principles of legality, honesty, loyalty, impartiality, and efficiency, together with a set of additional values: Public interest, respect, respect for human rights, equality and non-discrimination, gender equity, culture and environment, integrity, cooperation, leadership, transparency, and accountability.

In turn, a set of integrity rules complement the ethics code by specifying desired and undesired behavior in 13 areas:

1. public behavior
2. public information
3. public contracting, licensing, permits, authorizations and concessions
4. governmental programs
5. public procedures and services
6. human resources
7. administration of public properties
8. evaluation processes
9. internal control
10. administrative procedures
11. permanent performance with integrity
12. cooperation with integrity
13. decent behavior

Source: OECD 2017.

IMPLEMENTING A CODE OF BEHAVIOR: BUILDING A CULTURE OF INTEGRITY

While an explicit set of ethical standards or rules is fundamental to ensuring integrity, it is not, by itself, sufficient. The standards must be internalized by individuals to create a "culture of integrity" in the regulatory agency, and the workplace culture must support and encourage ethical behavior. This should aim at inspiring integrity through raising awareness of, and commitment to, ethics, public-sector values, and the public interest. The combination of a standards-based system (often known as a compliance-based system) with a values-based system that emphasizes self-policing and motivation, is far more effective than simple reliance on ensuring compliance with the standards (Whitton 2001).

Where a civil-service wide code of behavior already exists, the regulator should develop and release a policy that stresses the agency's commitment to the code and use it as the basis for its own code. The policy should:

- state that unethical conduct and behavior which breaches the code will not be tolerated;
- set out the responsibilities of the agency head, senior executives, other managers and employees to create a culture that supports ethical conduct;
- provide a clear view of, and strategies to promote, appropriate standards of behavior for employees at all levels;
- ensure all employees have easy access to the agency's policies on ethical conduct and behavior and regularly remind employees of their responsibilities.

The policy should identify clear channels for employees to report unethical or corrupt conduct and managers should inform employees, as far as possible, of any action they have taken to deal with their reports of inappropriate behavior. It is useful to nominate ethics officers to provide points of contact for employees to raise ethical issues, and to provide a forum for discussion of such issues in the agency.

Training in what constitutes ethical decision-making and behavior for all employees should be provided, making sure they understand and apply the code and the values it contains. It should be reinforced on a regular basis with further training and be a compulsory part of the induction process for new employees.

Individual managers and supervisors should model their own actions on the code's values, as this helps send clear messages to staff about expected behavior. In addition, they should be able to provide advice on:

- ways for employees to report concerns, including formal and informal processes and external avenues;
- where to go for advice and/or support, for example, employee assistance or counseling services, agency contact officers;
- relevant internal and external review mechanisms; and
- how to manage real or potential conflicts of interest.

Managers should also report on, and address misconduct and other unacceptable behavior in a fair, timely and effective way, declaring any personal interests that may impede ethical decision-making.

INTEGRITY IN THE POST-FRAGILE CONTEXT

Ensuring high standards of integrity is likely to be challenging in many post-fragile situations. Corruption typically flourishes in an environment of weak institutions and limited enforcement of legislative standards. At the same time, addressing corruption, and changing perceptions of corruption, is a crucial element in changing views of the attractiveness of the regulatory environment. Companies based in OECD countries typically face explicit legal prohibitions on payment of bribes, commissions and other incentives in their operations in third countries, thus establishing major disincentives to investment in countries with doubtful standards of integrity.

Recent work by the OECD[1] highlights the multidimensional nature of addressing integrity issues, with action needed in areas including prevention, detection and prosecution. However, it also underlines that a strong governance environment is a crucial component of the integrity toolkit.

In a context in which civil-service-wide integrity systems are likely not well-developed, it is particularly important that codes of conduct specific to regulators are sufficiently robust to both clearly set out the required standards of behavior and underpin enforcement action by officials within the regulator and externally. The role of top management in modeling the expected behavior is also likely to be particularly important.

As noted above, an integrity system that combines compliance-based and values-based elements is likely to be more effective than reliance on one or other of these approaches. Several formerly fragile states have achieved substantial reductions in the degree of corruption and perceived corruption by pursuing this strategy for example, Rwanda, Botswana, Mauritius and Cabo Verde.

INTEGRITY AND THE OTHER PRINCIPLES FOR GOOD REGULATORY GOVERNANCE

Integrity issues are closely connected with several governance principles. Hence, in evaluating a system of regulatory governance and, in particular, when considering possible changes to that system, it is important always to consider the possible impact of the changes on integrity issues.

Integrity and role clarity

Integrity should be explicitly addressed by the policy or statute establishing the regulator (as for Rwanda as in box 7.3); specifically, the policy or statute should state:

- that the regulator shall perform its functions with integrity;
- how the integrity of board members is to be achieved and sustained;
- that the existing code of behavior for the public service also applies to the regulator.

Integrity and independence

Independence is a means of reducing the risks to individual and organizational integrity, because it limits the extent to which the regulator is subject to undue influence and conflicts of interest. Establishing a regulator with a degree of independence thus creates greater confidence and trust that regulatory decisions

BOX 7.3

Founding legislation for the Rwanda Utilities Regulatory Authority emphasizes integrity

The key regulator in the electricity sector in Rwanda is the Rwanda Utilities Regulatory Authority (RURA). The importance of ensuring its independence and integrity was recognized in several ways by the law (No. 39/2001) which established it. The first was the law itself, for, in establishing a separate and independent regulatory agency, the government was sending a clear message to markets that it valued integrity highly in regulatory decision-making and was establishing an independent regulator to achieve it. Secondly, Article 13 explicitly requires that regulatory boards must at all times act in an independent, open, transparent and objective fashion and not discriminate in any way. Third, Article 23 requires all ministers to respect the independence of an agency and it's Regulatory Board in all cases.

will be made with integrity. Integrity should therefore be a major concern when deciding on the governance arrangements for a regulator.

The founding statute should also specify what constitutes appropriate grounds for the removal of board members and commissioners and should describe the required process, together with their rights of appeal. This protects them from unreasonable and inappropriate action by the minister or government as well as maintaining trust in their integrity.

Integrity, accountability and transparency

Accountability refers to the obligation for the regulator to accept responsibility for a decision or action and to report, explain and be answerable for the resulting consequences. In the context of regulatory governance, transparency refers to the degree to which the major decisions and actions of a regulator, together with the grounds on which they were taken, are open to scrutiny. Transparency is a fundamental requirement for achieving effective accountability. In turn, accountability and transparency are necessary to enable the integrity of a regulator to be assessed, since such assessments must be based on scrutiny of the regulator's decisions and actions.

Integrity and funding

In general, the ordinary fiscal controls, auditing policies and practices, and budgetary controls of the government must apply to the regulator, since these are fundamental controls aimed, in large part, at ensuring regulatory integrity. However, higher standards are likely to be required in some areas, as a balance to the greater independence granted to the regulator. Hence, it is vital that the law clearly sets out the obligations and responsibilities of regulators and the standards they must comply with.

It is also important to have a system of internal checks and balances on the regulator's finances, with some kind of arm's-length oversight of the system to reduce the risk of both "featherbedding" its budget and misappropriation of funds. Ideally this should be described in the statute establishing the agency.

Integrity and stakeholder engagement

While stakeholder engagement can contribute substantially to regulatory quality, it also entails integrity risks: where engagement is not conducted openly, with access available to all interested parties, the regulator risks giving too much weight to the interests of particular, influential stakeholders. Development of new forms of relationship between the public sector and the business and non-profit sectors, involving closer collaboration than in the past, including public-private partnerships and self-regulation, increases this risk.

Hence, it is important that stakeholder engagement be guided by clear policies and guidelines aimed at safeguarding regulatory integrity. Key requirements are to:

- **develop and publish an explicit stakeholder engagement policy** in consultation with representatives of stakeholder groups to ensure that engagement is both transparent and open to all stakeholders;
- **identify all groups who have a stake in the outcome**, or that are likely to be affected in relation to each engagement project. Understand their responsibilities, core motivations and interactions;
- **organize the type and level of engagement that is appropriate for the project** in question, keeping the process flexible so as to cope with changing circumstances while aiming to provide high levels of access;
- **allocate sufficient financial and human resources to make the engagement effective**, and share the information needed for decision-making, ensuring good information flows;
- **support stakeholder confidence in the value of participating in engagement** by ensuring that feedback is provided on their inputs and these are considered in decision-making, including explanations of why proposals have not been adopted, where appropriate;
- **regularly assess the process and outcomes of stakeholder engagement projects** to find out what went well and what did not, so as to improve future engagement projects.

Integrity and performance evaluation

As integrity is a primary element of good governance, it should be assessed during performance evaluation. This can help:

- convince supervisory bodies, legislators, journalists, citizens and stakeholders that the agency is performing with the required degree of integrity;
- establish what works and does not in relation to maintaining integrity, so that relevant processes and activities can be improved over time;
- improve staff morale by celebrating successes in sustaining integrity.

The policy and procedures related to integrity should be examined regularly as part of the routine evaluation of agency performance.

Integrity and "corruption proofing"

The underlying objective behind efforts to develop and implement a sound governance structure for regulators is to ensure systematically that they will carry out their functions effectively and efficiently, thus supporting the economic performance of the regulated sector. A major hurdle to effective regulation, particularly in post-fragile countries with relatively undeveloped institutional structures, is corruption. The growing danger of corruption has recently given rise to a body of literature which focuses on identifying and addressing that risk in relation to legislative drafting. *Corruption proofing* refers to the systematic assessment of the form and substance of draft or enacted legislation and regulation to identify and address provisions that risk giving rise to corruption. Box 7.4 describes how corruption proofing has been implemented on country-level.

Appendix D presents a corruption proofing checklist developed in the context of the *South-Eastern European Regional Anti-Corruption Initiative,* an

BOX 7.4

The growth of corruption proofing

Thirteen countries (Albania, Armenia, Azerbaijan, Kazakhstan, the Republic of Korea, the Kyrgyz Republic, Latvia, Lithuania, Moldova, the Russian Federation, Tajikistan, Ukraine and Uzbekistan) have put in place a method to be used to systematically assess whether their legislation may open the way to corruption. In some cases, corruption proofing is undertaken by the government during the legal drafting process, such as in Albania, where the ministry drafting the legislation is responsible. More often, an external body such as an anti-corruption agency is responsible for corruption proofing, preparing assessments that include recommendations to minimize the risk, as in Latvia and the Republic of Korea. Sometimes civil society reviews laws pertaining to corruption and develops its own methodology, as in Moldova and Ukraine, which requires that draft laws are published at an early stage and made available for public comment.

Source: Hoppe 2014.

BOX 7.5

Basic questions for guiding a desk review of integrity in a regulatory agency

1. Is there a national integrity policy?
2. Is there a reference to a code of behavior or standards code in the agency's statute and requirements as to its application?
3. Does the agency have an integrity and/or anti-corruption policy and associated processes?
4. Does the agency have a code of behavior as part of its integrity policy?
5. Does the agency's induction program for new staff include material and training in relation to integrity?
6. Does the agency have a unit or senior official responsible for integrity and corruption?
7. Are board members and senior staff required to make a declaration of their financial interests and, if so, how is this undertaken?

intergovernmental regional organization sponsored by the European Union and covering nine states: Albania, Bosnia and Herzegovina, Bulgaria, Croatia, North Macedonia, Moldova, Montenegro, Romania, and Serbia. The anti-corruption checklist may provide a useful additional resource when seeking to embed governance principles in new legislation or attempting to diagnose existing regulatory arrangements and address priority problems.

CONCLUSION

This chapter has outlined the need for a system of rules, or code of behavior, to help prevent improper conduct and maintain integrity among decision-makers. This is particular importance wherever corruption is deeply embedded or has become the norm. The chapter also briefly examined the relationship between integrity and the other principles of good regulatory governance, role clarity, requisite powers, independence, funding, decision-making and the governing body, predictability, engagement, accountability, transparency, and performance evaluation. Key questions that can help guide desk reviews of integrity are contained in box 7.5.

NOTE

1. See, for example, the OECD country surveys in relation to corruption and material in relation to anti-corruption at www.cleangovbiz.org.

REFERENCES

Hoppe, T. 2014. *Anti-Corruption Assessment of Laws ("Corruption Proofing"): Comparative Study and Methodology*. Southeast Europe 2020 SEE2020 Series. Sarajevo: Regional Cooperation Council.

OECD (Organisation for Economic Co-operation and Development). 2017. *OECD Integrity Review of Mexico: Taking a Stronger Stance against Corruption*. OECD Public Governance Reviews. Paris: OECD Publishing.

Whitton, H. 2001. *Implementing Effective Ethics Standards in Government and the Civil Service*. Berlin: Transparency International.

8

Predictability

ABSTRACT

Individual decisions made by regulators should, to a substantial degree, be predictable for regulated entities. Predictability adds certainty to their operating environment, thus favoring effective decision-making. It also enhances confidence in the impartiality and quality of the regulator's decisions. Predictability can be achieved by ensuring that the principles and rules that the regulator follows when making decisions are explicit, publicly available and well understood.

KEY TAKEAWAYS

General takeaways

- Predictability in regulatory decision-making is a commonly cited investor concern.
- Clear regulations enable individuals or organizations to judge what behavior is acceptable and what is not.
- Often, however, regulations do not provide sufficient detail on how the regulator will carry out its responsibilities. This creates uncertainty on the part of the regulated and of possible investors, which can be mitigated by making regulatory practices more explicit—through published policies, procedures, etc.
- While changes in regulatory policies or decisions (e.g., tariff methodology) may be required, changes, particularly significant ones, should only be introduced after significant public notice.
- "Predictability" should be committed to in the law; basic regulatory principles, practices, procedures should also be articulated.

Takeaways specific for post-fragile contexts

- Predictability may be hard to achieve in post-fragile environments, though establishing it should be a high priority. Taking the following actions can help:
  - establishing regulatory functions in law;
  - helping the regulator publish material on how it will carry out its duties;
  - providing regulator staff with clear guidelines so they know how to carry out their duties;
  - publishing formal written policies.

REGULATIONS AND PREDICTABILITY

Predictability in regulatory decision-making is one of the most commonly cited investor concerns (OECD 2015, 16). Regulations on what sort of behavior is permitted or prohibited often carry a penalty for those who break the rules and sometimes positive incentives for those who abide by them. They provide high-level criteria on which regulators base their decisions as to whether a person's behavior is in breach of the rules. They enable individuals and organizations to determine what behavior is acceptable and what is not, thus enabling them, if necessary, to modify their actions to make certain that they are acting within the law. However, a key issue is that regulations frequently fail to provide enough detail on how the regulator's key responsibilities must be exercised. This is likely an issue of concern in post-fragile countries, where specialist drafting skills are scarce and many regulatory structures are being developed for the first time.

For example, it is common for regulatory agencies in infrastructure sectors to be given, as an important part of their role, authority and responsibility for setting tariffs. However, sometimes the statute establishing the agency provides no details as to how, or according to what principles, tariffs should be calculated. This was the case in Brazil, where the method for valuing assets in the recalculation of electricity distribution tariffs was left entirely to regulator discretion. Private-sector distributors claimed they had been promised that the asset base would be purchased at the prevailing price at the time of sector privatization, whereas others countered that there was no such commitment. Both the law and the concessions were silent on the question. The result was ***uncertainty*** and a ***lack of predictability*** as to tariffs at a critical time in the development of the country's infrastructure markets. Both could have been minimized, if not entirely eradicated, if the basic methodology and criteria for calculating tariffs had been made explicit either in the law or in relevant contracts. This would have provided greater predictability for investors and consumers and, of course, guidance for the regulators.

While predictability can often be enhanced by ensuring the regulation provides high-level guidance on how to deploy regulatory powers, the need for regulators to exercise their own judgment and discretion necessarily remains. Predictability issues must also be addressed in these contexts. While formal legislation is almost always widely published and available for scrutiny, it is often not supported by formal policy statements from regulators giving their interpretation of the regulatory requirements that they must implement and providing clear guidance as to how they will be applied in practice.

The predictability of regulatory decision-making can thus be enhanced if the regulator develops and publishes additional material, such as formal policies, internal processes and guidelines. This material should always be consistent with the legislation governing the operations of the regulator and should focus on interpreting the law and its purpose, working to apply it effectively in practice.

The process of developing explicit policies, processes, guidelines and other such materials has benefits for both regulatory agency staff and regulated entities.

Regulatory agency staff and explicit agency policies

For regulator staff, availability of formal, written policies and procedures provides clear guidance on how to carry out their roles in ways that are legitimate and appropriate—that is, that are consistent with the law and broad government policy. This is likely to be particularly important in post-fragile environments where there is typically a lack of well-qualified staff and, in a context of newly established (or recently reformed) law and institutions, a lack of experience in the practical application of that law. From the perspective of a regulatory agency, the impact of such formal policies, internal processes and guidelines in enhancing the predictability of decisions is that they:

- give confidence to staff in undertaking their functions and making decisions and also help to provide organizational resilience (as opposed to undue dependence on a few experienced and well-trained individuals);
- provide an explicit framework for assessing staff decisions;
- enhance the perceived legitimacy of the regulator, through increased predictability, in the eyes of regulated enterprises, the public and the government—something particularly important for newly established or reformed regulators.

Making formal, written policies and procedures available to regulated entities

Publishing formal, written policies and procedures gives regulated entities a clearer understanding of the factors underlying the regulator's decisions. This enables them to predict the regulator's responses more reliably, (e.g., when approving applications), including its likely decisions and actions if regulated subjects break the rules. This predictability underpins investor confidence by providing a high level of assurance as to the expected outcomes of investment, operational and other decisions. It also enables regulated entities to clearly see when a regulator's decisions are inconsistent with its policy framework and standard procedures, and whether an appeal against a decision is likely to be successful.

CHANGING RULES AND PROCEDURES

To underline the value of predictability is not to argue that regulations should never change. Change is needed to respond to different circumstances and facilitate innovation, but significant changes should be introduced only after reasonable public notice and meaningful consultation with interested parties. Regulated entities should be given sufficient time to adjust to the impact of the changes on their operations and future investment plans. In particular, policy and regulation should never be retroactive.

PREDICTABILITY AND CONTRACTUAL COMMITMENT

Predictability, the law and agency decision-making

The basic regulatory principles, practices, procedures, and policies followed in infrastructure sectors should be articulated in law, preferably in a statute or primary law. The aim is to ensure stability and predictability in the entire regulatory system, leading to more rational, efficient decision-making by investors and consumers. Where these matters are not made explicit and enshrined in the law governing the agency, decision-making will generally be less transparent and decisions less predictable. This implies that investors face greater "regulatory risks" and, as a result, will be less likely to make investments. Where it is not possible or feasible to address these matters in legislation, they should, at a minimum, be included in policy and procedural documents developed by the regulator and made publicly available. Crucially, the regulator staff's actual decision-making practices should consistently be based on the content of these documents.

Predictability and contractual commitment

Part C of this manual examines the importance of contractual commitment in detail, notably in relation to attempts by governments and their agencies to renegotiate contracts. In summary, the maintenance of contractual commitment provides an important basis for predictability in decision-making and, in turn, in ensuring and maintaining investor confidence.

PREDICTABILITY AND THE RULE OF LAW IN THE POST-FRAGILE CONTEXT

While predictability is an important feature of all regulatory systems, it is usually in short supply in fragile and early post-fragile situations. In the period of fragility, regulatory decisions are typically unpredictable due to political, economic and social instability and conflict. There is also frequently a lack of transparency and participation in decision-making, making it difficult for stakeholders to predict government decisions. After a country exits from fragility and conflict it faces the challenge of rebuilding and reforming its regulatory system. This results in rapid changes to regulations and regulatory processes, resulting in further unpredictability, at least in the short term.

It follows that high priority should be given to establishing predictability, as it will be a key factor in creating a positive environment for domestic and foreign investment. If investors cannot be certain about the enforceability of their rights and obligations, this raises the cost of capital, thereby weakening firms' competitiveness and reducing investment. In addition, uncertainty and ambiguity in a regulatory system can also foster corruption as investors may be more likely to seek to protect or advance their interests through bribery, and government actors may seek undue benefits. These tendencies are only slowly reversed as trust, credibility and predictability are achieved. Hence, attention should be paid to predictability issues from the early stages of the reform process.

Box 8.1 provides an example of the problems that can arise due to a lack of predictability, specifically in the context of land acquisition for public projects, as well as a summary of reforms adopted to address this issue.

CONCLUSION: DIAGNOSING PREDICTABILITY ISSUES IN RELATION TO REGULATORY AGENCIES

This chapter examined the importance of the predictability of regulatory decision-making for agency staff and regulated entities, stressing the value of formal, written policies to guide behavior being made available to regulated subjects. Key questions for undertaking a desk review of predictability are contained in box 8.2.

BOX 8.1

Uncertainty and the expropriation of land in Indonesia

Many infrastructure projects require land to be expropriated, especially those involving the construction of roads and dams. Public-private partnerships (PPPs) in Indonesia were adversely affected by the laws governing expropriation and the delays that resulted from uncertainty as to their likely impact on road projects. Owners delayed selling their land to PPPs for as long as possible in the hope that their bargaining position—and hence the price—would be strengthened as the project progressed. Also, because of the drawn-out negotiation process involved in acquiring land, the long time between identifying land and purchase allowed speculators to drive up the price. This led to a significant escalation of total project costs.

A new, 2011 law regarding expropriation of land for public works and PPPs improved matters. From the perspective of the investor it made the timing of when the land would be available through expropriation more certain. The law set tight deadlines for appealing expropriation decisions and the level of compensation, to be based on the market price of the land.

Source: OECD 2012, 22.

BOX 8.2

Questions for guiding a desk review of predictability

Ideally, potential predictability issues should be identified when a policy and its related statute are being developed, particularly during the corruption-proofing process. Where a lack of predictability is believed to be an issue, key questions in diagnosing the issue and proposing solutions are as follows:

1. Are laws and regulations and their implementation and enforcement transparent and readily accessible? Do they set out key processes in sufficient detail? Are laws stable—that is, are they not changed very frequently?
2. How are the interests of investors taken into consideration when policy and regulations are amended?
3. What sources of information indicate that predictability is an issue and how reliable are the sources?
4. What are the specific issues identified by the available sources of reliable information and do they represent a major issue or constraint for business and investment?

5. How can the issue be resolved? This should involve thorough consultations with key stakeholders, especially those who have been affected by the alleged lack of predictability.

Where the review indicates that significant changes are required, the following steps should be taken:

1. Develop a preliminary action plan for resolving the predictability issue that is appropriate to the country's needs and context.
2. Support the action plan with key arguments, such as those related to private-sector investment, efficiency, effectiveness, communication, transparency and coordination.
3. If the action plan is endorsed, a communications strategy should be developed to ensure that all those inside and outside government likely to be affected by the reforms are informed of the changes in good time. This should include a selection of media, as well as more institutional means of communication, such as speeches by officials and ministers, publication in the Government Gazette and annual reports.

REFERENCES

OECD (Organisation for Economic Co-operation and Development). 2012. *Indonesia: Strengthening Co-ordination and Connecting Markets.* OECD Reviews of Regulatory Reform. Paris: OECD Publishing. http://dx.doi.org/10.1787/9789264173637-en.

——. 2015. *Policy Framework for Investment.* Paris: OECD Publishing. http://dx.doi.org/10.1787/9789264208667-en.

9

Engagement

ABSTRACT

Regulators should have established mechanisms for consultation and dialogue with stakeholders as part of achieving their objectives. Effectively drawing on the knowledge of regulated sectors and understanding the views of regulated businesses and citizens systematically improves the quality of regulatory decisions. Ensuring stakeholder views are heard and weighed also helps confer legitimacy on the regulator and its decisions and supports compliance. However, engagement processes must be designed in ways that avoid regulatory capture and conflicts of interest.

KEY TAKEAWAYS

General takeaways

- Stakeholder engagement is the process whereby a regulator discusses key regulatory issues with those affected by its decisions.
- Key purposes of such engagement include: (1) gathering information to allow the regulator to better analyze key issues; (2) helping promote confidence in the regulator and the decisions it takes.
- Regulatory issues that require engagement depend on the regulator's specific functions, though they should include broader issues like development of operational policies and significant regulatory decisions.
- A quality engagement process is: systematic; open; supported by the provision of adequate information; timely; characterized by feedback; sustained throughout the policy cycle; and evaluated.

Takeaways specific for post-fragile contexts

- Given civil society organizations are less common and generally less well-developed, identifying relevant groups to engage with might be more challenging. It may be appropriate for the regulator, or the relevant ministry, to help in the formation of such bodies.

INTRODUCTION

Stakeholder engagement refers to processes in which the regulator discusses key regulatory issues with those who are affected by its decisions. The primary stakeholders are the producers and consumers of the regulated industry's outputs. Other stakeholders include potential entrants to the industry, participants in downstream industries and final consumers. The aim of this chapter is to outline the value of effective engagement, with a focus on how to ensure a well-functioning engagement policy and process is put in place.

The purpose of stakeholder engagement is to:

1. gather information needed for a better analysis of key issues in the regulated industry to improve the quality of regulatory decision-making; and
2. promote confidence in the regulator and its decisions by ensuring that the opinions of affected groups are seen to be taken into account. This, in turn, promotes the legitimacy of the regulating body and its decisions.

The kind of issues requiring stakeholder engagement depend to some extent on the specific functions of the regulator. However, they should generally include both broader themes, such as the development of operational policies, and significant regulatory decisions.

In relation to policy development, the focus of engagement will likely be to obtain a clear understanding of what the community views as the key regulatory issues. This should inform the regulators' priorities. Where engagement relates to individual decisions, or specific sets of decisions, engagement will seek to obtain information to inform decision-making. This could include gathering specific data and improving the regulator's understanding of key market dynamics.

The use of formal advisory bodies

Constituting a formal advisory body is one option in implementing and demonstrating commitment to systematic engagement. Having an advisory body with legislative status can make stakeholders confident that the regulator will take account of their views. Where this is the objective, ensuring that a wide range of interests are represented will be paramount. Alternatively, these bodies can be structured with a focus on ensuring that a range of expertise is available to the regulator. An expert advisory body may provide significant benefits in the early stages of reform, when it might be difficult to recruit expert members to the regulator's governing body.

However, several risks are associated with this model. One is that the advisory board may be seen as a substitute for developing a strategy for wide-ranging engagement with stakeholders. This can result in the regulator hearing too narrow a range of opinions. A second is that reliance on an advisory board for expert input is ultimately a poor substitute for developing these capacities in-house. Associated with this is the risk of the advisory board becoming a mechanism leading to regulatory capture, as the regulator comes to depend substantially on the advice of the same interlocutors over a period in carrying out its functions. However, in a fragile context, while these are risks in the immediate post-conflict stage, the benefits of the advisory board's additional capacity outweigh long-term risks associated with the regulator never building those capacities.

These risks suggest that if an advisory board is adopted in the early stages of reform, consideration should be given to including a "sunset clause" in the relative legislation, thus setting a term for its existence or at least providing for its review after a certain period. This is consistent with the objective of gradually moving to reliance on internal expertise. Second, the membership of the board should be relatively broad so as to reduce the potential for its capture by specific interests. In addition, the legislation could also include specific requirements for the regulator to conduct broader and more open consultation besides the advice of the board.

QUALITY IN ENGAGEMENT PROCESSES

A high-quality engagement process should be:

- systematic
- open
- supported by the provision of adequate information
- timely
- characterized by the provision of feedback
- sustained throughout the policy cycle
- evaluated.

Systematic

The regulator should develop and publish a stakeholder engagement policy. This should explain in what circumstances it will conduct consultations and who will be consulted. It should also identify the general processes to be used, including how notice of consultation opportunities shall be given, what types of consultation mechanisms will be used (e.g., written submissions, public hearings, formal meetings) and what time will typically be allowed for responses.

Publishing a policy provides confidence among interested parties that they have a right to be heard and helps them understand how to engage. It also allows the regulator to be challenged if they do not engage with stakeholders in accord with the policy.

Openness

A key risk with stakeholder engagement is that it involves only selected interests, with which the regulator has established relationships. Where highly structured approaches to engagement, such as advisory boards, are used, this risk can be higher. Restricting the range of interests consulted will mean the regulator risks having a less sound understanding of the regulatory environment, opening it to greater risk of capture and detracting from its legitimacy by creating resentment among those excluded from the process.

These risks can be avoided if the regulator explicitly acknowledges the principle that any interested party can participate in consultation. Importantly, consultation practices should ensure this principle of open engagement is a practical reality. This means that the existence of opportunities to engage are made widely known, that enough time is allowed for submissions to the regulator and that efforts are made to identify and remove other impediments to less organized and resourced interests being engaged. Particularly in a low-income country context, the regulator

Engagement by the Georgian National Energy and Water Supply Regulatory Commission

The legislation governing GNEWSRC requires that all sessions, decisions, resolutions, orders, minutes and documents of the Commission are made available to the public and interested parties and stakeholders. This provides the basis for a very full engagement between the Commission and the public and a much-reduced potential for its regulatory capture and conflicts of interest. While the Commission does not appear to date to have developed a formal engagement policy, the requirement that a wide range of its key activities and documents be available to stakeholders and the public provides a mechanism for engagement by interested parties and a degree of expectation that consultation will be undertaken.

The Nepal Telecommunications Authority makes consultation information easily available

The Nepal Telecommunications Authority's (NTA) website includes a public notice page listing forthcoming consultations as well as the broader activities of the regulator. Detailed consultation papers, which explain the issue being addressed and identify a range of specific issues on which information and feedback are sought are also published on the website. The papers remain available for several years. The NTA has published an average of three consultation papers annually in recent years.

should take an active approach to this principle, trying to identify relevant interests and inviting their participation in the process in the least costly manner available.

Another element of openness is that stakeholders should have the opportunity to hear what views others have put to the regulator. This means it is good practice for written submissions to be published on the regulator's web page, that hearings are held publicly as far as possible, and that stakeholders should be able to challenge views put by other parties.

There will be circumstances in which the regulator seeks confidential material from some parties, and its sensitivity must be respected. However, there is a need to minimize any exemptions from the general principle of openness if engagement is to yield effective communication and retain the confidence of the stakeholders and the public. Box 9.1 provides an example from Georgia, showing how all documents should be made available to the public.

Supported by the provision of adequate information

A quality engagement strategy provides all parties with an equal opportunity to join in the process. However, where technically-based issues are being considered, less organized and well-resourced groups (e.g., consumer organizations) often have difficulty in engaging effectively. This means that regulators should support engagement by such groups by publishing relevant information in discussion papers or similar documents as the starting point for the consultation process. These should:

- provide relevant background information to enable the issue in question to be properly understood;
- identify the key focus of the consultation, possibly by including specific questions that stakeholders can address in developing their responses;
- be written in a way that is easily understood by people without a detailed knowledge of the issue in question.

This material must be made available in advance of the consultations so stakeholders can obtain and understand it before engaging. It should be published on the regulator's website and made available on request. The Nepal Telecommunications Authority, as outlined in box 9.2, has an engagement strategy which makes relevant information available in easy-to-understand form to interested parties.

Timeliness

Engagement must occur before regulators have decided an issue or determined a broad course of action. This means planning consultation initiatives at an early stage in the decision-making process and carrying out the necessary preparations, such as drafting discussion papers.

A common problem in relation to government policy development is that open, public consultation is seen as a formal obligation that must be complied with, rather than an important information source and integral part of decision-making. Very often, initial, informal discussions with key businesses and other powerful interests lead to policy directions being formed before broader consultation starts.

This is a major risk, for several reasons:

- The quality of decision-making is likely to be compromised where the regulator relies on limited sources of information and advice.
- There is a clear risk of capture if wider interests are excluded from effective engagement with the regulator.
- Stakeholders, seeing that their views are not weighed appropriately, often cease to engage, causing legitimacy problems and closing off sources of future information and advice.

Accountability mechanisms should be developed requiring the regulator to demonstrate that it has consulted appropriately and weighed the inputs received. This will help to develop a culture in the agency that sees stakeholder engagement as an important aid to carrying out regulatory functions more effectively.

Providing feedback

Even though the willingness of stakeholders to engage will quickly diminish if they do not see any benefits deriving from their involvement, their views do not necessarily need be adopted. However, the regulator should provide formal feedback after a consultation, indicating what views were received, how it weighed and analyzed those views, and how those views affected the final decisions.

This can be done at an aggregate level by publishing a single summary document setting out the key opinions put forward by each major party consulted and how they were assessed. However, there is also merit in responding directly to submissions by individual groups, particularly where less well-organized and well-supported groups have made significant efforts to engage.

Sustained throughout the policy cycle

It is important that the engagement policy cover stakeholder engagement at each stage of the regulatory governance cycle. This means that as well as consulting stakeholders when new regulations are being made, or regulatory decisions adopted, it is important to seek stakeholder views during regulatory implementation. Feedback from those directly affected by regulatory decisions can help to identify poor outcomes more quickly and enable any problems to be addressed promptly.

Evaluated

The regulator should ensure that its approach to consultation is assessed from time to time to identify and address shortcomings. This does not need to be a very detailed or formal process. However, ensuring that an independent body (e.g., an auditor-general) is given the task of undertaking evaluations, and that stakeholders can participate without fear of adverse consequences, is crucial to ensuring that accurate assessments are obtained.

ENSURING EFFECTIVE ENGAGEMENT IN THE POST-FRAGILE CONTEXT

The importance of engaging consumers and citizens, as well as producer interests, has been emphasized above. In the post-fragile context this engagement, while extremely important, is also extremely challenging. Data indicates that greater citizen engagement in rule-making is associated with higher-quality regulation, stronger democratic regimes and less corrupt institutions (Johns and Saltane 2016). However, in a post-fragile environment where the social contract is in flux and many lingering unaddressed grievances remain, ensuring that citizen engagement occurs and yields its desired outcomes may be difficult.

The flow of accurate unbiased information—such as between a regulator and relevant stakeholders—is key to rebuilding trust between the population and the state in post-fragile contexts. However, several barriers prevent information from reaching its intended audience. As mentioned throughout this guide, government institutions in these contexts often lack capacity, and this can affect their ability to ability engage with citizens. There may also be physical barriers— like destroyed communications infrastructure or pockets of lingering insecurity. On the receiving end, citizens are limited in their ability to receive and react to information from state institutions.

Furthermore, when the space for participation and engagement exists, the resulting interaction might not be meaningful or could even risk exacerbating existing forms of inequality or exclusion.

While these dynamics are challenging, finding a way to provide relevant information to stakeholders is, in general terms, fundamental in improving the quality of the feedback received. In the low-income/post-fragile context, where citizen and consumer organizations are less developed, paying attention to providing this background information in simple, easily understood form, is particularly important. It may also be important to keep the country's current context central to any engagement design. For example, does information need to be provided in multiple languages so as not to stoke existing social tensions? Or does reaching the most vulnerable infrastructure customers require an approach different from the standard one? Providing adequate time for developing responses is also likely to be a key factor.

Where citizen or consumer groups are yet to arise, it may be appropriate for the regulator or the minister responsible to help establish such bodies. While care should be taken that this does not lead to the creation of "dependent" groups, such initiatives may sometimes offer the only opportunity of obtaining real consumer feedback.

CONCLUSION

The aim of this chapter was to outline the value of effective engagement, with a focus on how to ensure that a good-quality engagement policy and process is put in place. A desk review of engagement should address key questions such as those listed in box 9.3.

BOX 9.3

Key questions for a desk review of engagement

1. Does the regulator have an explicit, written engagement policy?

2. Is engagement open to all interested parties? Is the regulator able to engage effectively with all interested parties (i.e., in terms of language, mode of engagement—not all places experiencing fragility will have access to internet or phones).

3. Likewise, does the regulator know who it needs to engage with?

4. Is engagement supported by the provision of adequate information for those interested?

5. Is the information provided in a timely fashion, enabling those interested to respond?

6. Is feedback characterized by a formal acknowledgement, with an explicit indication of whether or not it was used?

7. Is engagement sustained throughout the stages of the policy cycle?

8. Are the engagement policy and associated processes regularly evaluated?

REFERENCE

Johns, M., and V. Saltane. 2016. "Citizen Engagement in Rulemaking: Evidence on Regulatory Practices in 185 Countries." Policy Research Working Paper 7840, World Bank, Washington, DC.

10

Accountability and Transparency

ABSTRACT

Accountability and transparency are the necessary counterweights to independence. That is, regulators that enjoy a high degree of independence must be subjected to stricter accountability and transparency requirements to ensure that they are carrying out their functions appropriately. Regulators are accountable to the government (i.e., ministers and parliament), to regulated entities and to consumers and the public. Transparency—including publishing policies and guidelines, as well as important decisions, is one key element of accountability. The second key element is the existence of robust appeal mechanisms

KEY TAKEAWAYS

General takeaways

- Accountability implies that the objectives, functions and powers of regulators are clearly established and procedures for carrying them out specified.
- Transparency implies that a regulator is open about the way it operates.
- Regulators are accountable to multiple groups: Different accountability mechanisms are required for each:
  - The supervising ministry or legislature requires annual reports or statements of expectations.
  - Regulated entities require that the regulator conduct internal and external accountability reviews.
  - The public requires that the regulator publish major decisions, policies and procedures so that they can hold the regulator accountable.

Takeaways specific for post-fragile contexts

- In post-fragile contexts, key challenges include: The fact that regulators and the government itself have limited experience with effective regulation; that any appeals process will not be sufficiently detailed; that they will face capacity constraints.

- Nonetheless, systems should seek to ensure that relevant stakeholders have a clear right of appeal and that the process for lodging a complaint is clear and simple.
- Regulators should also ensure timely decisions to build confidence in the process.
- Appeals mechanisms should be detailed in relevant legislation.
- Given state judicial bodies in this context will likely have capacity constraints in handling appeals in good time, they could overcome them by:
  - Making legislative lists and expediting a review of the most economically significant cases. They can also facilitate the development of specific expertise within the court or tribunal by enabling judges to specialize in issues related to a regulated sector or sectors.
  - Establishing a specialist administrative or quasi-judicial body to oversee regulatory decisions.

INTRODUCTION

Accountability implies that the objectives, functions and powers of the regulator are clearly established, and the policies and processes it adopts to carry out those functions and exercise those powers are clearly specified. This provides the basis for assessment of its performance by the legislature or other responsible authorities and for action to be taken where it acts inconsistently. It also means that decisions can be challenged by regulated entities and consumers, using appeal mechanisms.

Transparency means that the regulator is open about the way in which it operates, publishing the policies, criteria and guidelines that guide its decisions and setting out the reasons for key decisions. Transparency also implies being open about the key results of the regulator's activities by publishing outcome indicators and other relevant material.

Regulators are accountable to the government (i.e., the minister and parliament), to regulated entities and to consumers and the public. Different mechanisms are needed to ensure that effective accountability to each of these groups is maintained.

ACCOUNTABILITY TO THE MINISTER AND THE LEGISLATURE

The regulator's role is to achieve public-interest objectives identified by the government. These objectives are usually identified explicitly in the laws establishing the regulator, as are the powers given to the regulator to achieve them. This means that the regulator is accountable to the legislature, either directly or through its minister, and thus should report regularly to these bodies.

Accountability mechanisms

A key way to hold the regulator accountable is to develop specific annual reporting requirements that clearly indicate what information is needed and when. These annual reports should be tabled in the legislature and made public to enable wider scrutiny and discussion. Also, their contents should demonstrate that the regulator is fulfilling its role efficiently, effectively, impartially and with integrity.

A second, commonly used accountability mechanism is the "statement of expectations." This is typically a formal document sent to the regulator's governing body, or to the CEO, by the minister. Such a statement is particularly important where the regulator is part of a ministerial agency, rather than an independent entity subject to specific legislation. However, even for independent regulators, a statement of expectations enables additional detail to be provided about the government's objectives for the agency and how it should operate, thus improving accountability.

A statement of expectations should identify relevant government policies and clarify the government's specific objectives for the regulator, including any expectations as to how it should do its job. It may be appropriate for the government to involve stakeholders in the development of this statement to ensure greater support and understanding of the regulatory structure. Importantly, however, the statement must be fully consistent with all statements regarding the functions, powers and objectives of the regulator established in the relevant legislation.

The regulator should respond formally to the minister, indicating how it will meet the expectations identified. This should include specific commitments and performance indicators, where possible. Where the regulator is required to address competing objectives, it should indicate how it will go about reconciling any conflicts and setting priorities.

Statements of expectations, and responses from regulators, should be published on the regulator's website, so that all stakeholders can assess the regulator's actions in the light of this information.

ACCOUNTABILITY TO REGULATED ENTITIES

Accountability to regulated entities involves ensuring that they can understand how the regulator goes about making decisions. Regulators should publish the policies and guidelines that they use to guide decision-making in key areas so that regulated businesses can reasonably anticipate the view that the regulator will take.[1] (See chapter 8, which addresses the principle of predictability.)

Accountability mechanisms

Where regulated businesses or citizens believe the regulator has not exercised its decision-making powers appropriately—that is, in accordance with the relevant legislation or its published policies and guidelines—they should have access to robust appeal mechanisms. A strong appeal process is fundamental to the accountability system and key in helping maintain trust. Appeal mechanisms should generally include internal and external elements.

Internal accountability mechanisms

Internal review often constitutes an appropriate first step in challenging a regulator's decision. Delegated decisions, such as those made by inspectors, can have significant impacts on regulated subjects and should be open to internal review on request. The regulator should inform regulated entities of these internal review mechanisms when they inform them of decisions made.

Internal review has the benefit of allowing rapid and low-cost reappraisal of the initial decision and can allow the regulator to self-correct poor decision-making. Internal review processes should be conducted by a separate group within the regulator's management structure that is at arm's length from those that made the original regulatory decision. Appellants should have the opportunity to explain, in writing and/or in person, the nature of their objections to the original regulatory decision. The response to the appeal should address these points and, where a decision is upheld, ensure that the basis for the original decision is explained and justified in terms of the relevant regulatory policies, principles and procedures.

However, internal review is likely not appropriate for major regulatory decisions involving much of the regulator's workforce. Moreover, where regulated entities are dissatisfied with the results of an internal review, it is important that they have access to an external review process considered to be independent and disinterested. This is essential to maintaining confidence in the robustness of the regulatory decision processes.

External accountability mechanisms

As a rule, external review of major regulatory decisions should be conducted via the judicial system. Appeals against major decisions should be heard in a senior court, since the issues raised can be highly technical and the financial implications large. A key concern is the need for appeals to be heard in a timely manner, since there may be important economic consequences, for example in terms of delayed investments, or market opening, which may affect wider economic development.

ACCOUNTABILITY TO THE PUBLIC

Accountability to the broader public is largely underpinned by transparency. In this context, transparency means that the regulator should publish:

- policies, procedures and guidelines it uses in regulatory decision-making; and
- major decisions made on individual matters, together with clear and detailed reasoning behind those decisions.

Some countries have gone further in this regard. For example, as noted above, Georgia's Law on Electricity and Natural Gas prescribes that the Georgian National Energy and Water Supply Regulatory Commission keep public records of all proceedings, decisions, orders and other documents and that the Commission's:

- sessions be open to the public, including sessions involving the grant, modification, revocation or suspension of licenses, as well as concerning the establishment, modification or revocation of tariffs;
- resolutions and decisions be published according to set rules.

ACCOUNTABILITY AND TRANSPARENCY IN THE POST-FRAGILE CONTEXT

Limited experience

A key issue in establishing appropriate appeals mechanisms in post-fragile contexts is that, in many cases, there will be little experience with challenging the decisions of government bodies based on clear rules and procedures. The legitimacy of such challenges may not be widely accepted, and there may also be concerns that challenges to government may have negative consequences. In such

BOX 10.1

Finding the right balance between expediting appeals and allowing sufficient time for external review

Indonesia allows applications for the court to review decisions of its Commission for the Supervision of Business Competition (KPPU) to the District Court within 14 days of the decision being announced. Appeals must be decided within 30 days of the start of a hearing. Similar deadlines are applied where a party wishes to appeal the District Court's decision to the Supreme Court.

While these time limits enable rapid review, they risk encouraging poorer findings as key questions in competition law cases often involve considering detailed, sometimes conceptually complex matters. Indeed, such reviews sometimes take 12–18 months to complete in other jurisdictions. This issue of ensuring adequate time is available to hear and determine appeals is made more significant by the fact that appeals against KPPU decisions are heard by generalist courts in Indonesia, rather than the specialist competition tribunals that some countries have created.

Source: OECD 2012, 120–21.

circumstances, it will be important to ensure that the right to appeal is clearly established and that processes for lodging appeals are simple and easy to follow. Timely resolution of appeals—particularly internal appeals—will also help establish confidence in the process, as will the provision of clear, readily understood reasons. That said, the need for timeliness in decision-making must be balanced against the imperative of ensuring that the appeal body has enough time to reach a well-considered decision. Box 10.1 provides an example.

Insufficiently detailed appeals process

Another key requirement is to ensure that appeals mechanisms are described in the relevant laws in sufficient detail to enable workable systems to be implemented. This includes that the grounds on which appeals can be made are clearly identified and the court or tribunal empowered to hear external appeals is specified. It should also include details of the circumstances in which both internal and external appeals can be initiated. Box 10.2 provides an example drawn from Rwanda of inadequate appeals provisions being subsequently strengthened.

Capacity constraints

A further issue of relevance to the post-fragile context is ensuring that the body nominated to hear appeals has adequate expertise and capacity. As noted in box 10.1, some appeals can turn on highly technical issues and may have major financial implications. This means that having robust institutional arrangements is essential to ensure sound outcomes and the development of confidence in the appeals mechanism among regulated parties. Achieving this may be difficult in a post-conflict context, where courts are likely to be overburdened and subject to substantial delays.

This may suggest the need to create specific "lists" within the court system, an approach with at least two significant benefits. Firstly, it can act as a triage mechanism, expediting review of the most economically significant cases.

BOX 10.2

The development of an appeals process in Rwanda

The multisectoral Rwanda Utilities Regulatory Agency (RURA) was established in 2001. The only direct reference to an appeal against RURA was contained in Article 47 of the relevant legislation, which specified that any person or organization aggrieved by a decision of its Board could appeal to the court. However, the legislation failed to specify to which court the appeal should be made or the procedures involved. Moreover, there was no specific mention of any internal review of the appeal process in the legislation.

In 2013 the RURA was reestablished by Law No. 09/2013 and the subject of appeals received greater attention. The Board was empowered by Article 20 to take decisions on any disputes referred to it and, upon request from the parties to a dispute, to conciliate. Article 47 empowers the Board to investigate any complaint made to RURA in relation to anti-competition activities. If the person or organization making the complaint is not satisfied by RURA's response, they may file a case with the competent court.

The Electricity Law (No. 21/2011) includes a similar generic appeals provision, with Article 15 stating that any applicant not satisfied with the regulatory agency's decision to refuse to issue a license may, after unsuccessfully attempting an out-of-court settlement, appeal before the competent court. Despite more robust appeals mechanisms, the new legislation fails to specify the court to which the appeal should be made, and the procedures involved. Moreover, there is no mention of any internal review or appeals process, other than that implied in Article 20. While such details are also absent from RURA's website, it provides details on how to lodge a complaint against the provider of a utility such as energy or gas.

Second, it can facilitate the development of specific expertise within the court or tribunal by enabling judges to specialize in issues related to a regulated sector or sectors.

One alternative to this model is to establish a specialist administrative or quasi-judicial tribunal to provide independent review of regulatory decisions. For example, decisions of the Australian competition regulator are appealed to the Australian Competition Tribunal.[2] A key benefit of this model is that membership of this and similar bodies typically includes a mixture of judges and expert lay people, which, combined with the specialized nature of the tribunal, helps ensure sound and rapid decisions in respect of highly technical matters.

There are likely to be challenges in establishing such tribunals in the immediate post-fragile context, given both resource and capacity constraints. One solution is to establish a single tribunal with jurisdiction to hear appeals in respect of regulatory decisions across a wide range of infrastructure sectors, as well as competition issues and other economically significant regulatory appeals. It may be possible to coopt expert lay members on a part-time basis from domestic academic institutions or foreign governments or universities to help ensure such tribunals are adequately resourced.

A further alternative is to establish an arbitration mechanism whereby an independent person can hear the parties to a dispute on a largely informal basis and make a binding decision. However, it should be noted that arbitration systems generally require both parties to agree to be bound by decisions, while some measure of appeal to the courts is also typically provided for. Thus, while arbitration may make for a timely decision in the first instance, it may not provide finality for the parties.

At a fundamental level, having an effective appeals process requires minimizing the number of appeals that need to be heard. This highlights the importance of predictability, and decisions being made in accordance with clear, published policies, principles and guidelines, so that appeals with limited prospects of success are less likely to be initiated. It also requires that initial regulatory decisions may only be overturned on appeal on limited, clearly specified grounds, principally when the regulator:

- acted outside the scope of its lawful authority;
- failed to follow proper procedures;
- acted arbitrarily or unreasonably; or
- acted against the clear weight of available evidence.

CONCLUSION

This chapter examined the importance of accountability in regulatory governance. It outlined accountability and mechanisms for its achievement in relation to ministers and the legislature, regulated entities and the public. A checklist of key questions for a desk review of accountability is contained in box 10.3 below.

BOX 10.3

Checklist for applying the principles

Applying the principles—accountability and transparency

Accountability to minister and the legislature

1. Has the minister or other oversight body published a written statement of expectations to the regulator? If not, how have the expectations of the regulator been provided?
2. Has the regulator published a formal response to this statement, explaining how it intends to respond to the priorities set out in it?
3. Is there a mechanism to make sure that the statement of expectations is renewed or updated regularly?
4. Is there a legal requirement for the independent regulator to produce an annual report to the legislature?
5. Does this requirement set out the major performance indicators and other information required to be included in the report?
6. Do the agreed performance indicators provide sufficient information to enable meaningful assessment of the regulator's performance in meeting its responsibilities?
7. Do the performance indicators help the government and the legislature to monitor and assess the performance of the overall regulatory framework?
8. Is there a legislative requirement for all major measures and decisions to be published in a timely manner?

Accountability to regulated entities

1. Does the regulator provide easily accessible and understood guidance material on appeals processes and systems to regulated entities?
2. Does the regulator have a clearly established process for internal review of significant delegated regulatory decisions?
3. Are regulated entities advised that internal review of significant delegated regulatory decisions is available when they are informed of the outcome of the decision?

continued

Box 10.3, *continued*

4. Is the internal review unit as operationally separate from the decision-making body as possible?
5. Is the right of appeal through judicial process available for regulated entities? Under what circumstances?
6. Can a successful appeal result in the original decision being reversed?
7. Is the appeal process transparent, timely and conducted at arm's length?

Accountability to the public

1. Has the regulator published its main operational policies, principles and processes?
2. Is information on reviews and appeals processes easily accessible and readily understood?
3. Are all major decisions made by the regulator published, together with a clear account of the underlying reasoning?

NOTES

1. An exception to this general principle is that in circumstances where publication would allow regulated businesses to game the regulatory system, limiting transparency is justified in order to avoid such gaming.
2. Canada also has a Competition Tribunal, which similarly has a mix of judicial and expert lay officers.

REFERENCE

OECD (Organisation for Economic Co-operation and Development). 2012. *Indonesia: Strengthening Co-ordination and Connecting Markets.* OECD Reviews of Regulatory Reform. Paris: OECD Publishing. http://dx.doi.org/10.1787/9789264173637-en.

11

Performance Evaluation

ABSTRACT

Evaluation is an essential part of the policy cycle. Evaluations of the performance of regulators should consider both their effectiveness in carrying out the functions assigned to them both in legislation and through other directives, and the fitness for purpose of the regulatory structures that are in place. That is, the results should distinguish where changes to the way a regulator carries out its responsibilities are required and where more fundamental change may be needed to the governance arrangements under which the regulator operates as well as the market rules it administers

KEY TAKEAWAYS

General takeaways

- Regulator performance evaluations should be carried out internally (to determine how successfully it is meeting its objectives) as well as externally (to assess whether its strategic goals are being met).
- Key characteristics of a good performance evaluation include:
  - pre-scheduling them
  - having a review body
  - developing a good review process and methodology.
- A regulator's performance should be evaluated against a set of indicators directly linked to the regulator's objectives and functions.

Takeaways specific for fragile contexts

- Performance evaluation is very important in the post-fragile context where new institutions and market structures dominate infrastructure industries. This may require refinements to initial arrangements.

- However, developing a robust performance evaluation system takes time. It is advised that regulators in these contexts start with internal evaluations; external evaluations conducted by an Auditor-General should be prioritized so that capacity constraints are managed.

INTRODUCTION: PERFORMANCE EVALUATION IN THE FRAGILE CONTEXT

Performance evaluation is particularly important in the post-fragile environment, where new institutions and market structures are likely to dominate the infrastructure industries and it is very likely that refinements to the initial arrangements made will be needed. Even where new institutions are working well, evaluation is important to help determine whether it is feasible to move to the next stages of reform.

Performance evaluation is an essential feedback mechanism that provides information on what is being done well or badly. This can reinforce positive behaviors and provide incentives to address problems. Performance measurement also enables the regulator and the government to demonstrate the benefits of reform to stakeholders and helps validate the regulatory model chosen.

SCOPE OF PERFORMANCE EVALUATION

Performance evaluations should be carried out internally and externally. Those carried out within an organization form part of good internal governance practices, as they provide key information to underpin changes in management strategy and approach. These evaluations should focus on how well the regulator is performing its functions and how well the specific systems, processes and procedures it has adopted for this purpose are contributing to its performance.

While internal evaluation is a core activity for a well-functioning organization, the strategic importance of infrastructure regulators means that independent, external evaluation is also needed. External reviews should have a broader focus and aim primarily to assess the extent to which the regulator's strategic goals, such as increasing competition and service reliability, are being met. Where there are shortcomings, these reviews should where and how they originate. This implies that external reviews should primarily address systemic issues, identifying any problems with governance arrangements, the regulator's integrity and the broader regulatory environment for the industry in question. This can also include examining key decisions by the regulator that have strategic significance.

In addition, a key focus of reviews should be to evaluate the practical impact of recent changes to the legislative framework or other key elements of the regulator's operating environment.

KEY CHARACTERISTICS OF A GOOD EXTERNAL REVIEW PROCESS

External reviews should, in general, be initiated by a body other than the regulator itself—typically the minister or cabinet, or the legislature. The regulator's governing body may determine it is appropriate to initiate an external review itself in certain circumstances, such as where no external review has been conducted for a long time. An external review is likely to be more widely perceived as credible and independent.

The key characteristics of a high-quality independent review process

1. Pre-scheduling of reviews

There is often opposition to conducting performance reviews within the public sector. This may be due to concern that negative conclusions will create political problems. In addition, reviews of an independent regulator by the supervisory ministry may be seen—or at least presented—as amounting to political interference.

These factors suggest that pre-scheduling reviews to be conducted at specified future times can help ensure that they are undertaken. Review clauses are frequently included in the legislation that establishes, or governs the operation of, the regulator. A legislated review requirement, typically stating that a review must be completed by a certain date (or that reviews should be conducted at specified, minimum intervals), arguably provides the highest level of assurance that a review will proceed. Alternative approaches include having government pre-announce future reviews as part of major policy statements in respect of the relevant sector; and assigning responsibility for developing a program of performance reviews of key public bodies to an appropriate body with the requisite skills, experience and independence, typically the Auditor-General's department.

Reviews should be conducted more frequently in the early stages of reform implementation, when significant changes to regulatory governance or other matters affecting the regulator's operations will more likely occur. Addressing such changes and issues in a timely way is important for successful reform. Reviews can be scheduled for specific dates (e.g., 3 or 4 years after a new regulatory agency starts operations, or after it takes on responsibility for regulating a new sector) or can be triggered by specific events (e.g., a review may be required within, say, 2 years after a mobile phone spectrum auction has occurred).

2. A Review Body

The key characteristics required of the review body are that it should be independent and have sufficient technical expertise. Reviews should be undertaken by a body that is (and is seen to be) independent of both the regulator and other major interests in the industry, particularly those of the main regulated entities. Some possible models include:

- **Review by an independent expert body**. Responsibility for developing a program of performance reviews can be given to an independent body, such as an auditor-general, not subject to government direction.
- **Review by expert consultants**. This approach may be attractive in low-capacity environments, due to its potential to bring high-level expertise to bear. Having international consultants conduct the review will minimize any perceived problems of conflict of interest. However, care will be needed to ensure that the consultants understand the low-income (or post-fragile) environment and the key issues arising from it. Cost may also be prohibitive, although support may potentially be available from donor bodies.
- **Review by ministerial panel**. The Minister responsible for the regulator may appoint an ad hoc review panel. In this case, the composition of the panel is particularly important. At a minimum, there should be representation from central agencies (i.e., Finance department, Chief Minister's department) to ensure a "whole-of-government" perspective is taken. Independent regulatory experts (e.g., academics) and those from international agencies should

also be considered. Box 11.1 provides an example of a performance evaluation by a ministerial committee in Nepal.

- **Review by a parliamentary committee**. This model is likely to be used where the prescheduled review requirement is included in legislation. A parliamentary committee can second experts to work with it during the inquiry and can take evidence from sector experts as part of public hearings.

Reviews conducted by an independent expert body, such as an auditor-general, are likely to have high levels of credibility among stakeholders, as they are usually free from political influence. Conversely, where a supervising minister appoints expert consultants or a review panel to conduct reviews, transparency in the appointment process and in the setting of terms of reference for the review will be important to ensure credibility. Box 11.2 exemplifies how different models for review of a regulator were used at different points in time.

Review by a parliamentary committee may give rise to concerns regarding independence, especially in circumstances in which the government has a substantial parliamentary majority. In addition, there may be problems in ensuring that adequate technical expertise is available, particularly if budget constraints prevent the appointment of external experts to assist the process. Care is thus needed in assessing whether such a model is likely to yield credible results.

3. Good review process and methodology

Following a good review process is essential to ensure that the outcome both identifies key issues

---

BOX 11.1

Performance evaluation at the Nepal Telecommunications Authority

The Nepal Telecommunications Authority recently reappointed its CEO for a second, 5-year term. Prior to that, the Ministry of Information and Communications formed a committee to review his performance during his initial term. While this review appears to have been an ad hoc decision, scheduling performance reviews prior to discrete, major events affecting the regulator, such as the appointment of a new CEO, can help ensure that such reviews occur with appropriate frequency.

BOX 11.2

Australia's Essential Services Commission Act develops review mechanism and timing of review, which lead to mandate changes for the regulator

The Essential Services Commission (ESC) is a multisectoral infrastructure regulator established under the Essential Services Commission Act (ESCA). Section 66 of the ESCA. requires the responsible minister to ensure that the Act was reviewed within 5 years of it coming into operation. Specific review objectives identified were:

1. to determine whether the objectives of the Act and of the Commission are being achieved and are still appropriate; and
2. whether the Act is effective or whether it required amendment to "further facilitate" the objectives or to insert new objectives.

Section 66 also requires the minister to table the review report and the government's response to it in parliament within a set time. A review was conducted in 2006–07 by a retired civil service department head, assisted by a group of Ministry of Finance officials.

The ESC was given progressively broader functions by government and its operating environment changed in many ways. While no subsequent review requirement is contained in the Act, the government commissioned a second review, which reported approximately 10 years after the first. This review was conducted by a Ministry of Finance team, assisted by specialist consultants.

and potential solutions and is seen as credible by stakeholders. A fundamental requirement is that the review body has sufficient time to undertake a thorough assessment. Also, in a rapidly evolving market and regulatory environment, conclusions and recommendations need to be delivered in a timely manner. Where major reviews are undertaken, a review period of 6–12 months is quite likely appropriate.

The review should be open to stakeholders and the public. This means the review body should seek written submissions from stakeholders and the public and that enough time should be allowed for these to be developed. Participation through public hearings is also a key good process element, since it:

- enables the reviewers to question interested parties and engage in dialogue on key matters;
- provides opportunities for those who may not be well-placed to make written submissions to participate. This can include community organizations, small local government bodies and the general public.

To enable interested parties to participate effectively, the review body should publish a discussion paper which briefly describes the main issues to be addressed in the review and identifies key questions on which stakeholder input is invited. This can include requests for quantitative data as well as qualitative information and opinions.

Finally, the review should identify the criteria according to which it will assess the performance of the regulator and (where relevant) the regulated sector. These criteria should be derived directly from the objectives, functions and responsibilities of the regulator, as identified by the government and often, by legislation. These should be supported by the development of relevant indicators, discussed below.

DEVELOPING INDICATORS

Regulators should develop performance indicators, directly linked to their objectives and functions, as part of their ongoing performance management function. These indicators should avoid creating perverse incentives—that is, encourage staff to act in a certain way to achieve a high score on an indicator—when this is not necessarily consistent with achieving the underlying objectives of the regulator.

Identifying indicators early in the regulator's development helps ensure that data collection starts early, thus maximizing data availability. However, it will usually be necessary to refine the indicators, or add new indicators over time, as weaknesses or gaps in existing indicators are identified. Public bodies frequently pursue multiple, conflicting objectives, (e.g., affordable electricity, self-funding sector and an attractive investment environment). This implies that a range of indicators is needed to ensure performance is measured against all relevant objectives, and conclusions can be drawn about which trade-offs to make.

The indicators developed should include those that relate to:

- final outcomes sought; and
- matters over which the regulator has direct control.

That is, both the regulator and the external reviewers should have information to allow good assessments to be made of both the extent to which the government's reform objectives for the sector are being met and the extent to which the regulator is helping to achieve them.

Over the long term, and where possible, the analysis of indicators should draw on time series and cross-sectional data, including international comparisons. Expert interpretation of indicators may be helpful, particularly where performance is being assessed against multiple indicators. However, this level of analysis may not be feasible in the post-conflict stage.

The regulator should publish indicator data as part of its annual reporting cycle, in addition to using them as part of the review process. This helps stakeholders scrutinize the regulator's performance and to advocate for review or change where they identify significant problems.

A regulator's performance should be assessed by quantifiable indicators of activities. For example, a key indicator for many regulators may be processing times for regulatory approval or other decisions. These are important because undue delays in regulatory processes impose additional costs on business and the community, so regulators should measure their processing times for key decisions against specified benchmarks (Victorian Competition and Efficiency Commission 2012). Changes in the size of the regulator's budget over time should also be monitored and assessed in the context of changes in the extent of its regulatory responsibilities.

Indicators of the final outcomes sought are likely to include increases in investment and output in the regulated industry, as well as average prices. The regulator can clearly not be held fully accountable for these outcomes. However, reporting on these indicators can focus on key elements of the regulator's performance influencing them. For example, the time taken to assess and approve license applications is one partial measure of the attractiveness of the business environment.

BOX 11.3

Evaluation of the Rwanda Utilities Regulatory Authority

In common with all Rwandan public institutions, RURA is subject to regular external performance evaluation, as required by Organic Law No. 06/2009 OL, Article 5. RURA's performance is evaluated under a performance contract agreed between its Board and the Ministry of Infrastructure, its supervising ministry. These performance contracts have specified durations, but are renegotiated on expiry.

In addition to this external review requirement, RURA has, since 2013, been required by its Board to develop an annual action plan that is, among other things, used by the governing body as the basis of an internal performance evaluation.

USING PERFORMANCE EVALUATION

Performance evaluation is a tool that enables performance improvements to be achieved progressively over time, enhancing governance and individual capacity. Publishing reviews contributes to this outcome, since making available assessments of existing performance to all stakeholders will put pressure on the government to adopt review recommendations. A requirement for government to respond formally to the review, including in legislation, can contribute toward the executive taking ownership of review recommendations and acting on them. This is a frequently overlooked element of a performance evaluation system. For example, while the statutory requirement for all Rwandan public bodies to be subject to regular performance evaluations against the terms of an agreed performance contract (discussed in box 11.3) represented an important step forward in the post-fragile context, the system does not yet require making public the results of the evaluation. This means the performance evaluation system is not backed up by an effective public accountability and feedback mechanism.

In the long term, the criteria used in performance evaluations should form the basis of individual performance assessments of key regulator staff, helping to ensure that their performance is aligned as closely as possible with the regulator's overall performance objectives.

DEVELOPING PERFORMANCE EVALUATION OVER TIME IN POST-FRAGILE COUNTRIES

A fully developed performance evaluation system as described above requires significant expertise and resources and is unlikely to be feasible in the immediate post-fragile context, although governments such as those in Rwanda have made impressive progress. Thus, an important consideration is how to implement a set of feasible but useful requirements in the short term and build progressively on them over time.

One aspect of this issue is the scope of evaluation. Starting by requiring regulators to conduct internal evaluations will help to instill a culture of performance assessment into these organizations from an early stage. In the short term, expert resources to conduct external assessments are likely to be in short supply. Hence, if an independent agency such as an auditor-general is tasked with conducting external evaluations, the range of regulatory bodies it can evaluate is likely to be limited due to capacity constraints. Thus, government must identify priority regulators based on their strategic importance to the wider economy and society, and focus external evaluations on them.

Early performance evaluation systems should be restricted to a relatively narrow range of indicators, with the initial focus being on assessing the regulator's effectiveness and efficiency in carrying out its specific functions, rather than seeking to measure its larger strategic impact. Such indicators can typically be measured more easily, while it should be possible to obtain inputs from regulated entities to assist in developing assessments.

Finally, publication of the results of performance evaluations can be undertaken from the outset and are likely to add significant value by enabling discussion and critique of these reports by stakeholders and experts, both domestically and, potentially, internationally.

CONCLUSION

This chapter has outlined the importance of performance evaluation as an essential feedback mechanism that provides information on what is being done well and or badly. It argues that it can reinforce positive behaviors and provide incentives to address problems. Further, it enables the regulator and the government to demonstrate the benefits of reform to stakeholders and helps to validate the regulatory model chosen. Box 11.4 contains several aspects to consider with regards to instituting performance evaluations for regulators.

BOX 11.4

Applying the principles for performance evaluation

1. All major regulators should be subject to regular, independent external reviews, in addition to any internal review activity.
2. External reviews should be prescheduled—the dates for the completion of future reviews should be fixed in advance. These review schedules should be set out in legislation or in a substantial, publicly available policy document.
3. In a fully functioning review process, the scope of the review should cover both the effectiveness and efficiency with which the regulator carries out its functions and meets its objectives and the regulator's impact on the broader infrastructure sector. However, in early post-fragile contexts, the scope of these reviews should be limited to the former.
4. Where capacity constraints limit the number of reviews that can be undertaken, the most economically significant regulators and those believed to be experiencing significant performance problems should be given priority.
5. Substantial regulatory changes should be a priority matter for assessment as part of the review process.
6. Regulators should be required to establish internal review processes at an early stage and embed a culture of feedback and self-improvement. These processes should continue even where regular external reviews are undertaken.
7. Regulators should identify indicators that can be used to assess key elements of their performance within the context of the review process. These should include both "input" indicators, relating specifically to the regulator's actions, and "outcome" indicators, which focus on the government's key objectives for the sector (e.g., growth in infrastructure investment).
8. Time series and cross-sectional (i.e., international) comparisons and peer expertise and evaluation should be used as part of the review process.
9. The performance evaluation criteria and results of the reviews should be published.
10. The performance evaluation criteria should be reflected in performance assessments of regulator staff, where possible.

REFERENCE

Victorian Competition and Efficiency Commission. 2012. *Annual Report 2011–12*. Melbourne: Victorian Competition and Efficiency Commission.

C Implementing Reforms to Regulatory Systems and Governance

Part B identified and explained the importance of applying a set of principles in designing and assessing systems of governance for regulators and examined some key elements related to their practical implementation, particularly in post-fragile contexts. Part C provides more strategic advice on adopting and maintaining a program of regulatory reform in one or more infrastructure sectors, including the establishment of a regulatory agency in accordance with the principles set out in Part B.

It is not possible to address the whole range of implementation issues in a manual this length. However, the following chapters discuss some of the most common and significant:

- **Chapter 12** examines the need to gain and mobilize support for reform, how to engage stakeholders in the development of regulatory policy, and the importance of transparency in the consultation process.

- **Chapter 13** points out the value of, and need for, coordinating reform at the center of government and the merits of developing a broader, government-wide regulatory policy.
- **Chapter 14** discusses capacity requirements for successful reform.
- **Chapter 15** indicates how to develop a reform strategy and the challenges faced. And
- **Chapter 16** concludes by highlighting how to ensure that the reform strategy is sustained over time, including ongoing commitment, continuity and policy stability.

Mobilizing and Engaging Pro-Reform Forces

INTRODUCTION

This chapter aims to explain the importance of mobilizing and engaging pro-reform forces to support planned and actual reform projects and to provide strategies for achieving this goal. The Public Utility Research Center (PURC) at the University of Florida and the World Bank's *Body of Knowledge on Infrastructure Regulation* notes:

> It is commonly understood that 75 percent of people in authority need to "buy into" a change for it to be successful. Furthermore, any significant change needs a critical mass of supporters who formulate and guide the strategy from beginning to end.
>
> (BoKIR 2019)

Plans for major reform to the market structure and regulation of major infrastructure industries almost always face substantial opposition from different groups:

- **Citizens and civil society groups** may object to reform due because of the possible consequences on consumers (particularly vulnerable ones) when government monopolies are broken up and/or competition from private companies is introduced.
- **Government monopoly providers** also typically oppose reform. The establishment of a competitive market creates substantial new challenges for them and diminishes their political and economic influence.
- **Several political actors** will also likely oppose reform, since appointments to major state-owned infrastructure enterprises are often important sources of patronage, and revenues from regulatory taxes can be used to fund activities unrelated to infrastructure.

The lengthy periods required to fully implement major reforms create ample opportunities for opponents to frustrate the process. Their actions can lead to government reform plans being delayed, in design changes that compromise underlying reform objectives, and even in the abandonment of reforms altogether. This dynamic is present in virtually all countries, but is particularly acute in the post-fragile context due to weaker institutions, less transparent politics and more pervasive networks of patronage and corruption.

Consequently, working to address concerns about the potential negative impacts of reform, as well as mobilizing groups and organizations to support reform, is a key strategy in improving its prospects of success. Engagement should be undertaken on a sustained basis with a wide range of officials and stakeholders, including NGOs and community service organizations, as outlined in chapter 9. This should aim to identify and discuss implementation issues and consider options for achieving the required goals more effectively and at least cost. The process should include ministers, relevant senior officials, civil society organizations and interested donor agencies. Importantly, this process should involve consumers from the sectors affected, including both businesses and households.

Mobilizing support within the public sector

Gaining the support of the boards and senior managers of state-owned enterprises for major reform in the infrastructure sector is typically a major challenge. Indeed, these groups often actively oppose reform. Moves to introduce competition and the privatization of state enterprises are typically seen as threats by the boards and senior managers affected, particularly if they have benefitted illegally from their positions. Box 12.1 illustrates this problem with the case of Georgia's electricity sector after independence.

It is therefore important that reform include, as far as possible, incumbent infrastructure providers as a key part of the reform process. In many cases, support can only be gained with the replacement of opposing board members and managers—politically challenging where board members or senior managers were appointed as a reward for political support. For example, in Nepal, the government responded to long-standing opposition to reform by the Nepal Electricity Authority by appointing a new, reformist CEO and removing two Board members who were seen as particularly obstructive. However, this then obliged the government to defend its actions in the Supreme Court. This case highlights both the need for governments to be willing to take strong action to address systematic attempts to frustrate reform and to ensure that such actions

BOX 12.1

The power sector in Georgia after independence

The centrally planned economy of the USSR was largely integrated with the economies of the constituent republics. Georgia's power sector was thus not designed for independent operation. Private enterprise was not allowed and state management inefficient. The power system was run by Sakenergo, a state-owned monopoly roiled in economic crisis, political unrest, internal conflict, and corruption. Political upheavals frequently disrupted the generation and supply of power, which was further impaired by widespread theft of power, equipment, and materials. An extremely low (5 percent) collection rate of fees led to a lack of revenue and resulted in an absence of capital for investment and for the repair and maintenance of infrastructure. The system became unstable, further damaging plant and equipment, and planned reforms were often delayed because of the opposition of board members and senior officials (Lampietti, Banerjee, and Branczik 2007).

have a legal basis strong enough to withstand powerful challenges from vested interests. Box 12.2 illustrates the point.

While governments can and do take strong action against state-owned enterprises seeking to undermine reform, questions about the durability of these changes inevitably arise. The problem is that in the absence of systemic changes to the management of these SOEs, the underlying incentives to oppose reform remain and the possibility of the changes being reversed is real. Infrastructure reform measures should thus target not only the agencies involved but also the underlying governance issues in respect of these organizations. Replacing individual CEOs and/or Board members with appointees more favorable to reform is not enough. Only by addressing the governance of these organizations will enduring, systemic change become feasible. This involves assessing the governance arrangements of the key SOEs in the sectors undergoing reform against principles similar to the ones set out in Part B.

BOX 12.2

Reform in the Malagasy electricity industry

When, after 5 years of political instability and declining economic performance, Madagascar returned to stability in 2014, the electricity system was in a poor state. Jirama, a vertically integrated state-owned utility governing Madagascar's electricity sector faced a deteriorating operational and financial situation. The utility was unable to collect sufficient revenues to meet expenses and faced rising input costs, primarily for imported fuel. Customers suffered frequent load shedding.

The country needed better sector management and more investment. Political interference and an absence of accountability, combined with a lack of sector planning, led to non-transparent, inefficient, and costly decisions. For example, in responding to private companies offering to generate power, Jirama frequently agreed to buy electricity at a price higher than what it could sell it for.

To resolve these issues and promote private investment in power generation, the Government, with substantial World Bank support, embarked on a major reform program in 2015–16. In the short term, the program aims to improve Jirama's performance. The Government appointed a new Energy Minister in April 2017 and recruited a new Director-General and Deputy Director-General for Jirama via competitive and transparent processes. New board members were appointed, and a new Chairman elected in May 2017. Jirama's new Board of Directors has developed detailed job descriptions for all senior management positions, forming the basis of a competitive recruitment process launched in 2018 for all positions reporting directly to the Director-General.

Nonetheless, the reform's success will depend upon continuing Government commitment. In the short to medium term, this will largely involve supporting the new Board of Directors and senior management in overcoming the resistance of most existing private-sector operators (who fear the loss of unduly profitable power purchase agreements) and addressing excessive staffing levels while assuaging the unemployment fears of union members.

In the longer term, success will depend substantially on the Government's ability to pass legislative changes that can both improve Jirama's governance and strengthen the hand of the industry regulator, ORE. More broadly, strengthening ORE's authority and financial resources will help, as it will underpin the development of a more open and competitive industry and spur Jirama to be effectively managed.

Source: World Bank 2016.

Mobilizing consumers as pro-reform forces

The beneficiaries of reform include many domestic consumers and businesses to whom telecommunications and electricity services, for example, are production inputs. Such clients typically stand to benefit from lower prices, greater reliability of supply and more innovative service offerings. Hence, it should be possible to mobilize significant support for reform from both these groups, although low-income customers typically fail to benefit in the short term and may require continuing subsidies for the purchase of electricity.

A key requirement here is to communicate how and how much stakeholders will benefit from reform in ways that are readily understandable to them. These messages are likely to have greater credibility if it is explained to them why the reform process will lead to better outcomes.

Attempts to mobilize stakeholder support should ideally commence as early as possible—that is, after a proposed reform program has been announced and prior to detailed reform design being undertaken. This is important because successful efforts to mobilize stakeholder support in these early stages will help change the political dynamics of reform, increasing the actual and expected benefits and reducing the costs. This will increase the likelihood that systematic reforms will be adopted in practice, rather than being abandoned or diluted as opposition is mounted by vested interests. The larger the pro-reform constituency mustered, the greater the political cost to governments of failing to carry through their reform proposals.

One major complicating factor must be highlighted. This is that in post-fragile contexts, reforms in some sectors often lead to significant price rises in the short to medium term. This usually happens if prices in a given sector have been set at artificially low levels for political reasons and price regulation is removed.

For low-income consumers the prospect of significant price rises is a major concern, which can be used by vested interests to stir up feeling against reform. This can make the task of gathering support for the reform agenda from consumers challenging. However, given that during conflict many users may have paid more for intermittent, suboptimal services from informal service providers, they could well be more amenable to reforms than assumed.

Potential strategies to engage these consumers include:

- focusing on the benefits expected from reform, including reliability of service;
- adopting measures to protect the interests of low-income consumers.

In some cases, it may also be necessary to correct distorted regulated prices before the reform process begins in order to prevent reform being seen as the cause of the price rises and consequently being opposed by key groups.

ENGAGING STAKEHOLDERS IN THE EVOLUTION OF REGULATORY POLICY

In addition to seeking to enlist key stakeholders, including consumers and business users, as supporters of the reform process, it is essential to engage them in the design and development of the reforms.

Ongoing stakeholder engagement, as outlined in chapter 9, is a key element in regulatory review and reform. However, the need for adequate stakeholder interaction is particularly acute in post-fragile countries. This is because a key objective here is to obtain private (and largely foreign) investment to underpin the development of the system. Concerns about the quality of the regulatory environment often deter such investments. Thus, engaging with stakeholders to ensure their concerns are understood and that proposed reforms are supported is all-important in improving investment prospects.

Stakeholder engagement should therefore start at an early stage in the development of the proposed reform program. This will help to ensure that its design reflects their priorities and concerns and will help create an attractive investment environment. Such engagement should be sustained over time, with additional opportunities for stakeholder input as the proposed regulatory scheme is developed in more detail.

Engagement should also be a significant part of the ongoing policy review and revision process. For major regulatory reforms are rarely "one-off" processes. Instead, it is typically necessary to closely monitor and review the performance of the reforms to identify blockages and design further reforms to address these. Stakeholder engagement is likely to be at least as valuable in this "*ex-post*" context, in which investments have already been made and market participants can speak credibly about the conditions they face, the unanticipated impacts of government policies as they relate to their investments, competition issues and other factors bearing on the ability of the reform to achieve its objectives.

However, as in any consultation process, it is necessary to guard against specific voices becoming unduly influential, potentially leading to capture. Developing formal mechanisms to undertake consultations and ensuring that the stakeholder engagement process is as open and transparent as possible constitute significant safeguards, as examined in chapter 9.

In principle, stakeholder engagement during the policy review and revision process should be simply one element of a larger, continuing process. Box 12.3,

---

BOX 12.3

Stakeholder engagement by the Georgian National Energy and Water Supply Regulatory Commission

Georgia's Law on Electricity and Natural Gas (LENG), requires a high degree of transparency in GNEWSRC's activities, as well as continuous stakeholder engagement in relation to a wide range of GNEWSRC activities. The legislation requires that GNEWSRC's sessions, decisions, resolutions, orders, minutes and documents are all available to the public and interested parties. This provides the basis for a very full engagement between the Commission, stakeholders and the public, since they have access not only to substantial information on the work of the Commission but also to the reasoning behind it. The high level of transparency provided also greatly reduces the potential for regulatory capture and conflicts of interest.

The LENG also establishes rules for meetings of the Commissioners and their employees with interested parties, with a Commissioner being required to notify stakeholders in advance, and in writing, of consultations, and to provide them with an opportunity to take part. The LENG and the Law of Georgia on the Conflict of Interest and Corruption in Public Service also ban Commissioners and their staff from having any direct or indirect stake or economic interest in any licensee, importer, exporter, supplier or market operation, or hold any positions in such enterprises.

below, highlights the approach taken to stakeholder engagement by the Georgian National Energy and Water Supply Regulatory Commission.

Ensuring adequate stakeholder representation

As suggested above, effective and credible stakeholder engagement requires consulting a wide range of interests and weighing their opinions. This is essential to avoid regulatory capture by major stakeholders, and to assure that policymakers benefit from all relevant inputs.

Making certain that the consultation process is open to all interested parties is a basic requirement for credible engagement. However, a significant issue in many post-fragile contexts is that there may not be groups organized to represent stakeholder interests or, where such groups exist, their membership and resources may be very limited.

This implies a need for governments to consider providing active support for such groups, with the aim of encouraging their growth and ability to engage on policy and reform issues. It also underlines the importance of providing key information on reform plans and options in a clear, easy-to-understand form.

Using the principles as the basis for stakeholder engagement

The principles for the governance of regulators set out in chapter 9 can be a useful basis for structuring stakeholder engagement. The principles constitute a framework for reform proposals that clearly identify the underlying logic and purpose of the reform program. By receiving clear information about a reform's rationale, stakeholders will be better able to assess the appropriateness and effectiveness of key reform elements and offer alternatives where needed.

Transparency of the consultation process

In addition to being open to the views of all parties, consultation processes must be transparent. Effective consultations provide complete information about which institutions and individuals have engaged and what opinions they have put forward. Wherever possible, submissions made during consultations should be published, as should summaries of meetings with stakeholders and the public.

CONCLUSION

Consultations provide a cost-effective way of identifying the strengths and weaknesses of reform proposals as well as of gathering any further information needed. They also help identify faulty reasoning and those parts of the proposal (and in some cases the entire proposal) that are likely to fail because unacceptable to major stakeholders. Any changes made can be incorporated in the final reform proposal.

This chapter stressed the importance of mobilizing and engaging with pro-reform forces. It focused on the need to secure support in the public sector as well as from existing infrastructure providers and the public, emphasizing the need to guarantee adequate and effective representation from all major stakeholders at all stages.

REFERENCES

BoKIR (Body of Knowledge on Infrastructure Regulation). 2019. "A Narrative: Developing and Improving Infrastructure Regulation in Fragile and Conflict-Affected States: Revitalizing and Reforming Regulatory Governance for Infrastructure in post-FCV Environments." http://regulationbodyofknowledge.org/a-narrative-developing-and-improving -infrastructure-regulation-in-fragile-and-conflict-affected-states/.

Lampietti, J. A., S. G. Banerjee, and A. Branczik. 2007. *People and Power: Electricity Sector Reforms and the Poor in Europe and Central Asia*. Washington, DC: World Bank.

World Bank. 2016. "MG-Electricity Sector Operations and Governance Improvement Project (ESOGIP) (P151785)." Implementation Status and Results Report PAD1147, World Bank, Washington, DC.

13

Central Coordination of Reform

INTRODUCTION

The previous chapter argued that developing and implementing a robust reform proposal is challenging, with numerous vested interests acting to oppose and/or undermine change. Working to build and maintain coalitions of pro-reform forces can help address this dynamic, while formal engagement processes can help clarify, and apply scrutiny to, the arguments of those opposed to reform, and to counter these arguments effectively.

Building support for reform requires communicating, monitoring and building capacity within government as well as working and communicating with stakeholders outside government. Establishing a *central coordinating body* with cross-sectoral responsibilities related to the reform agenda can help:

- consolidate and coordinate support for the reform agenda, including overall responsibility for the continuing engagement process;
- promote efficiency, as many challenges to be addressed in implementing reform will be broadly similar across different sectors, or industries;
- promote consistency, as the principles underlying the reform program will be similar across sectors.

Giving oversight and coordination authority to a single body at the center of government helps to ensure the overall consistency of reform across sectors and to boost the reform agenda.

ESTABLISHING A SPECIALIST BODY TO COORDINATE AND MONITOR REFORM

Such a body is most appropriately located in a ministry at the center of government, with broad, "whole-of-government" coordination responsibilities. This is most likely a Prime Minister's/President's office or a Ministry of Finance, but could also be a separate Ministry for Infrastructure established for this purpose, as in Georgia, Kosovo, Madagascar and Rwanda (see box 13.1). Locating the reform body in a central ministry increases its authority and helps ensure that a broad view of key issues is taken. Establishing a separate Infrastructure Ministry, if it is provided with the leadership of a senior minister and appropriate resources, can do the same.

BOX 13.1

A ministry for reform coordination

In Georgia, one of the most prominent members of the Government, the Minister for Economic Development, Khaka Bendukidze, was appointed as State Minister for Reform Coordination in 2004, with wide-ranging responsibilities embracing reform of both the public sector and the regulatory system. His appointment ensured that reform efforts in different sectors were effectively integrated at the political level and exercised by a Minister with strong authority within the government. The Minister was supported by a new Office of the State Minister for Reform Coordination. During the following years, Georgia rose substantially in the World Bank's Doing Business rankings, at 100 in 2006, 37 in 2007 and 18 in 2008. Unfortunately, while a wide-ranging program of regulatory reform was adopted, it was not guided or coordinated by an explicit policy on systemic regulatory reform or governance during this period. Thus, while responsibility for reform was handed to a single, powerful minister, the absence of an explicit, overarching reform strategy meant that there was no explicit policy to guide the design and implementation of consistent reform efforts.

Key functions of a central reform body

As suggested above, establishing a central reform body helps to promote consistent approaches to reform, while also lifting the profile of the reform agenda and strengthening it within government (see the example of Rwanda in box 13.2). The central reform body can contribute to these outcomes by undertaking a range of reform-related activities such as:

1. Advocacy

Key to the central reform body's role is promoting understanding of the benefits of reform, and the ways through which the reform of key infrastructure and other sectors will achieve wider benefits for society. This function should be undertaken both within government and externally.

2. Monitoring and feedback

A central body responsible for individual regulators can take an independent view of reform progress and function as a source of unbiased advice to government about the performance of the reform agenda. This can contribute to more rapid identification of key problems and the development of effective solutions.

3. Capacity development

Access to staff with relevant expertise is frequently a problem for newly established regulatory agencies, and one particularly acute in post-fragile environments. A central coordinating body can help here in at least two ways. First, it can help provide training to ministries and regulatory agency staff and publish relevant materials and resources. Second, it can improve the ability of the civil service to recruit expert staff by undertaking recruitment centrally.

DEVELOPING A REGULATORY GOVERNANCE POLICY FOR THE INFRASTRUCTURE SECTOR

A key function of a central coordination body is to develop an explicit regulatory governance policy statement covering the entire infrastructure sector.

The Rwanda Development Board—A central reform body to encourage private-sector investment

The Rwanda Development Board (RDB) was formed in 2008 from the merger of eight different bodies. RDB brings together all government agencies responsible for the investment environment, that is: Key agencies responsible for business registration, investment promotion, environmental clearances, privatization; and specialist agencies which support information and communications technologies and tourism as well as small and medium enterprises and human capacity development in the private sector. Independent and influential, the RDB reports directly to the President and is guided by a board that includes all key ministers.

RDB has managed to improve several areas related to the country's investment climate. The country was a top reformer in the World Bank's Doing Business report in 2010 and 2014, and the country's ranking improved from 158 in 2007 to 41 in 2018. At the same time, the number of registered firms increased by 24 percent between 2011 and 2014 and employed 24 percent more workers.

Sources: Rwanda Development Board Website (https://rdb.rw/); World Bank 2016, 2018.

Infrastructure investments are typically characterized by large sunk costs, low mobility of assets, and site specificity, all of which mean they are vulnerable to sovereign risks due to major and unexpected changes in government policies. Hence, infrastructure investors assess the effectiveness and integrity of a country's legal and regulatory institutions as a vital part of their due diligence process. They are looking for governments and agencies that have a clear infrastructure strategy and that operate within a well-designed and effective legal and regulatory system. This poses a major challenge for most fragile and post-fragile countries, as they typically do not possess, or are only beginning to develop, clear infrastructure strategies and well-developed regulatory systems. In addition, major infrastructure assets have often been destroyed, badly damaged or neglected during the conflict, making the task of restarting investment urgent.

Explicit policy statements that provide a broader framework for understanding the focus and priorities of the regulatory reform agendas being adopted are relatively common in developing countries. In some cases, such as that of Rwanda[1] and Mauritius (Government of Mauritius 2007) the focus has been on elaborating sectoral plans. A still broader approach, addressing all infrastructure industries in a single policy statement, can potentially yield significantly greater benefits in terms of consistent, strategic policy orientation and consequent increases in investor confidence.

Such policies and plans are typically examined in detail by domestic and international investors considering buying into a country's infrastructure networks. In particular, such investors pay attention to a government's expressed intentions in respect of private participation and the policy elements that support them (or, conversely, which fail to do so, as, for example, in Tanzania [OECD 2013]). A well-developed policy and/or plan, maintained over the lifespan of several governments, clearly signals to investors that the country is committed to infrastructure development with private participation.

However, many such policy statements fail to focus on the importance of developing and maintaining good regulatory systems for infrastructure development. In Rwanda, for example, despite strong policies encouraging foreign private infrastructure investment, none of the sector plans for infrastructure listed on the Ministry of Infrastructure's website mention regulatory governance policy. Consistent feedback from actual and potential investors in many low-income and post-fragile countries indicates that the quality of the regulatory system helps shape their view of the attractiveness of the investment environment. A regulatory policy within these plans can greatly improve their practical effectiveness and help attract investment.

Elements of a regulatory governance policy statement for infrastructure sectors

An infrastructure-specific regulatory governance policy statement should:

1. Focus on the organization, processes, tools and norms of interaction, decision-making, monitoring and evaluation used by government organizations and their counterparts in the private sector.
2. Follow a sound strategic approach to infrastructure planning that reflects clear views of how the relevant industries are expected to develop over time and what the key objectives are in the short-, medium- and long-term.
3. Set out in broad terms the basic elements of the regulatory regime for infrastructure, specifying what regulatory agencies will be established and/or modified, with a clear allocation of roles between the institutions involved, providing a high degree of certainty for the various actors, while retaining a degree of flexibility to meet changing circumstances.
4. Encourage development, management and renewal of infrastructure that is sustainable and affordable.

The need for flexibility is important if the aim is to make one or several infrastructure sectors more competitive for private investors. Indeed, the regulatory governance policy will have to vary, depending upon the government's choice of delivery modes for infrastructure. What is appropriate for a system of state ownership of infrastructure will differ from that needed for one increasingly dominated by public-private-partnerships, or one that is entirely privatized.

The statement should specify the:

- objectives of the regulatory governance policy statement for each infrastructure sector in relation to the government's infrastructure policy and plans, particularly its choice of delivery modes;
- need to establish a small, expert advisory unit in the ministry responsible for infrastructure policy, with a description of its role, responsibilities and authority;
- responsibilities and authority of the regulatory agency or agencies responsible for infrastructure regulation;
- principles of regulatory governance that will be applied to the infrastructure sector, including those examined in Part B of this manual;
- requirement for periodic assessments of the performance of infrastructure sectors by the expert advisory unit where regulation has been recently reformed, and any recommendations for change.

In addition, there should be a less frequent requirement for a regular, major report on the regulatory governance policy statement and the system put in place to implement that policy.

A LONGER-TERM PERSPECTIVE—DEVELOPING A GOVERNMENT-WIDE REGULATORY POLICY

A key medium-term benefit of an explicit infrastructure sector policy, supported by a central coordinating body, is that it fosters a view of regulatory reform as a strategic activity taken across government, rather than a series of sector-specific initiatives. This broader view of regulation can help to pave the way for the development of a whole-of-government regulatory policy in the medium term.

While such policies are rarely adopted in the post-fragile context, and are often not feasible in the short term, moving in this direction provides the basis for broadening and deepening the reform process and achieving significantly greater benefits.

Adopting the above architecture in the context of infrastructure reform will cement several important steps that can form the foundations for a whole-of-government policy. In particular:

- Developing a policy statement and coordinating approaches to regulatory reform on the basis of guiding principles (such as those elaborated in Part B), introduces key regulatory policy principles to major stakeholders, facilitating their acceptance.
- A coordinated approach to infrastructure reform can help develop essential capacities within ministries and regulatory agencies.
- Developing a track record of effective reform in the infrastructure sector, based on principles and approaches consistently applied by a central body, can help demonstrate the benefits of applying such pathways to the reform of government regulation more broadly. Thus, it will assist in helping to develop a constituency in favor of adopting a whole-of-government regulatory policy.

The elaboration and implementation of a whole-of-government regulatory policy is largely beyond the scope of the current manual. However, given the importance of regulatory policy and the clear links with the subject of this chapter, an outline of some key considerations is provided in appendix C.

CONCLUSION

This chapter has argued the need for, and value of, a reform monitoring body at the center of government, guided by the development of a regulatory governance policy statement for the infrastructure sector. The next chapter examines the governance and individual capacity needed for successful reform.

NOTE

1. http://www.mininfra.gov.rw/index.php?id=188.

REFERENCES

Government of Mauritius. 2007. *Outline of Energy Policy 2007–2025: Towards A Coherent Strategy for the Development of the Energy Sector in Mauritius.* Port-Louis: Ministry of Public

Utilities. http://publicutilities.govmu.org/English/publications/Documents/OUTLINE%20ENERGY%20POLICY.PDF.

OECD (Organisation for Economic Co-operation and Development). 2013. OECD *Investment Policy Reviews: Tanzania 2013*. Paris: OECD Publishing. http://www.keepeek.com/Digital-Asset-Management/oecd/finance-and-investment/oecd-investment-policy-reviews-tanzania-2013_9789264204348-en#.WjMXU1WWZIw#page151.

World Bank. 2016. *Rwanda Economic Update: Rwanda at Work*. February 2016, Issue 9. Kigali: World Bank.

——. 2018. "Institutional Mechanisms for Business Environment Reforms." Unpublished note. Indicator-Based Reform Advisory, World Bank, Washington, DC.

14

The Capacity for Reform of Regulatory Governance

INTRODUCTION

Chapter 13 described the value of establishing a reform monitoring body at the center of government, together with a regulatory policy for the infrastructure sector. Both constitute a valuable, ongoing resource to ensure maintenance of a high level of regulatory performance, providing an important part of the **governance capacity** of the state. This chapter continues the emphasis on the need to establish or develop a **capacity for reform and, with it,** improved regulatory governance.

The effective reform of any regulatory system requires that there is the capacity to undertake the work involved in the following four stages of the reform process:

1. **Identifying and assessing strengths and weaknesses** in the existing system or part of the system based on the use of the 10 principles discussed in Part B of this manual, or similar instruments.
2. **Designing a strategy for reform**, including an implementation plan, such as outlined in Part C.
3. **Implementing** the strategy for reform.
4. **Monitoring and assessing** ongoing regulatory performance.

This chapter discusses the governance capacity needed in the enabling environment supporting the regulatory reform process as well as the capacity needed inside the regulator itself.

The governance capacity needed at the level of the enabling environment relates to the quality of the roles, relationships and distribution of powers and responsibilities between the legislature, the minister, the ministry, the judiciary, the regulator and the regulated entities. Internal governance dimensions include the regulator's organizational structures, standards of behavior, compliance and accountability, oversight of business processes, financial reporting and performance management.

When an infrastructure sector or several infrastructure sectors undergo reform, both the external dimensions governing the process as well as the internal dimensions must have sufficient capacity to ensure that the reform proceeds. This chapter evaluates the "external" and "internal" capacities needed.

WHOLE-OF-GOVERNMENT CAPACITY REQUIREMENTS FOR REGULATORY REFORM

This section discusses "external" governance capacity requirements for regulatory reform, identifying what is needed from the government, including regulatory agencies, supervising ministries and key actors in the infrastructure sector, representatives from regulated entities and consumers. The discussion of these requirements is laid out against the steps in the reform cycle.

To ensure that there is sufficient external governance capacity to handle infrastructure reforms, different parts of government should be mobilized and involved in the process. Establishing a set of committees like those outlined below, together with an initial schedule of meetings (a major task, given the number and seniority of the persons involved), can help facilitate this process.

Possible committees include:

- **Ministerial Coordination Committee (MCC).** Could help ensure continuing political authority for the reforms and effective coordination. It could be chaired by the Prime Minister or President, or by the Treasurer/Minister of Finance. The Minister of Economic Development/Business Affairs and the Minister of Justice should also be members, as well as the supervising ministries and the Environment Ministry. Such a committee could help vet and approve the reform, providing a powerful focal point to drive assessment, strategy design and implementation. The committee could also resolve differences between ministers and ministries and review any progress reports pertaining to the reform.
- **Reform Steering Committee (RSC).** Could help coordinate the activities, expertise and support of numerous ministries and agencies involved in the reform process. This type of whole-of-government coordination is helpful in the entire reform process, but especially in the strategy design and implementation stages. Such a committee should be chaired by a very senior official, with a representative from each relevant ministry and agency who will also be responsible for liaising with their ministry or agency. The RSC would be the key body within the governance structure for the reform project. The functions of the committee would include approving the budgetary strategy, defining and realizing outcomes, monitoring risks, quality and timelines, making policy and resourcing decisions, and assessing requests for changes to the scope of the project.
- **Project Advisory Committee (PAC).** Is helpful for large, multisector reforms with expert members drawn from top business associations, consumer associations, universities and, where relevant, project donors. It would report to the RSC, acting as a conduit for expert advice and a feedback mechanism in relation to progress, results and key problems arising. The Committee could also be useful in helping develop continuing support for, and commitment to, the reform project and wider regulatory reform in general.
- **Reform Unit (RU).** A small RU led by an experienced manager, with administrative support staff, would be heavily involved in the early stages of the reform—namely identifying any issues with an existing system of regulation and developing a reform strategy.

Whole-of-government capacity needed for the first stage of reform

The first stage of a reform process includes a detailed assessment of existing weaknesses in the system of regulatory governance. To conduct this assessment adequately, it is helpful to have a reform (or similar) unit, or a small team of individuals with:

- a thorough understanding of regulatory governance involves;
- a thorough understanding of the infrastructure sector's place in the national economy;
- familiarity with the existing system of regulatory governance in the infrastructure sector;
- the ability to use the 10 principles or similar instruments to assess strengths and weaknesses in the regulatory governance of the infrastructure sector, gained through training and previous experience in the application of the principles;
- substantial experience in both desk-based research and field research, including interview skills. Experience and skill in developing and administering an opinion survey is also often required but can be contracted out to an expert in another government agency, or a private-sector consultant working under the supervision of a member of the unit;
- substantial experience in strategy design and implementation planning;
- high-level legal, economic, budgeting, accounting and auditing skills and experience;
- experience in liaising with a range of ministries, agencies and regulated entities.

In addition, the team will require the authority and resources to:

- access the relevant records of the supervising ministries and regulatory agencies;
- undertake a survey of the senior officials in the ministries, regulatory agencies and staff of regulated entities, as well as the general public;
- interview a selection of senior officials in the ministries, regulatory agencies and staff of regulated entities.

In fragile contexts it is likely that only a few persons will have the necessary qualifications. Where this is the case, one or more consultants should be recruited and major donor agencies such as the World Bank Group can be of assistance. However, it is important that local staff be drawn upon as far as possible and, where necessary, provided with relevant training before project startup. They can later act as a small core of experienced staff that can be drawn upon for a variety of regulatory reform projects, as well as to provide advice and training in regulatory reform for all government bodies.

Whole-of-government capacity needed for the second stage of reform

Capacity required to design the reform strategy varies according to:

- Type and extent of the strengths and weaknesses identified in the first, assessment stage of the reform process. Where more weaknesses are identified, then more organizational and individual capacity will be needed to develop a strategy to address them.
- Likely support for, and resistance to, reform from key actors in the infrastructure regulatory system. In general, the greater the reform proposed, the greater resistance to the reform strategy. Hence, the latter should include consideration of how to deal with such resistance to ensure successful implementation.

Fragile countries have limited human and financial resources, so it is important that the reform strategy developed is not overly ambitious and, ideally, is broken down into stages that can be modified in due course as resources become available and opportunities reveal themselves. It is particularly important that the human and financial resources necessary for each of the stages be identified. Where the reform demands human resources that are not available, appropriate training and/or recruitment processes should be outlined and agreed in the strategy.

This stage of the reform process requires the active involvement of individuals with significant strategic planning and budgeting experience, and ideally include people who were involved in the first stage of reform.

The strategy should comprise a detailed implementation plan. In large-scale reforms the development of such a plan requires an RU team member with experience of the development of government- sector implementation plans and the capacity to liaise effectively with the ministries and agencies involved.

Also, given the need to gain approval from the highest level of government (e.g., at the ministerial level) someone active in the reform strategy development process should have significant, high-level, policy advocacy skills and experience, and have sufficient credibility with ministers and senior officials.

Whole-of-government capacity needed for the third stage of reform

During reform implementation, the RU steps back and the relevant ministries and regulatory agencies involved take a more prominent role in accordance with the implementation plan.

This phase presents three major challenges:

1. **coordinating** the range of actors and activities involved;
2. ensuring the necessary **cooperation** between different ministries and agencies, especially where substantial change is involved;
3. gaining the necessary, agreed **feedback** on implementation progress from ministries and regulatory agencies in good time.

Capacity required to implement the reform strategy varies according to:

- The extent and type of reforms to be implemented. For example, changes requiring significant drafting of existing legislation and regulation, the creation of new legislation, the creation of new regulatory agencies, or the substantial modification of existing agencies, will require considerable capacity spread across the RU, supervising ministries and regulatory agencies.
- The number of levels of government involved. Where only one level of government, for example, the national government, is involved, the capacity required is less than if individual federal state levels are also affected.
- The number of ministries and regulatory agencies involved.
- The implementation plan and schedule—a slower schedule, in general, will require less capacity because there is enough time to train members of the RU, ministries and regulatory agencies.

At this stage it is vital that appropriate, planned, human and financial resources are available in the ministries and regulatory agencies. Since relatively few of the available staff are likely to have experience in reforming regulatory governance, prior training will be required.

Whole-of-government capacity needed for the fourth stage of reform

It is important that after completion of the reform project, the reform process should have the capacity to monitor and assess **regulatory performance** at the cabinet, ministry and agency levels.

Monitoring and assessing a reform process requires:

- monitoring the routine administration of the reformed activities at the ministry and agency levels on the basis of agreed performance indicators;
- providing advice and support, particularly training, to individuals and units in the ministries and regulatory agencies;
- providing regular reports on regulatory performance to the minister and cabinet, including proposals for further regulatory reforms.

There also needs to be capacity, possibly in a reform or similar unit, to provide:

- continuing advice as to the ongoing impact of infrastructure regulation;
- a continuing source of external pressure for regulation and the need for regulatory reform, encouraging transparency and accountability.

REGULATOR CAPACITY REQUIREMENTS FOR REFORM

The regulator is a key component of the system of regulatory governance and needs appropriate capacity to administer (i.e., manage and enforce) regulation effectively—and to do so in ways that steer the behavior of target groups, such as businesses, public sector providers, consumers and citizens, that are consistent with public policy purposes. Moving from a situation where key infrastructure services (e.g., electricity, telecoms) are provided by a government monopoly to the establishment of a competitive market necessarily gives rise to substantial challenges.

The fact that sectoral reforms are usually implemented progressively, with competition spreading progressively through the various parts of the sector, means that the scale of the regulatory capacity challenge will continue to increase as time goes by. This means that a strategic approach is needed to ensure that existing regulatory capacities are identified and leveraged effectively and that they are developed over time as the size of the regulatory task expands. The development of regulatory capacities is a crucial priority to support improved regulatory governance, while failure to address this issue can have significant negative implications.

Identifying relevant capacities

A fundamental requirement is that the regulator's staff should have a clear understanding of the:

- **Technical realities of the regulated industry**. Even in fragile contexts, these capacities are likely to be in reasonable supply, since they are also needed by ministries responsible for the supervision of government monopolies. However, regulating in a developing competitive market requires a range of skills, which go beyond those required in the monopoly context.
- **Principles of competition and their application in a regulatory context**. Such skills are likely to be in short supply in the civil service in post-fragile countries, given that competition policies are often either yet to be adopted or only recently

implemented and competition authorities are, clearly, not well established, if at all. However, it may be possible to seek access to this expertise via academic institutions or via recruitment from the broader corporate sector.

- **Technical aspects of regulating a developing, competitive industry**. This includes expertise in price regulation (or, in a more developed market, in price monitoring/approvals) and the associated issue of addressing community service obligations (i.e., ensuring that the poor are protected when undertaking tariff reform). As discussed in the next section, this is likely to be an area where the assistance of external bodies, such as donor organizations, in developing and implementing training programs can help develop the needed skills.

The principles set out in Part B also emphasize the importance of establishing and maintaining systems of continuing stakeholder engagement. This is another area in which relevant expertise is needed to ensure effective implementation. Such skills are again likely to be in short supply in the civil service in post-fragile countries, suggesting the need to target other, relevant industries such as marketing and advertising to obtain access to the expertise required.

Moreover, good organizational design and management are required to ensure that a "critical mass" is achieved.

Recruiting and retaining staff

A key challenge in many developing countries is that of recruiting and maintaining staff with relevant expertise. Particularly in contexts where people with the right skills are likely to be found outside the civil service, rigid recruitment and remunerations policies can be major barriers to regulators recruiting and retaining skilled staff.

Given the strategic economic importance of ensuring good regulatory performance, seeking to include agency-specific staffing rules (e.g., offering higher salaries) within the governing statute of the regulator can be an effective way to address the capacity issue. For example, at the time of the establishment of Indonesia's competition authority (the KPPU), agency-specific staffing and remuneration rules were adopted to enable it to recruit and retain high-quality staff.

Leveraging existing capacities

A second set of capacity issues concerns the need to use scarce human resources effectively. One means of doing so, discussed briefly in Part B, is to favor the development of one or more multisectoral regulators, rather than sector-specific agencies. This option may be attractive where one infrastructure sector has already been reformed and an independent regulator established as part of this process. Where such a regulator has already developed expertise and experience, this can be leveraged by expanding its responsibilities to include a newly reformed sector. While some sector-specific expertise is necessarily required, many of the required regulatory capacities will be broadly transferable between sectors, meaning that regulatory staff who have already developed key skills and experience in one sector can be deployed into the regulation of a newly reformed sector. This can provide a core of expertise around which further staff development can be built.

This dynamic will tend to make it more likely that expanding the remit of an existing regulator will yield better regulatory outcomes in the short term than establishing a new regulator. This dynamic is likely to be a key part of the explanation for the empirical finding, noted in Part B, that expanding the scope of an existing regulator to include a newly reformed sector is a common strategy in many countries (Jordana and Levi-Faur 2010).

As suggested above, expanding the scope of an existing regulatory agency can facilitate capacity development by providing greater opportunities for staff with regulatory expertise to conduct internal training and mentoring of new recruits, particularly in a continuous and informal way. However, consideration should also be given to establishing training programs under the auspices of central government agencies which use existing regulatory expertise to provide broader training opportunities across other elements of the civil service. The World Bank Body of Knowledge highlights the importance of "knowledge gaps" as constraints on the implementation of infrastructure sector reforms in post-fragile contexts and argues that these limited professional capacities can be addressed by regulators "...organizing training, speaking at public meetings and via media, and hosting education events" (BoKIR 2019).

As noted above, the task of identifying and developing necessary capacities is one which may be greatly facilitated by strategic input from donor organizations. World Bank research highlights the importance of a context-specific approach to regulatory reform in the fragile context in particular, but notes that this approach must be developed within the context of consistent principles:

> Regulation in FCSs [fragile and conflict-affected situations] is nonstandard, because motivations, specific goals and instruments, and institutional arrangements must be peculiar to the unique circumstances of each FCS. No standard model exists for FCS, but clearly laid out principles of how institutions and businesses function, stakeholder engagements, and basic strategies appear to consistently improve outcomes.
>
> (BoKir 2019)

In this context, a collaborative approach with key international organizations may help to ensure that training is both tailored to the specific needs of the individual post-fragile context and reflective of sound regulatory principles, such as those outlined in this manual. Importantly, donor bodies can help to identify key capacity gaps and mobilize specialist expertise to address these via targeted training programs.

BUILDING GOVERNANCE CAPACITIES FOR REFORM OVER TIME

As regulatory reform programs progress, the nature and extent of the regulatory capacities required for successful implementation will continue to change and increase. Thus, the provision of capacity development programs must be a continuing process and should involve both identifying available external sources of training and developing tailored training programs within government.

A key source in the former category is that of programs provided by major donor bodies. For example, the World Bank has a well-establish *International Training Program on Utility Regulation and Strategy*, which provides intensive training aiming at enhancing economic, technical and policy skills for managing regulatory reform in the infrastructure context, as well as providing a forum for international exchange of ideas and experiences.[1]

Where tailored training is to be developed and provided within government, this should be guided by ongoing monitoring of performance and key capacity gaps. Again, external bodies may be able to assist in the diagnosis of major capacity issues and the design of appropriate programs to address them.

Communities of practice

One important mechanism in addressing these capacity development needs is participation in regional "communities of practice," which bring together infrastructure regulators from a range of similar countries. The broader role of these organizations is discussed in chapter 16. However, a key benefit of participating in them lies in the opportunity they provide to leverage expertise for key capacity development initiatives, by delivering seminars and longer-form training programs to regulators from a number of participating countries. This can enhance opportunities to benefit from knowledge transfer from academics, donor organizations and the like.

For example, since 2007, the East Asia Pacific Infrastructure Regulatory Forum has developed a core training program on the economics of infrastructure regulation, which is aimed at mid-level regulatory staff, as well as training on advanced topics for higher-level staff. Other specific training topics include public-private partnerships, stakeholder consultation, competition policy, and quality of service. Berg and Horrell (2008) highlight the fact that many regional communities of practice partner with academic institutions to provide structured training tailored to the needs of their member regulators. The authors note that a broader role of regional regulator networks in this regard can be to share information about the cost-effectiveness of different training programs and the quality of support materials.

The opportunity to share experiences and lessons through subsequent interactions via the communities of practice can also help to consolidate lessons and deepen learning. The community of practice model can also potentially be used to identify mutual assistance opportunities. For example, one member country that has made recent progress in developing expertise in a particular area may agree to provide training assistance to another member facing similar challenges.

The community of practice model can also be developed on a domestic basis. This is particularly common in federal countries, where much regulation is undertaken at subnational level, so there are often several regulators covering a particular sector within the same country.[2] However, this model can also be adopted in unitary countries. Where there are several, sector-specific regulators with responsibilities for infrastructure regulation, the development of such a forum or association can provide another mechanism for leveraging scarce regulatory capacities, enabling knowledge and experience to be shared, key issues to be discussed and approaches to high-level regulatory issues to be coordinated.

Another form of capacity-building program identified by the World Bank focuses on engagement between the regulator and a range of stakeholders to help develop a shared understanding of the views, priorities and objectives of different stakeholders (BoKIR 2019). Initiatives in these areas can help to improve communications between regulators and regulated entities and enhance the predictability of regulatory decisions by providing industry participants with a better understanding of regulators' priorities and perspectives.

CONCLUSION

This chapter highlighted the capacities needed within the system of regulatory governance, or the "external" dimensions of regulatory governance, highlighting the various structures that should be in place to ensure that a reform has the support to proceed. It also highlighted the capacities needed within the regulator itself, or the "internal" dimensions of governance to manage a reform process. It closed with a discussion of the need to adopt strategies to develop and expand regulatory capacities, starting at an early stage of the reform process. These strategies should identify relevant external sources of training and capacity development, as well as developing means of leveraging existing capacities as effectively as possible. Capacity development should remain a key concern of reform policy in the longer term, since the role of regulators generally develops and changes over time with reform implementation and the advent of more competitive markets.

The next chapter addresses the need to develop a reform strategy and key challenges in its implementation.

NOTES

1. See, for example: https://bear.warrington.ufl.edu/centers/purc/docs//PAPERS /TRAINING/ITP/Program_Brochure.pdf.
2. For example, Australia's Utility Regulators' Forum was established in 1997 to encourage cooperation between utility regulators. It aims to facilitate information exchange and the development of shared understandings of regulatory issues, promote more consistent regulatory approaches and provide a forum for discussion of new ideas about regulatory practices. See: https://www.accc.gov.au/about-us/consultative-committees/utility-regulators -forum.

REFERENCES

Berg, S., and J. Horrell. 2008. "Networks of Regulatory Agencies as Regional Public Goods: Improving Infrastructure Performance." *Review of International Organizations* 3 (2): 179–200.

BoKIR (Body of Knowledge on Infrastructure Regulation). 2019. "A Narrative: Developing and Improving Infrastructure Regulation in Fragile and Conflict-Affected States: Revitalizing and Reforming Regulatory Governance for Infrastructure in post-FCV Environments." http://regulationbodyofknowledge.org/a-narrative-developing-and -improving-infrastructure-regulation-in-fragile-and-conflict-affected-states/.

Jordana, J., and D. Levi-Faur. 2010. "Exploring Trends and Variations in Agency Scope." *Competition and Regulation in Network Industries* 11 (4): 342–60.

15

Developing a Strategy for Reform and Putting It Into Practice

INTRODUCTION

Part B provided detailed guidance on evaluating the strengths and weaknesses of existing systems of regulatory governance in relation to each of 10 principles. Chapter 12 outlined the need to make the case for reform among stakeholders within and outside government and mobilize support for the reform agenda for infrastructure regulation. Chapter 13 highlighted the potential benefits of establishing a dedicated coordination body at the center of government to promote, facilitate and monitor reform and respond to identified issues in the implementation program. It also discusses the benefits of having an explicit reform policy covering a range of infrastructure sectors. Chapter 14 outlined the need to ensure that the capacity required for effective reform was in place. Each of these factors is an important element in the development of a reform program.

This chapter addresses the next step, which is to develop and execute a strategy to improve regulatory governance in one or more infrastructure sectors. It draws upon the evaluation advice provided in Part B and provides examples.

The development of a strategy is important because it:

- Helps ensure that all relevant factors are taken into consideration in an organized and effective fashion when working to implement government policy decisions, especially when they involve substantial institutional and market change.
- Enables the relevant minister and/or the cabinet to make an informed judgment about whether and how to proceed in light of the risks involved and the resources required.
- Helps ensure the desired outputs and outcomes are delivered by making it clear who has responsibility for doing what, when and how.

As noted above, constraints such as lack of political support and technical capacities may mean that the scope of the reform program may be limited in the immediate term. However, major reform, leading to the creation of competitive infrastructure sectors that are effectively regulated by a competent, adequately resourced independent regulator must remain the longer-term goal. This means that the strategy should be based on identifying a coherent reform process that takes account of current constraints and provides a sound basis from which to move toward a comprehensive reform outcome.

Any strategy adopted needs flexibility to respond to unforeseen challenges and opportunities. A change of government, for example, might bring with it a president or prime minister strongly committed to regulatory reform, providing an opportunity to deepen and/or accelerate the pace of reform, or again achieve a particular, strategic reform outcome previously blocked. Similarly, sudden economic crises such as those experienced by several states following the global financial crisis, confront governments with the need to develop and implement new policies. In this type of situation, accelerating a strategy of regulatory reform as one element of crisis response could make sense. Having a long-term, regulatory governance reform program in place means that there is a clearly defined reform path as well as a set of objectives that can be drawn upon to respond to opportunities and challenges as they arise.

STAGING REFORM

As the above suggests, a threshold issue is whether reform is most likely to succeed if implemented as a series of distinct stages, or whether an immediate move toward a competitive industry regulated by an independent entity is feasible and appropriate.

A "one-off" reform process has the potential benefit of reducing opportunities for reform to be undermined, delayed and/or reversed by opponents. Conversely, legislating to establish a fully disaggregated infrastructure sector, with open entry for competitors and an independent regulator, may cause substantial short-term problems in many post-fragile environments. For example, where the financial position of the incumbent is poor and its ability to invest limited, it may be largely prevented from competing effectively.

In practice, varying approaches may be adopted in different infrastructure sectors, reflecting the practical differences in the technical and economic environments between sectors. Thus, for example, reform has frequently progressed more quickly in the telecommunications sector than in the electricity sector. This reflects the fact that the size of the investment required is typically substantially smaller, and the time required to develop new assets and infrastructure typically much shorter. The dominance of wireless infrastructure for voice telephony and, increasingly, internet access, has been a significant factor in this regard, enabling competitive markets to develop quickly and favoring rapid reform.

Conversely, establishing workable competition in the electricity sector is frequently found to be a longer-term and more challenging process. While a starting point of vertically integrated government monopolists is common in both sectors, an important difference is that electricity tariffs are frequently not cost-reflective in post-fragile (and other low-income country) environments, with incumbent electricity providers often in financially precarious positions and reliant on substantial subsidies from the budget sector. Other distortions also frequently exist, notably including major cross-subsidies between different consumer groups (e.g., households vs. business, or different types of commercial users).

These different starting points for reform can have major implications for reform strategy. For example, some key reform elements can have perverse effects where basic problems exist such as pricing which is not cost-reflective. In Kosovo, vertical separation of the electricity industry has apparently increased the financial pressure on the electricity-generating utility (see box 15.1).

This reflects the fact that vertical separation has led to cost increases that have not been offset by efficiency gains in downstream sectors, due to a lack of effective competition. At the same time, there is no longer any possibility of cross-subsidizing between the different elements of electricity supply.

Strategically, a key problem in moving rapidly to reform the electricity sector in such contexts is that price increases are likely to be seen as the product of reform, rather than as reflecting the removal of artificial pricing underpinned by non-transparent subsidies. In such situations, opposition to reform is likely to develop quickly. This implies there may be substantial benefits in staging reform by addressing key governance issues in relation to the incumbent monopolist **before** undertaking market restructuring.

For example, moves to make prices cost-reflective can be combined with the adoption of explicit subsidies to protect the position of priority groups such as low-income households. At the same time, working to improve governance and accountability within the incumbent electricity authority should help to achieve cost reductions due to efficiency gains and reductions in corruption and in economic losses, thus paring the size of the necessary subsidies. Corporatizing the incumbent, including adopting functional separation of key activities (i.e., generation, transmission, distribution, retail) can also provide a sound basis for future disaggregation and privatization of elements of the system, together with the introduction of market rules to enable competition.

BOX 15.1

Electricity reform in Kosovo

Kosovo has undertaken a rapid unbundling of its government-owned electricity monopoly. It started in 2008 with the separation of generation and distribution functions and was essentially completed by 2016. The government continues to own the electricity generator, KEK, while the assembly has taken the ownership interest in the transmission-system operator, KOSTT. The distribution system operator KEDS was unbundled from supply activities in January 2015 and the supply operator KESCO has been privatized. A major package of laws including the Law on Energy, Law on Electricity and the Law on the Energy Regulator was adopted in 2016. The early adoption of this reform was driven by a strong determination to achieve an industry and regulatory structure consistent with the European Union's *Acquis Communautaire* so as to participate eventually in the Energy Community—facilitating regional integration of electricity networks, with potentially significant economic gains.[a] This fact is noted explicitly in Article 1 of the Law on Electricity, which states that the

legislation was adopted *"partially in compliance with"* three electricity-related EU directives. The broader goal of eventual accession to the Energy Community itself was also a significant factor driving the reform program.

However, some industry participants have argued that the disaggregation of the electricity sector was premature and cost-increasing. They cite limited prospects of short-term entry into the generation and retail sectors in such a small market, while the substantial financial weakness of the incumbent generation entity was compounded by this move, particularly in a context in which key retail prices continue to be regulated while upstream prices are not. Thus, while the government adopted a full-scale reform for the sector, complete with unbundling and an independent regulator, market participants seem to suggest that the scale and scope of the reforms was excessive. Delaying the implementation of these changes and adopting a more staggered approach could arguably have avoided placing additional stresses on the sector.

a. Energy Community 2017.

A key consideration is that the role and functions of the regulator, and the legislation under which it operates, are appropriate to the structure and the capacity of the sector at each stage of the process. Box 15.1 highlights a case in which rapid changes in the legislative framework have been undertaken, giving rise to concerns regarding the short- to medium-term impact on the industry.

Scanning the environment

As part of the development of the reform strategy, conducting a detailed scan of the political, economic, social and legal environments will help to identify phenomena that might impact, positively or negatively, on the implementation of the program. This information can then be used to help design the reform program itself. The self-assessment tool available at the World Bank's *Body of Knowledge on Infrastructure Regulation*,[1] portal provides a useful checklist for scanning the environment and identifying relevant factors. These can be assessed for their likely impact on each of the core principles of regulation examined in Part B of the manual, as illustrated in box 15.2.

This environmental scan should be repeated periodically, as key elements are likely to change over time, requiring reconsideration of aspects of the reform program in order to respond to new opportunities or address key threats. The concept of the "policy cycle" implies that, as a general rule, major policy initiatives should be subject to regular review and reassessment. This is particularly important in the context of infrastructure sector reform, which constitutes a major paradigm shift in government policy in most post-fragile contexts.

As the aforementioned discussion on mobilizing stakeholder support underlines, it is important to engage key partners in the scanning process, especially where those developing the implementation plan lack expertise as regards one or more of the infrastructure sectors. The above checklist can function as a useful vehicle for this engagement: stakeholder group representatives can be asked to complete the self-assessment checklist and the environment scanning/principles of regulation matrix, the responses compared and analyzed, and follow-up meetings with groups of stakeholder representatives used to explore the findings and develop an overall perspective. This is particularly important where the process reveals significant differences in stakeholder views.

BOX 15.2

Scanning and principles of regulation matrix

FACTORS IDENTIFIED IN THE SCANNING PROCESS	THE CORE PRINCIPLES OF REGULATION									
	P1	P2	P3	P4	P5	P6	P7	P8	P9	P10
Economic	+	0	0	−	+	−	−	−	−	+
Political	+	−	−	−	+	0	0	0	+	0
Social	0	−	−	−	0	−	+	0	+	0
Law and Justice	−	−	+	+	+	0	0	−	+	−
Governance	0	−	+	+	+	0	0	0	+	−
Other	−	0	+	+	+	0	0	0	+	+

Note: P = principle of regulation; + = supportive of reform; 0 = neutral; − = challenge to reform.

As well as helping improve the performance of the plan by drawing on available expertise, this engagement process can:

- help ensure a continuing awareness of the progress of the reforms embodied in the plan among all stakeholders;
- provide an opportunity to enhance consensus on the need for the reforms among those likely to be affected, helping to legitimize the government's plan;
- promote "ownership" of the plan and its reforms.

Selecting and training the implementation team

A major reform program requires a small implementation team of persons with experience in regulatory policy, infrastructure operations and/or regulation and large-scale project implementation. The team should be, or become, an essential part of the reform monitoring unit described above. As expertise in these areas is likely to be in particularly short supply in fragile and post-fragile countries, the selection and the training of officials for the implementation team is a key challenge. Given the strategic importance of this group to the policy's success, the assistance of experts from major donor agencies such as the World Bank Group should be sought where possible in selecting and training team members and providing continuous advice and assistance.

Organization and governance

Governance arrangements for the implementation of the policy, including the design and functions of key organizations, should be established in the early stages of the project, in consultation with key stakeholders. The arrangements will provide an essential framework to support those responsible for the implementation of the plan. Given the duration of the project, governance arrangements should be reviewed and adjusted at scheduled points, especially where there is a change in senior members of the implementation team. The following section provides examples of the organization of the key units and members of the bodies involved in a reform plan.

Substantial, ongoing political commitment is needed to ensure the success of projects of this nature. This suggests, as indicated in chapter 14, the need for a standing Ministerial Coordination Committee to ensure both continuing political authority for the reforms and effective coordination. The Ministerial Coordination Committee (MCC) could be chaired by the Prime Minister or President, or by the Treasurer/Minister of Finance. The Minister of Economic Development/Business Affairs and the Minister of Justice should also be members. In a federal state, the MCC might also include the prime ministers of each federal state. In addition, it would be valuable to have a standing "Stakeholder Advisory Group," reporting to the MCC, acting as a conduit for expert advice and a feedback mechanism in relation to progress, results and key problems arising.

Appropriate functions of an MCC include:

- vetting and approving major new policy initiatives in relation to regulation, thus providing a powerful focal point to drive implementation and reform;
- reviewing progress reports in relation to regulation and regulatory policy;
- endorsing ministry action plans to reduce administrative burdens on business; and
- monitoring progress and assessing the need for modifications to the plan.

Developing the first draft of the detailed reform plan

The content and layout of the detailed plan will vary from country to country, depending on the extent and type of regulatory policy to be established, and the local requirements for major submissions to the cabinet or the equivalent body. However, in all cases the following items should be included:

- a summary that clearly relates the regulatory policy to existing government objectives, policies and plans concerning the infrastructure sector, explaining how regulatory policy will contribute to their achievement;
- a brief description of the regulatory policy and each of the planned reforms (the deliverables) that it contains. This should focus on the need for a small, expert unit working under a senior minister to drive, coordinate and implement the policy, with an advocacy and training role. It should also examine the role and importance of assessments of proposed regulation;
- a statement of the priority to be given to each reform, with an estimate of the expected costs and benefits, and the expected risks involved;
- identification of groups that can be expected to support or oppose each key reform;
- a list of the major stages, activities and timelines in the reform plan, noting the deliverable(s) to be achieved at each stage and the key milestones;
- description of the roles and decision-making responsibilities of each key person or group, together with the hierarchy of authority, accompanied by an organigram.

Integrating the regulatory policy into established policy processes

If the processes associated with the regulatory policy are not integrated with established policy processes, they will tend to be regarded by line departments and agencies as an "add on," something imposed on them from the center of government. Integration is a long-term process that should begin by ensuring that senior officials have a thorough understanding of what is involved in implementing the principles underlying the regulatory policy within their departments and agencies. It is also useful to highlight successes and the benefits this can bring to the departments and agencies involved.

PUTTING THE PLAN INTO PRACTICE

Assigning authority and responsibilities

As discussed above, implementing key reforms is a long-term process, in which monitoring results, identifying possible policy modifications to address key problems and looking for opportunities to expand the breadth and depth of the reforms are key elements. At the same time, opposition to the reform process can be expected from a variety of vested interests.

All these factors point to the need for a clear allocation of political and administrative responsibility for the implementation of reform, preferably to a coordinating body at the center of government, as discussed in the previous chapter. In addition, it is essential that those with responsibility have adequate resources to support continuing policy implementation and development.

Designating a senior minister

Allocating specific responsibility for the reform program to a senior minister will help to ensure that it is seen as having political support and authority and ensure that the reform policy has an advocate in cabinet and political debate. The likelihood of significant opposition makes it important that a top-ranking minister is given political responsibility. The main risk in making an individual minister responsible is that he or she may be isolated from other cabinet members in supporting the policy. This can suggest broadening responsibility somewhat through the establishment of a cabinet committee or other structure. Conversely, having reform responsibilities split between different ministers can undercut the effectiveness of political advocacy.

Establishing a reform monitoring, support and coordination unit within the administration[2]

As noted above, ensuring that there is a champion of regulatory policy and reform within the administration has several important benefits. At a basic level it helps to ensure consistency. While changes of government (or within government) may mean that the minister responsible for the policy is frequently replaced, the existence of an administrative body with policy coordination functions helps ensure that a body of knowledge and experience can be developed and maintained over time.

A model that has been adopted in some countries, like the Business Environment Delivery Unit in Kenya described in box 15.3, involves broadening the scope and expertise of the reform monitoring and oversight body by appointing a board to direct its operations. This can include—and indeed can often be dominated by—appointees from outside government. The approach can be useful in the post-fragile context as a means of both addressing capacity constraints and improving accountability for achievement of reform objectives. Members can be drawn from academic institutions, industry and consumer or citizen groups, etc.

The coordination function performed by such a unit can be particularly important in implementing major sectoral reforms in post-fragile contexts, where several ministries often have responsibilities with significant influence on reform implementation. For example, until recently foreigners seeking to invest in hydro-electricity generation in Nepal needed licenses issued by the Ministry of Energy, while many license-related functions were dispensed by the Ministry of Electricity Supply, and water supply fell under the authority of the Ministry for Water Resources. Moreover, the Ministry of Finance had responsibility for the tax treatment of investments in the sector and ruled in relation to repatriation of profits.

Another approach to coordination, adopted in Nepal's 2017 National Electricity Regulatory Commission Act, is to require representatives of a range of ministries with key interests (in this case including the Ministry of Finance, the Ministry of Energy and the Ministry of Water resources, as well as the Executive Director of the NEA and key external resources) to be represented on the board of the independent regulator. However, as noted in Part B, there are disadvantages in placing civil servants on boards.

Reform units can also help to improve understanding of the reform agenda's purpose and rationale throughout the administration and improve capacities over time, both by promoting the reform generally and by providing specific training to officials on key issues. Such bodies can also function as internal consultancies, helping to provide expertise to ministries engaged in essential reform tasks. Importantly, such bodies ensure that there is a strong and consistent

The Kenyan Business Regulatory Reform Unit

Kenya established the Business Regulatory Reform Unit (BRRU) in 2007 as part of a broad regulatory reform that initially focused on reorganizing business regulations and, in particular, license, permit and certification systems. The BRRU was located at the Ministry of Finance, ensuring that it had strong authority within the administration and access to senior ministers. It was given a range of high-level functions, including "keeping track of all regulatory regimes" and liaising with regulators to conduct Regulatory Impact Assessments (RIA). The government noted that a key reason for creating the BRRU was the need to institutionalize these reforms within its wider regulatory reform strategy and ensure that gains were not eroded over time by "creeping reregulation."

The BRRU was reconstituted in 2014 as the Business Environment Delivery Unit (BEDU), within the Department of Industrialization and Enterprise Development. This was a less powerful location in that it was not at the center of government. However, the structure of the BEDU included representatives from all ministries, as well as private-sector experts. In addition, it was required to develop performance indicators to measure the contributions of each ministry to regulatory improvement. These measures sought to make the improvement of regulatory arrangements a shared responsibility across government, while also enabling the reform body to benefit from the knowledge of key experts from outside the administration.

Notably, the reform of business licenses and permits was identified as a key challenge for the new BEDU—even though license reform had been a central element of BRRU's remit 7 years earlier. This highlights the fact that even quite specific regulatory changes can be challenging and time-consuming.

pro-reform voice inside the government. This function is likely to be particularly important during the implementation of major reforms, as these often provokes strong opposition from vested interests.

Monitoring and evaluating progress against milestones

Because implementing major reform is a medium-/long-term process, progress must be monitored regularly against milestones. These should be established in the implementation plan, early in the reform process, and should reflect a realistic pathway toward the achievement of the ultimate goals of the reform program.

The main purpose of undertaking regular monitoring and evaluation of progress is to identify in good time when outcomes are falling short of expectations and to determine why. This includes:

- identifying unanticipated impacts of the strategy;
- identifying unexpected impediments to the achievement of key goals; and
- identifying institutional problems, such as situations in which reforms are consistently blocked by opposition from particular public bodies.

It is unlikely that a completely fit-for-purpose reform path can be designed and legislated at the beginning of the reform process. This means policymakers must continuously subject the reform program to critical scrutiny during its implementation and be ready to modify it to ensure it can meet its objectives. That said, frequent, major changes to policies and legislation can have their own costs, particularly as they can give rise to uncertainty and associated planning difficulties on the part of investors. Foreign investors, who are less familiar with the government and economic environment in a country, may be most affected. These issues, and the means of minimizing negative impacts, are discussed in chapter 16, which addresses the need for policy commitment and stability.

As suggested above, a regulatory monitoring unit frequently oversees the process of monitoring and measuring reform policy performance. Allocating responsibilities to such a body has important benefits. Importantly, it is more likely to take a whole-of-government perspective in assessing progress. This can be important where the reform policy has multiple objectives which entail trade-offs and even conflicts. For example, policy reform in the electricity sector is likely to aim to expand generation and access to electricity on the one hand, while maintaining affordable tariffs on the other.

Similarly, a regulatory monitoring unit with broad governance responsibilities is more likely to identify governance problems in key bodies responsible for sectoral reform policies (e.g., independent or arm's-length regulators). They are also more liable to advocate for needed changes than are the ministries to which these bodies report. This role can be reinforced if a board structure, involving members from a range of non-government backgrounds, is adopted as part of the management.

Conducting the review process

As suggested above, reviews should be conducted by an appointed body that has sufficient expertise and is, as far as possible, at arm's length from the reform policy subject to review. As noted, the review should benchmark performance against criteria that were identified and agreed when (or soon after) the reform policy was adopted. The review process should be as open as possible and should, at the very least, require significant consultations with a range of stakeholders.

Responding to the conclusions

Ensuring that the results of the evaluation are reported widely—ideally, published for general consumption—can help to mobilize support for needed changes. Thus, governance arrangements in respect of the reform policy should include requirements—possibly legislated—for the publication of progress reports and for formal responses to them to be published by government. Providing for parliamentary scrutiny and debate is also likely to create additional pressure for policy responses to be widely discussed and adopted.

External reviews

While the above describes a series of good practices in reviewing the ongoing implementation of reform programs, it is clear that policy review is a systematically under-resourced activity in most countries—both developed and developing. There are clear political disincentives to thoroughgoing reviews being undertaken in most contexts, with governments reluctant to be confronted with—and bear the political cost of—the failures of past and present policies.

Recognizing this suggests that a key strategic step can be to encourage, or create circumstances, in which external reviews will be conducted. Where significant resources have been provided by donor organizations to assist in the implementation of reform, formal review of the outcomes achieved will often be a requirement. Inviting engagement with the reform program by such organizations can thus be a useful means of ensuring that reviews are undertaken, as well as making sure that assessments are made by disinterested parties. There may also be opportunities for reform bodies within governments to work with donor organizations to see to it that the timing and focus of such reviews are as favorable as possible to the long-term development of the reform program.

Modifying the strategy on the basis of regular evaluations

Where performance reviews show that little progress is being made toward the goals set for the regulatory reform program, a credible response is needed to maintain (or, arguably, to restore) the confidence of the public and key stakeholders that reform outcome will be achieved. This highlights the importance of a thorough, analytically robust and transparent review process. Stakeholders must be able to understand the key problems responsible for lack of progress and be confident the proposed policy changes can resolve them.

At the same time, making substantial change to a previously announced, long-term policy can give rise to perceptions of "sovereign risk" among investors if these changes can potentially damage their interests. Thus, the way in which changes to the policy are developed, announced and implemented must be considered carefully, to minimize such risks. Key issues in this regard include consultation, the timing of changes, and the communication of their expected impact. As discussed in chapter 13, governments may, in any case, need to weigh the costs of a perceived lack of policy commitment against the benefits of changes that are expected to improve reform outcomes.

Opportunities to advance reform

While the above has focused on the issue of unanticipated problems of implementation in reform programs, reformers should also be alert to the possibilities of making significant steps forward in a multi-stage reform process should favorable opportunities arise. For example, a change of government, or of the minister responsible, may provide the opportunity to move forward more quickly, as was the case in Georgia in 2003–04 (see box 15.4).

BOX 15.4

The Rose Revolution as an opportunity for reform

As noted by the World Bank, the initial regulatory reforms put in place or proposed by the Georgian government of President Eduard Shevardnadze during and after 1995 had, by 2003, sputtered to a halt and Georgia was a near-failed state. Political power was increasingly fragmented, corruption and crime rampant, there were massive arrears in pension payments and teacher's salaries, and infrastructure was in a state of near collapse. Most of the country lacked power and the road network increasingly deteriorated. There was mounting public opposition to President Shevardnadze and many reforms stalled in the face of growing parliamentary opposition to his rule.

After a period of increasing civil unrest, Mikhail Saakashvili, who had been the Minister of Justice in the Shevardnadze Government, was elected President in January 2004, during the "Rose Revolution," on a strong anti-corruption platform, with approximately 96 percent of the vote. The new Saakashvili Government took immediate advantage of the public's demand for reform and proceeded to rapidly put in place a wide range of regulatory reforms, set out in its Economic Development and Poverty Reduction Program (EDPRP), linked to the UN's Millennium Declaration. The reforms focused on the creation of a market economy, with rapid deregulation, privatization and a dramatic reduction in the size of the public service (for relevant details see IMF 2003b). Energy, transport and communications were identified as key sectors for reform (Macfarlane 2013).

Another source of opportunities can be the involvement of donor organizations. For example, efforts to create an independent regulator in the electricity sector in Nepal had been unsuccessful for well over a decade prior to the prospect of the US-based Millennium Challenge Corporation making a major investment. Millennium Challenge sought the establishment of a credible, independent regulatory body as a prerequisite for its investment, being convinced that this was a key element in ensuring a successful outcome. Pro-reform forces were thus able to develop and implement legislation quickly, due largely to this opportunity arising from abroad.

In some situations, the disappointing performance of an initial reform initiative may be used as an argument in favor of moving quickly to adopt bolder reforms that were initially seen as belonging to a later stage in the reform process.

CONCLUSION

This chapter has outlined key issues in developing and putting into practice a strategy to improve regulatory governance in one or more infrastructure sectors. The next chapter examines how to maintain that strategy over time, regularly evaluating its performance and modifying it as circumstances change.

NOTES

1. See http://regulationbodyofknowledge.org/self-assessment-tool/#/home for a copy of the self-assessment tool, as developed by the Public-Private Infrastructure Advisory Facility (PPIAF), the World Bank, and the Public Utility Research Center at the University of Florida.
2. Allocating responsibility to a specific Minister and establishing an oversight body for the regulatory policy are consistent with the 2012 OECD Council Recommendation on regulatory policy, which states the governments should "establish mechanisms and institutions to actively provide oversight of regulatory policy" (OECD 2012).

REFERENCES

Energy Community. 2017. *Annual Implementation Report*. Vienna: Energy Community Secretariat.

IMF (International Monetary Fund). 2003. "Georgia: Poverty Reduction Strategy Paper." IMF Country Report 03/265, IMF, Washington, DC.

Macfarlane, S. N. 2013. "Georgia and the Political Economy of Statebuilding." In *Political Economy of Statebuilding: Power after Peace*, edited by M. Berdal and D. Zaum, 309. London /New York: Routledge.

OECD (Organisation for Economic Co-operation and Development). 2012. *Recommendation of the Council on Regulatory Policy and Governance*. Paris: OECD Publishing.

16

Maintaining the Strategy Over Time

INTRODUCTION

The reform process should seek to develop a credible market and regulatory architecture which enables private, and particularly foreign, investors to develop confidence in the regulatory environment and makes them willing to maintain and expand their investments. The principle of predictability, highlighted in Part B, is an important contributor to this outcome. A significant aspect of predictability is that policy positions should be maintained over the medium term and any significant changes made through a proper process involving advance warning and adequate consultation with affected parties. Two closely related concepts needed to achieve this type of reform process are policy commitment and stability, which are discussed below.

COMMITMENT, CONTINUITY, AND POLICY STABILITY

A fundamental principle of good regulation is that of credibility. Stakeholders must be confident that the regulatory system will "honor its commitments"— that is, will function in the expected manner consistently over time. In a post-fragile environment, the establishment and maintenance of credibility poses particular challenges, which must be identified and addressed carefully.

Commitment

Maintaining credibility requires commitment. Commitment implies that contracts and other agreements with investors in regulated sectors continue to be honored and that regulatory frameworks remain stable over time. However, a frequent dynamic in developing countries is that government agencies seek to renegotiate such agreements, or revise regulatory provisions, within relatively short periods. In some cases, renegotiations can be imposed unilaterally, while in others the initial agreements require both parties to accept a renegotiation. However, given the extent to which investors in any country are dependent on government decisions, there may be little difference in practice between these two scenarios.

Such renegotiations inevitably create uncertainty for investors, introducing "sovereign risk" into their investment calculus. In addition, the need to adapt to a new regulatory and/or commercial environment itself causes disruption costs, which can be substantial. Estache and Wren-Lewis (2010) report data which shows that such renegotiations tend to both reduce the amount of investment and increase the risk premium (hence, the total rate of return) required by investors over the medium to long term. Both of these impacts are necessarily welfare-reducing, in economic terms. Hence, governments must be cautious when considering a renegotiation of existing agreements.

Nonetheless, there are sound reasons for governments to seek renegotiation of such agreements. Particularly in post-fragile countries, a key dynamic is that the original contract may have substantial deficiencies, often because of the relative lack of commercial sophistication of government negotiators and/or drafters. Such deficiencies can often mean that agreements do not contain adequate provisions to protect the interests of government entities, taxpayers and/or consumers. Where it becomes evident that outcomes unreasonably favor investors over these other groups, whose interests' government must protect, there may be a strong motive for renegotiation.

Alternatively, outcomes that are unfairly weighted toward investors may result from unforeseen, material changes in the economic and/or commercial environment. Such changes are especially likely to occur in the post-fragile context, where institutions, industries and other key social infrastructure are being rebuilt, or built anew.

Governments in these circumstances have clear responsibilities to safeguard the interests of consumers. The benefits of infrastructure investments must be widely distributed across society to maintain and strengthen support for regulatory and structural reforms over time. While equity goals are often more efficiently pursued via budgetary measures in developed countries, low fiscal efficiency in post-fragile states can mean that the regulatory system is the only feasible/effective means of pursuing distributional goals.

Further, the outputs of infrastructure industries provide inputs to production in the great majority of economic sectors. This means that a failure to ensure that consumers of infrastructure services obtain substantial benefits from reform will imply significant welfare losses in other parts of the economy. Box 16.1 summarizes key reasons for governments to consider contract renegotiations or to change regulatory provisions.

Thus, there are clear and legitimate reasons for governments to seek to renegotiate contractual arrangements and/or vary regulatory provisions. However, policymakers should approach these questions cautiously and adopt a benefit/cost framework to determine when and how to conduct such renegotiations. Broadly speaking, the costs associated with the sovereign risk that renegotiation introduces to investors' views of investment must be weighed carefully against the expected benefits to taxpayers and consumers from renegotiation.

The means by which renegotiations are conducted can have a significant impact on this balance of benefits and costs. Some key considerations in this regard are:

BOX 16.1

Recap of reasons governments may want to pursue contract renegotiations or change regulatory provisions, despite breaking "continuity"

1. Original contract may have substantial deficiencies;
2. unforeseen, material changes in the economic and/or commercial environment;
3. to safeguard the interests of consumers;
4. possible substantial welfare losses in other parts of the economy fueled by contract structure or regulatory architecture.

- **View the agreement as an outline of commitments**. Large-scale and complex agreements involving several parties are common in relation to infrastructure. These agreements should be seen as an outline of commitments, detailing the major responsibilities of each party as specified in the contract. When a party has difficulty in servicing the contract due to unforeseen conditions, it should communicate and share this with the other side as soon as possible. In some cases, a relatively simple modification, such as rescheduling shipments or extending payments, can be enough to ensure implementation without major renegotiations. However, where larger changes with significant impacts on other parties are required, an open and timely approach will help to maintain trust and help achieve an outcome that benefits all parties.

- **Be aware of cultural differences**. Contracts often involve parties from widely different cultures with differing views on the role of negotiation and the content of contracts. American firms, for example, often prefer lengthy, detailed contracts with little flexibility, attempting to identify all possible factors that could influence the contract and incorporating clauses to specify what should be done in each case. In addition, strict penalties for non-compliance are often included. Other cultures, such as the Chinese, often see a contract as only the beginning of a business relationship, considering that negotiations can be reopened. These differences should be taken into consideration in the negotiations and the design of the contract, with negotiators repeatedly asking, "What does this section of the proposed agreement mean to the other party?" and, "To what extent is the other party committed to the agreement?" Where there are clear differences of interpretation and commitment, answers should be sought in the negotiations. Sometimes a shorter contract that acknowledges the possibility of eventual renegotiations and amendments may be more appropriate, although penalties and other deterrents should always be included to avoid potential abuses.

- **Predictability**. Include, as far as possible, provisions identifying the circumstances in which renegotiation can occur and how it will be conducted to reduce uncertainty and cost. These are often known as "intra-deal" renegotiations and are likely to be smoother if the initial agreement contains a clause that permits them, due to unforeseen events. Their acceptance will often help reduce tensions and misunderstandings. Including in the initial contract some rules or guidance as to how matters to be negotiated will be addressed may also reduce opportunities for disagreement and conflict.

- **Continuously monitor progress and consider incorporating scheduled reviews in the agreement**. At the time of signing the contract the parties often assume that the negotiations are over whereas, in practice, bargaining has only completed the first stage. A negotiation is not complete until the resulting agreement is fully implemented and, in reality, unexpected changes are the norm so that a smooth implementation is the exception rather than the rule. When a long-term agreement is put in place, both parties can decide to meet regularly to identify potential problems. This provision of a specific mechanism for addressing issues can reduce conflict due to "unexpected" claims for modifications to the contract.

- **All parties should build in renegotiation costs**. As renegotiations are expensive in time and money, the anticipated costs should be incorporated in the agreement as far as possible.

Continuity

A common problem during the implementation of new regulatory systems as part of infrastructure- sector reform is that of a lack of continuity. This problem often arises in relation to the governing bodies of recently established regulators but is also sometimes seen in relation to incumbent public enterprises. Parties that oppose a new regulator's reform agenda often bring strong pressure to bear on government to appoint more "flexible" board members. At the same time, however, political struggles within government and/or parliament can make it difficult to agree on such appointments. Extended paralysis of this kind can make boards largely unable to take key regulatory decisions, giving rise to substantial blockages in the broader reform process. Box 16.2 highlights an example of this problem drawn from Kosovo.

It is important to have an appointments process that minimizes the risk of appointees lacking requisite technical qualifications and experience due to political considerations. The process should also ensure that appointments can effectively be made in a timely manner. Legislation establishing independent regulators frequently seeks to address this issue by including requirements setting out the qualifications that individuals must possess in order to be eligible board positions. However, excessively prescriptive provisions can give rise to vexatious challenges, as noted in Part B. For example, in Nepal, following a change of government a challenge was made, in 2012, to the appointment of the new Chairman of the National Telecommunications Authority on the basis that he did not meet the qualifications criteria set out in the Telecoms Act 1997. The Supreme Court stayed the appointment in early 2013, finding that, while a

BOX 16.2

Lack of continuity on regulatory boards in Kosovo

Recent EU reports[a] on Kosovo have highlighted the tendency for appointments to the boards of many regulatory authorities and state-owned enterprises to be made on political grounds rather than on the basis of professional competence. One consequence is that there have frequently been very long delays in completing appointment processes as different groups sought to have their candidates nominated and approved by parliament. This kind of jockeying often resulted in major organizations postponing important decisions for years.

For example, the Kosovo Competition Commission was unable to take major decisions for over 3 years until five board members were finally appointed in mid-2016. Similarly, the appointment of three board members to the Energy Regulatory Office in November

2015 ended a long period in which key decisions regarding the electricity market were blocked, including the approval of licenses for new suppliers. However, May 2017 saw the number of board members again fall to two—short of the necessary quorum of three—and the board was consequently paralyzed again

The telecoms regulator (the Regulatory Authority of Electronic and Postal Communications [RAEPC]), previously faced the same problem. However, this led to a subsequent change in the law on telecommunications, which now provides that existing board members whose terms have expired continue in office pending the appointment of new members. This change has ensured board continuity at RAEPC, enabling key decisions to be made and the regulator to carry out its functions.

a. European Commission 2016.

mechanical engineer, he did not meet the requirement that the appointee should be "qualified and experienced, as prescribed in the technical and administrative, market management, accounts and auditing or legal field relating to the Telecommunications Service." The court finally upheld his appointment in October 2014 (Kathmandu Post 2014)—after the regulator had been without a chairman for almost 2 years.

A further factor in relation to appointments is the question of the involvement of parliament in the process. In some countries, such as Kosovo, parliament must formally appoint members to the boards of a range of regulatory agencies and public enterprises from names put forward by the government. This process is typically favored as tending to stop governments filling top posts with political appointees. But it has often led to long delays, as in the case of Kosovo, and raises concerns about the ability of parliaments to appointing candidates to often highly technical positions.

A potentially preferable alternative is to give parliament a safeguard role, that is, parliament can reject government appointments on limited grounds specified in relevant legislation. This can speed up the filling of high-level posts, while still imposing some official discipline on the process.

Policy stability

A related issue is that of policy stability. A key risk in recently reformed sectors of the economy is that the often initially disappointing performance of newly created or reconstituted regulators leads to pressure to make further changes to the institutional architecture within relatively short periods. Such short-term changes may then be repeated if the revised architecture fails to deliver improved outcomes in the medium term. An example of this dynamic is illustrated in box 16.3.

However, frequent changes in institutional architecture can result in significant costs. It is important to recognize that the development of regulatory capacity takes time. It involves recruiting and training a critical mass of competent, dedicated staff who need to build expertise in the specific regulatory environment through experience. A key risk arising from major institutional changes is that this process is likely to be disrupted so that a newly appointed regulator is less-equipped to embark on its task than its predecessor.

Important considerations are that:

- Key staff are likely to be discouraged by the abolition or fundamental restructuring of the original regulatory structure, considering it an implicit criticism of their performance. As a result, they may not seek reappointment in the new regulatory body.
- Equally, the attractiveness of roles in the new regulator for well-qualified staff can be diminished by the perception of career risk stemming from changes in the regulatory structure.
- In any organization, the early years of a new or substantially reformed entity are characterized by large quantities of resources being devoted to the establishment of the new body, including developing standard procedures and processes, agreeing lines of authority and responsibility and clarifying the nature of the body's relationships with other key entities in its operating environment. Developing an organizational structure and undertaking major recruitment are also significant tasks. What it adds up to is that a new or reconstituted regulator is likely to under-perform for perhaps 2–3 years.

The importance of these costs should therefore be weighed against the gains expected from implementing major change to regulatory arrangements. Careful consideration should be given to whether problems with the performance of the current regulator can be addressed through smaller, more targeted changes over a period of time.

Maintaining the integrity of the reform process—exemptions and exceptions

A common problem in post-fragile environments is the creation of exemptions from the newly adopted regulatory processes implemented as part of the reform agenda. Such exemptions are often justified as being needed to meet urgent needs, or address particular issues. They are therefore often framed as "emergency exemptions" or as streamlined approvals for "strategically important projects."

However, when such exemptions from the standard processes are granted, there is a clear risk of undermining the integrity of the newly established regulatory systems. The potential for unfair treatment of different current or potential operators is evident while the mere suspicion of bias has obvious negative impacts on investor confidence. Such exemptions, which typically rely on the approval of a single minister or a small group of ministers, also clearly creates significant opportunities for corruption, further undermining the regulatory system.

BOX 16.3

A lack of policy stability in the Rwanda infrastructure sector—2003–10

In 2003, Rwanda's major state enterprise, Electrogaz, was placed under a management contract with Lahmayer International for 5 years, with the aim of eventual privatization. In 2006 the contract was terminated when the Rwandan Government became aware of misconduct in Lahmeyer contracts in Lesotho. The World Bank later "sanctioned," in effect "blacklisting," or "debarring," Lahmeyer International for 7 years from World Bank-funded contracts following the Lesotho incident.

The Electricity Law of 2008 was introduced shortly thereafter, with Electrogaz split into the Rwanda Energy Corporation (RECO) and the Rwanda Water and Sewerage Corporation (RWASCO). RECO assumed all Electrogaz's electricity-related activities, assets, and liabilities. However, the decision to split Electrogaz was not deemed a success and in December 2010 Law No. 43/2010 established the Rwanda Energy, Water and Sanitation Authority (EWSA), with both RECO and RWASCO reintegrated into the new entity.

In October 2013, the Rwandan Cabinet, dissatisfied with the performance of EWSA following a very critical review by the Auditor-General, decided to terminate the organization and create three new companies, though this time under company law, rather than by statute. The first was an electricity utility, the Electricity Utility Corporation Limited (EUCL); the second an energy development company, the Rwanda Energy Development Corporation Limited (EDCL); and the third a company to be responsible for water supply and sanitation services development and operations, the Rwanda Water and Sanitation Corporation Limited (WASAC).

While the aim was to develop increasingly efficient infrastructure sectors, with growing private involvement, the extent and type of largely unpredictable changes also created ongoing, institutional instability that at times had an adverse impact on staff and performance.

BOX 16.4

Presidential projects in Madagascar

In Madagascar, Law 98-032 provides for electricity generation licenses to be awarded to private firms by tender, with the criteria used to assess submissions and projects subject to the required legislative processes (e.g., environmental approval). However, some entries, if given the status of "Presidential Projects," need not go to tender or, in some cases, undergo feasibility studies. Such exemptions from normal practice is authorized under Article 19 of Law 98-032, which states that "The State guarantees the continuity of the public service of electricity in case of deficiency by holders of Concessions or Authorizations, or in the absence of the holders. To this end, it may take any urgent measures in accordance with the terms and conditions specified by decree."

There is no definition of what might constitute an "urgent measure," leaving room for considerable discretion at political level. As a result, the "Presidential projects" can contain technical flaws serious enough to endanger public safety. Also present is the risk of corruption due to insufficient scrutiny of relevant provisions such as the prices at which power purchase agreements are concluded.

Source: Rafitoson 2017.

Consequently, one should be skeptical about allowing such exemptions or exceptions within the regulatory structure. Where they are adopted, several principles should be observed in order to minimize any negative consequences:

- The exemption process should be established in law, so that its existence and key features remain transparent.
- The purpose and scope of the exemptions from, or exceptions to, normal approval processes should be clearly specified, or the details of any alternative processes should be clarified.
- The nature of the decision-making process to be used in "exceptional circumstances" should also be made explicit, as should the identity of the decision-maker.
- Transparent criteria and/or thresholds should be established to determine when the exceptions process can be used: it should be consistent with the stated objectives of the system.
- The decision-maker(s) should be required to publish an explanation of why it was decided to use the exceptional process and what results can be expected.

In addition, the law should include a provision requiring exempted projects to be independently reviewed (e.g., by an Auditor-General or a parliamentary committee) within a specified period (e.g., within 3 years of coming into operation). The review should assess the value added by projects approved under these alternative arrangements, the probity of the process and any impact on confidence in the impartiality of treatment of investors.

ADDRESSING THE "IMPLEMENTATION GAP"

A key concern in the early years of the implementation of a reform program is that of a major gap emerging between the policy objectives and the outcomes of the practices implemented. This is often referred to as the "implementation gap" and is likely to require attention in low-capacity environments. The implementation gap typically arises due a combination of factors, although the relative importance of each can vary.

Key contributors to the implementation gap include:

- **Policy deficiencies**. The policy adopted may lack elements that come to be seen as crucial to its success. This can often happen because specific elements of the policy environment are not well understood at the time policy is developed. Recognizing policy deficiencies will help develop and tailor the policy to address context-specific factors and ultimately help achieve policy objectives.

- **Unanticipated impacts**. The implementation of the policy may have important unanticipated effects, particularly where sectoral policies are poorly coordinated with each other or, as above, a lack of understanding of aspects of the policy environment causes problems in policy design.

- **Lack of resources/capacities**. Post-fragile environments will likely lack adequate resources or capacities. This can create a significant gap between the formal analysis and process requirements established by policy and the content achieved in practice. Recognition of capacity constraints is obviously important at the policy design stage. However, following implementation, a clear focus on key areas in which policy elements are not being delivered in practice, and are significantly compromising the achievement of policy objectives, is needed. Responses should include consideration of whether and how additional resources can be applied in key areas of failure and assess whether changes in the policy are needed to achieve better practical outcomes. For example:

    - **Overly demanding impact assessment (IA) requirements** focusing on quantified analysis could mean that resources are focused on completing a small number of assessments, with the IA requirement not being met in many other cases. Modifying the requirement to establish a more manageable level of analysis could help ensure that all relevant proposals receive at least a minimum of assessment (e.g., the World Bank's "RIA Lite" approach, which aims to tailor the Regulatory Impact Assessment discipline to suit the realities of developing country environments [World Bank 2010]).

    - **Consultation periods that are too short**, meaning that effective participation by stakeholders is often very limited, or narrowly based. Possible policy responses could include extending consultation periods, providing additional material to help stakeholders participate effectively and improving the consultation methods used to make it easier to participate.

    - **Poor coordination**. Performance problems may result from gaps in the allocation of responsibility or, alternatively, unclear responsibilities for key program elements, potentially including overlap between different ministries, regulators, or other entities. These issues may be addressed by agreeing and adopting clear protocols setting out the relative roles of the major bodies with responsibilities for the reform program, but legislative change may also be required to establish clear lines of responsibility.

    - **Governance issues**. As discussed elsewhere, deficiencies in the governance arrangements of key institutions can mean that they do not consistently focus on achieving the goals of the reform program. Even where sound governance principles formed the basis for developing these arrangements, compromises will often have been made. Practical experience in implementing the reform policy will often highlight the real impacts of these and indicate where change is needed if the policy is to better achieve its goals.

Careful and coordinated policy design will help minimize the extent of the implementation gaps that arise. However, significant gaps will most certainly appear during the early stages of major policy reform. Ensuring that efforts are made to identify and address such gaps is therefore a key part of the "policy cycle"[1] and essential to making certain that reforms are sustained and expanded over time.

The use of the Part B principles in such situations will assist in both identifying and clarifying the specific gaps, or issues that arise and developing changes to regulations that will help bridge them. Scheduling review activity on a regular basis and using the principles as the basis for the review will both help to ensure that a systematic and rigorous approach is taken, thus improving the quality of the outcomes achieved.

Developing and participating in communities of practice

Many regulators and supervising ministries responsible for the reform of infrastructure regulation have found participation in international associations of regulators an important way to address implementation gaps and improve practice over time. These associations can function as "communities of practice," in which regulators can identify and discuss key issues, share experiences and lessons learned and provide mutual support. They can also be important mechanisms for knowledge transfer from experts in academia, donor organizations, etc.

These associations are often organized on regional lines and offer the advantage of enabling regulators to exchange experiences with their counterparts in countries with relatively similar socio-economic systems and levels of development, thus potentially providing a particularly relevant source of advice and assistance. Box 16.5 provides an example of such a forum for regulators.

BOX 16.5

Regional forums for utility regulators

The African Forum for Utility Regulators (AFUR)

AFUR was established as part of the African Union's socio-economic program, the New Partnership for Africa's Development (NEPAD). It focuses on issues involving the regulation of the energy, telecommunications, transport, and water and sanitation industries. Members include 33 regulatory authorities from 21 African countries, while regulators from four more African countries are represented among its seven observers.

AFUR emphasizes issues that are common across the sectors regulated by its membership, but has also established four sectoral committees (for communications, energy, transport, and water and sanitation) which focus on sector-specific issues. Partnerships with the European Union and the World Bank's PPIAF program provide opportunities for knowledge transfer and technical support, such as the EU-supported *Guidelines for Electricity Supply Cost, Tariff Level and Structure* (AFUR 2016). AFUR holds regular forums and workshops and hosts a web discussion forum. https://www.afurnet.org/en/.

The East Asia and Pacific Infrastructure Regulatory Forum (EAPIRF)

EAPIRF was established in 2003 with support from the World Bank Group (notably PPIAF). It is intended to foster capacity-building and knowledge exchange among infrastructure regulators in the region to support enhanced regulatory decision-making. It also

continued

Box 16.5, *continued*

seeks to facilitate the development of training and capacity-building opportunities for regulators.

EAPIRF covers the energy, water/sanitation, telecoms/broadcasting and transport sectors. It has a two-tier structure, in which regulators are core members while institutions with related interests, such as NGOs, donor bodies and universities are able to join as affiliate members. EAPIRF's activities include conducting workshops, conferences and training activities and the publication of a range of materials such as regulator and country profiles and academic papers. http://www.eapirf.org/about-eapirf.

Other regulators' forums

The website of the International Confederation of Energy Regulators (www.icer-regulators.net)

provides a list of regionally based associations of energy regulators, including the South Asian Forum for Utility Regulators, the East Asia and Pacific Infrastructure Regulatory Forum, the Organization of Caribbean Energy Regulators and the Regional Electricity Regulators' Association of Southern Africa.

Regional associations of telecoms regulators include the Telecoms Regulators' Association of Southern Africa, the West Africa Telecoms Regulators' Association, *Le Réseau francophone de la régulation des télécommunications,* Latin American Telecommunications Regulators' Forum and the South Asian Telecommunications Regulators' Council.[a] The International Telecommunications Union also hosts meetings of regional regulators' associations (see www.itu.int).

a. For a fuller list of regional regulators' associations, focussing on the telecoms field, see: http://www.itu.int/ITU-D/treg/Documentation/Table_region_reg_assoc.pdf.

Training and professional development

The importance of investing in structured programs of training and professional development has been noted at various points in this manual, especially in relation to ensuring adequate capacity for reform. Resources must continue to be devoted to this task throughout the implementation of the reform program, as improving technical capacities within regulatory agencies and supervising ministries constitutes an important means of addressing implementation gaps over time. As noted above, participation in communities of practice at the regional level are one significant way of ensuring knowledge transfer and capacity development. However, this should be supplemented by internally developed programs, with the central coordination bodies responsible for the reform program taking the lead in identifying needs and ensuring the delivery of relevant and appropriate training.

CONCLUSION

This final chapter has focused on the work involved in maintaining an appropriate strategy for regulatory governance over time and modifying it to suit changing circumstances. It has stressed the need for commitment, continuity and policy stability in helping to ensure good regulatory governance and to address the implementation gap often faced by reformers.

NOTE

1. The "policy cycle" refers to a concept of public policy as circular, with the key stages being policy development, implementation, review/outcome assessment, policy analysis and further policy development. This process of analyzing outcomes and refining and modifying policies is particularly important when major new policies are being implemented. However, the constantly changing policy environment means that the conception of policy-making as a cyclical process has a broader importance and relevance.

REFERENCES

AFUR (African Forum for Utility Regulators). 2016. *Electricity Supply Cost, Tariff Level and Structure*, by Alain Doulet. Final Version: December 2016, AFUR Secretariat, Pretoria.

Estache, A., and L. Wren-Lewis. 2010. "On the Theory and Evidence on Regulation of Network Industries in Developing Countries." In *The Oxford Handbook of Regulation*, edited by Robert Baldwin, Martin Cave, and Martin Lodge, 371–406. Oxford: Oxford University Press.

European Commission. 2016. "Kosovo 2016 Report." Accompanying the document: "Communication from the Commission to the European Parliament, the Council, the European Economic and Social Committee and the Committee of the Regions. 2016 Communication on EU Enlargement Policy." {COM (2016) 715 final}. Commission Staff Working Document, European Commission, Brussels. https://eur-lex.europa.eu/legal-content/en/TXT/?uri=CELEX:52016SC0363.

Kathmandu Post. 2014. "Apex court upholds Jha's appointment as NTA chief." *Kathmandu Post* 2014-10-29. http://kathmandupost.ekantipur.com/printedition/news/2014-10-28/apex-court-upholds-jhas-appointment-as-nta-chief.html (accessed June 24, 2019).

Rafitoson, K. 2017. *La Lente March vers La Transition Energetique A Madagascar: Etat Des Lieux et Perspectives*. Friedrich-Ebert-Stiftung. http://library.fes.de/pdf-files/bueros/madagaskar/15155.pdf.

World Bank. 2010. *Making It Work: 'RIA Light' For Developing Countries*. Better Regulation for Growth: Governance Frameworks and Tools for Effective Regulatory Reform. Washington, DC: World Bank. http://documents.worldbank.org/curated/en/184141468167049021/pdf/55636-WP-REPLACEMENT-RIALightNov2009.pdf.

Glossary of Key Concepts Used in the Manual

The following concepts are used in a variety of sometimes overlapping and/or inconsistent ways by authors from different disciplines. To avoid confusion, the following definitions clarify their meaning as used in this manual.

KEY CONCEPTS RELATING TO REGULATION

Governance

In its broadest sense, governance refers to all processes of governing, whether undertaken by governments, corporations, professional or industry association, etc. It relates to the dynamics whereby actors interact and make decisions, giving rise to institutions and social norms, and change them over time.

Policy

Policy, in the current context, refers to the objective(s) being pursued by government and the general approach being adopted to their implementation. In a broader sense, policy can mean similar things in relation to a wide range of organizations—that is, the objectives they seek and the broad means of pursuing them.

Public policy

Public policy refers to broad courses of action adopted or proposed by a government in pursuit of public-good objectives.

Regulation

In its broadest sense, regulation encompasses any exercise of authority intended to modify the behavior of another group. Under this definition, both governments and various private bodies (e.g., industry or professional associations) engage in regulation. However, for present purposes, we are concerned with government regulation.

The regulatory process: A recurrent cycle

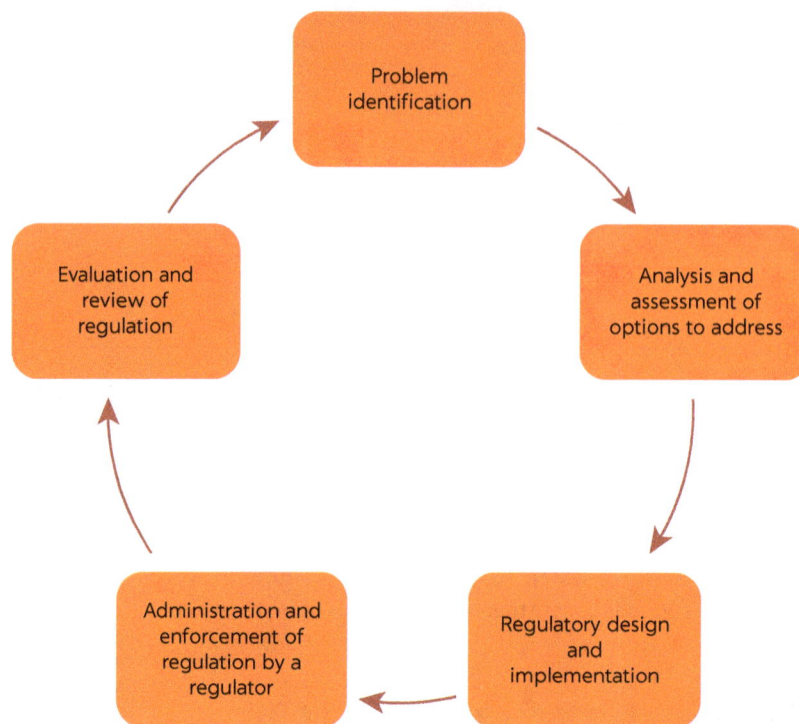

Government broadly has three sets of tools available: the first allows it to levy taxes, the second enables it to spend the resulting revenue, while the third concerns regulation. In this sense, regulation encompasses all laws, ordinances, decrees and other legal or legislative instruments that either prohibit certain actions or require groups within society to act in certain ways or become subject to certain constraints.

Considered in this manner, regulation can also be viewed as a process. The regulatory process involves a recurring cycle of activities, often referred to as the "regulatory cycle" (see figure A.1), which involve: problem identification; analysis and assessment of options to address the problem; regulatory design and implementation; administration and enforcement of regulation by a regulator, and evaluation and review of regulation (which, in turn, leads back to a new problem-definition phase).

The term regulation can also refer specifically to subordinate legislation—that is, rules (often called "regulations") made under the authority of an Act of Parliament/Congress. Common types of subordinate legislation are: regulations, ministerial orders, codes of practice and local laws and bylaws.

This manual is primarily concerned with the regulatory process carried out within government and with all the different instruments that result from this process.

Regulatory capture

Regulatory capture refers to a situation in which a regulator or regulatory agency advances the interests of one or more group rather than the broad public interest. In many cases, regulators act in the interest of one or more regulated party (e.g., industry), rather than the broader interests of consumers, taxpayers and the public. An example is industry persuading the regulator to defend the status quo and thus preventing competitors from entering the market.

Regulatory compliance

Regulatory compliance refers to an organization's or individual's adherence to laws, policies, regulations and guidelines. Compliance strategies may be adopted by government to ensure adequate levels of adherence to new regulations or to maintain or increase levels of compliance with existing or modified regulations.

Regulatory governance

Regulatory governance refers to the policies, tools, processes and institutions that are primarily concerned with developing, implementing, administering and enforcing new regulations and reviewing and revising regulation over time. To put it another way, regulatory governance is the process of regulating regulations and regulators.

Regulatory independence

Regulatory independence in the context of governance refers to a regulator's (or regulatory agency's) ability to act in accordance with the law (usually its founding statute) and without direction from government other than that which is specifically authorized by that law.

Regulatory management or regulatory management system

A regulatory management system is the set of formal and informal institutions, processes and actors that is responsible for oversight of the development and implementation of government regulation. In most senses it is a synonym for regulatory governance.

Regulatory policy

Regulatory policy refers to any government policy that is intended to have an impact on the system of regulatory governance.

Regulatory quality

Regulatory quality refers to the efficiency, effectiveness, transparency, accountability and, ultimately, the legitimacy of a body of regulation.

Regulatory strategy

A regulatory strategy is an explicit government policy aimed at maintaining or increasing regulatory quality. In practice it often takes the form of government endorsement of a set of "good practice" or "best practice" regulatory principles. In federal states there may be differing regulatory strategies at the federal and state levels and, less often, at the level of local government.

KEY CONCEPTS RELATED TO FRAGILE AND CONFLICT-AFFECTED STATES

Definition of fragility stages[1]

Stage 1. Crisis

A situation of crisis can refer to a period when there is acute instability in a country, with increased levels of violence and the potential for more generalized violent conflict, or when there has been a natural or man-made disaster. Frequently, there are major political divisions in this period and often conflict among communities, leading to widespread mistrust and fear. Security forces may be committing generalized human rights abuses amid endemic corruption so that the public has little confidence in the security apparatus. The security sector is typically fragmented and often being reformed. Rule of law is typically eroded and politicized, and the economic sector is severely constrained. During this phase, justice is only upheld at national, and not at local or regional level, and the country faces many human rights violations that the state fails to address. As a result, violence is used increasingly as a means of settling disputes. Basic government services are likely to be weak or nonexistent, and the international humanitarian and aid community may have stepped in to provide emergency relief. International organizations may also be supporting security through police or peacekeeping missions. Government revenues are often low or nonexistent, and countries often suffer illegal or informal exploitation of natural resources and weak enforcement of regulations governing natural resources.

Stage 2. Rebuild and reform

During this phase, renewed efforts at engaging in political dialogue to resolve political differences may be made. However, power is often shared inequitably between groups. There may be some progress on disarmament, but security remain a challenge, with a high proliferation of small arms. Institutions are often weak and deliver services sporadically. As compared to the crisis phase, the intensity of conflict and of political disputes is more manageable and efforts are made to establish stronger security institutions and to recruit personnel. However, in this stage, the efficacy of the security apparatus is likely to be limited. Justice institutions start to make their presence felt beyond national capitals but are often ineffective so that the rule of law is not enforced. As for the foundations of economic activity, basic infrastructure and an enabling economic environment are beginning to be put in place, but high unemployment rates are still to be found, particularly among young people. During this phase, large potential sources of domestic revenue may have been identified (e.g., natural resources and/or customs), but these are poorly accounted for, benefiting only a small part of the population. While the process of reforming public financial management may have begun, budget execution problems remain and accountability is weak.

Stage 3. Transition

This stage is often associated with the signature of agreements and an overall situation of stability. There is more space for formal dialogue between parties, which leads to the creation of institutions, including electoral institutions, to support the talks. While there should be increased stability in the country, there is also likely to be corruption and problems in working with strong opposition groups. Oversight capacity from the legislature is often weak. In comparison to the previous phases, there is improved oversight and advocacy from civil society and some initial media freedom. There may be an improvement in security provided by the state. And although lack of resources and capacity may still pose problems, there is also increased confidence in security and justice institutions, with a corresponding reduction in the use of violence for settling disputes. Efforts to decentralize the mechanisms of justice may be made, including the adoption of alternative dispute resolution mechanisms. During this stage, there may be increased access to basic infrastructure, but mainly in urban areas. While government usually remains the largest employer, there are signs of more jobs being created in the private sector and of an increase in government revenue, particularly from natural resources (if they exist), tax collection and other revenue streams. Stronger basic services are provided, with a sturdier but poorly implemented regulatory framework.

Stage 4. Transformation

In the transformation stage, a country may have increased social resilience, with conflicts more often resolved peacefully. Credible, non-violent and democratic political processes start to make their appearance. Civil society begins to play an active role in political and societal debates, and, increasingly, good governance principles are adhered to. However, in this period there may also be a lack of public understanding of those principles. During this phase, the security situation has typically remained stable for a considerable time, often at least 5 years. One is more likely to encounter security personnel across the territory, albeit in small numbers and with limited capacity. Usually there is also increased public confidence in security institutions, and potential abuses are more frequently sanctioned. Economically, an enabling environment for business may be found, with more job opportunities, including in the private sector. Public institutions may be capable of managing domestic revenues better through improved tax and customs collection. Very often, decentralization is undertaken to extend access to basic services to the whole country.

Stage 5. Resilience

Resilience may be understood as a society's capacity to deal with challenges and to absorb shocks without entering into crisis. Every stage in the Fragility Spectrum represents progress toward that end, but at this stage resilience has been institutionalized in its social customs, cultural practices, social contract and formal state institutions to such a degree that a relapse into crisis is so unlikely that the country in question can no longer be considered a post-conflict nation. The focus thus shifts away from socio-political consolidation to long-term social and economic development. During this period, political stability has existed for a long time, typically more than 20 years, and the country should have created a strong culture of democracy and good governance. The country may also have made it possible for its citizens to gain a better understanding of the political process. The government should be active in combating corruption with transparent and inclusive processes. Fundamental rights are more likely to be upheld, and the role of civil society should have been defined. There should be sufficient security personnel throughout the country and a high level of confidence among the population. There is evident political will to fight elite impunity, and widespread awareness of how the formal justice system operates. Good infrastructure now connects different parts of the country and the private sector represents a large share of the labor market. Systems are likely to be in place for properly managing natural resources while enough revenue is generated to provide essential services to citizens. Public institutions function both at national and subnational level, and the state increasingly becomes the main service provider for basic needs.

NOTE

1. Source: g7+ 2013.

REFERENCE

g7+. 2013. *Note on the Fragility Spectrum*. Dili: g7+ Secretariat. https://www.pbsbdialogue.org /media/filer_public/17/43/17434d29-eb70-425b-8367-7ccef13bfb0b/g7fragility _spectrum_2013.pdf.

A Review of the Literature Related to Regulatory Governance

The following summarizes the state of knowledge regarding regulatory governance as it relates to the objectives of the manual. It deals primarily with the following areas:

- regulatory governance, including the governance of regulators;
- governance relating specifically to infrastructure regulation, particularly in fragile countries;
- regulatory management capacity; and
- instruments and strategies for improving and maintaining good regulatory practice.

There is an extensive and rapidly growing literature on regulation and governance in the developed and developing world and the material covered in this review can only cover part of it. Readers are encouraged to seek out this broader literature, as it contains much that is of value to the practice of regulatory governance.

The material discussed below is relevant to *evaluating and strengthening regulatory governance* and largely excludes the much more extensive literature on the development, implementation and review of specific regulations, except where the focus of the regulation in question is to improve regulatory governance or regulatory management capacity. The literature review examines multiple themes or issues and several of the references are relevant to more than one.

Why study the literature?

There are three major reasons for providing a short review of the relevant literature in a manual such as this. First, it underpins the analysis and recommendations made in the manual. Second, it helps provide context for the manual by identifying and briefly discussing relevant material that has not been included. Third, a literature review provides references that can be followed up by readers who wish to learn more about a topic.

THE LITERATURE EXAMINING THE IMPACT OF REGULATORY GOVERNANCE ON DEVELOPMENT

Why should regulatory governance be examined? Fundamentally, because regulatory governance has a significant, measurable impact on economic development. A rapidly growing body of empirical and theoretical research shows that poor regulatory governance impedes economic development. Stern and Holder (1999), for example, studied 12 infrastructure industries in six developing Asian countries and found that "structural liberalization" (that is, the opening of these industries to competition), was an important catalyst for developing good practice regulation. The authors also highlight the importance of transparency for effective regulation. Most importantly, they found that the clarity of roles and objectives, autonomy, participation, accountability, transparency, decision-making and predictability of regulatory governance were important determinants of industry performance. Similar conclusions have been reached by Andrés, Guasch, and Staub (2007), Stern and Cubbin (2005), Jacobzone et al. (2010), Cordova-Novion and Jacobzone (2011), Gutiérrez and Berg (2000), Gutiérrez (2003), Ros (2003), Cubbin and Stern (2006), Maiorano and Stern (2007), Andrés, Guasch, and Lopez Azumendi (2008) and Estache, Goicoechea, and Trujillo (2009).

Laffont (2005) was among the first to address regulatory governance in developing countries. He stressed that regulatory institutions and policies cannot be simply transferred from developed to developing countries, as has often been done. Minogue and Cariño (2006), similarly, found that existing policy models of regulatory reform were inappropriate, ineffectual, and too narrowly conceived to address the requirements of developing countries. They proposed that these models should be evaluated and reshaped within the broader context of poverty reduction and developmental programs.

Kirkpatrick (2014) reviewed the empirical evidence on the impact of regulatory reform in developing countries and found that there was a positive relationship between regulatory reform and improved economic performance. However, he qualified this finding by pointing to various methodological and data problems that limited the robustness of his conclusions and pointed to the need to broaden the range of designs and methods for evaluating the results of regulatory reforms in developing countries. IFC (2010) found that while effective regulatory governance was important for development, and was much needed, its implementation was often ineffective.

In summary, while each of the studies have weaknesses, most find that regulatory governance matters when it comes to economic development. However, the limited evidence available suggests that many attempts to improve regulatory governance have had limited impact, often because they draw too heavily on the experience of reforms in more developed countries. This latter conclusion necessarily underlines the importance of careful design and implementation of such reform programs in developing country contexts generally, and fragile states in particular.

THE LITERATURE EVALUATING SPECIFIC ASPECTS OF REGULATORY GOVERNANCE

Regulatory governance encompasses a variety of policies, tools, institutions and processes and raises numerous issues and challenges. Reflecting this, there is a growing literature that focuses on individual elements of the regulatory governance matrix, rather than the whole picture. Elements that have received the bulk of attention include:

- sequencing of regulatory reforms
- regulatory capacity
- regulatory independence and capture
- roles, functions and relationships
- decision-making bodies and decision processes
- appeals and reviews of decisions
- accountability and transparency
- engagement and credibility
- funding, and
- measuring and evaluating performance.

Sequencing regulatory reforms

Which regulatory reforms should be implemented, and when, are two of the most difficult questions to be addressed and have long been discussed by bodies such as the World Bank and the IMF, particularly in relation to the financing of planned reforms in developing countries (see Rihani 2002). A significant literature attempts to provide practical answers to these questions. It is characterized by a lively debate as to appropriate sequencing for reforms, although few doubt its importance (see, for example Branch and Cheeseman 2009; Carment, Samy and Landry 2013; Carothers 2007; Herbert 2014; Rao 2014; Wallsten 2002). Diamond (2012), for example, believes firmly in the value of appropriate sequencing and provides a set of "good practice" guidelines for the sequencing of reforms to public-sector financial management, though he stresses that such reforms should always be tailored to meet the unique circumstances of each country. He further argues that "leapfrogging" can be dangerous: for example, attempting to improve service delivery by introducing results-based budgeting reforms when adequate financial control is lacking, or there is undue instability in resource availability, is unlikely to be successful and could prove counterproductive.

Painter (2014), however, takes a contrary view, arguing that the good governance orthodoxy that proposes a particular sequence of reforms as a necessary component of development is misguided. He cites the examples of China and Vietnam, two authoritarian one-party states that have disregarded this orthodoxy in favor of "leapfrogging" and "retrofitting." His article examines the case of the rapid marketization of public service delivery to illustrate his arguments and concludes that the lesson from these two countries is that good governance can be addressed later in the development process.

Historically, most studies of sequencing have focused on proposing or assessing reform sequences for macroeconomic reform. More recently, reform sequences for public-sector management, and public- sector financial management reforms, have been the focus of this literature. However, to date, few, if any, published studies deal with the actual or ideal sequence of reforms to systems of regulatory governance, and more research is needed. Importantly, sequencing can be a sensitive political and administrative issue in relation to the reform of regulatory governance. Given that the literature strongly suggests that the restoration of essential infrastructure is a precondition for transition out of fragility, reforms of regulatory governance for infrastructure must be a priority.

Decisions regarding the sequencing of reforms must take the strengths and weaknesses of the current arrangements into account, as well as the type and amount of resources available to implement reform. However, they must also take account of broader local circumstances, including any specific impediments to reforms.

Regulatory capacity

The extensive literature that discusses the improvement of capacities in fragile states has been usefully reviewed by Christoplos, Engstrand, and Hedqvist (2014). The authors point out the key limitations in the various approaches to identifying gaps and strengthening capacity, noting that the literature predominantly addresses the capacity of governments and public administrations.

There is no discussion of regulatory governance as such, a fact that reflects the limited amount of research conducted in this area. However, the authors do make a number of points relevant to those attempting reforms to regulatory governance. They stress the need to be aware that prevailing systems of incentives in governments are often skewed against genuine reform. Systems of patronage and bureaucratic fiefdoms can make introducing formal norms and principles of regulatory governance extremely difficult as they involve a loss of power and control over incentives for those in authority. In such situations, "least bad solutions" are often the best available and for fragile countries experiencing high levels of violence and civil strife, reform to regulatory governance is very difficult. Indeed, the authors go so far as to suggest such reform efforts should be confined largely to countries that have developed more stable systems of public administration and focus on those elements with a greater capacity for change.

Barma, Huybens, and Viñuela (2014), reach more positive conclusions. In a recent study of state capacity-building in fragile states, they find that successful institutions share and deploy a common set of internal and external operational strategies, leading along three "pathways" to institutional success. First, some succeed on the basis of strong elite commitment. Second, others seize a window of opportunity to lock in reforms. Third, yet others succeed by more actively cultivating broad support from clients and key stakeholders. The pathways constitute the strategies and practices that are pursued to link largely internal, "micro-organizational" changes with the broader, or "macro" socio-political fragile context. While the study was based on a small sample[1] and did not focus on regulatory governance, its findings are of considerable relevance. It identifies the shared causal mechanisms underpinning institutional success in fragile states, focusing on both internal and external factors.

Roll's study of "pockets of excellence" in state capacity (Roll 2013) (areas of government that work relatively efficiently) focuses on the reasons such pockets form and suggests that there might be potential for such pockets to be built upon by those pursuing reforms to regulatory governance.

While the need to assess and develop regulatory capacity is fundamental to achieving successful regulatory governance reform, the literature addressing this specific issue is quite limited. However, the broader literature on state capacity provides relevant lessons that can be adapted to the regulatory governance context. In particular, regulatory governance reformers can draw on the literature addressing capacity, particularly as regards undue influence, decision processes and organizational structure in relation to regulatory independence, accountability, funding and performance evaluation.

Regulatory independence and capture

The literature on regulatory independence is perhaps the largest single body of writing related to regulatory governance and is too broad to summarize in detail in this review. Hence, only a short overview of selected studies is provided here, and readers should take the opportunity to explore the wider literature. A key reason for the extensive development of this field of study lies in the findings of numerous works, concluding that lower levels of independence are closely associated with poorly performing systems of regulatory governance, and vice versa (see, for example, to list only few, Andrés, Schwartz and Guasch 2013; Cubbin and Stern 2006; Gilardi 2002, 2008; Johannsen 2003; OECD 2015, 2016a; Trillas and Montoya 2013). This has promoted a literature focusing on the question of *how* to promote regulatory independence. There is also a distinct literature related to regulatory independence and infrastructure, particularly as regards telecommunications and water (see, for example, Bartle and Vass 2007; Baudrier 2001; Estache 1997; Estache and Wren-Lewis 2010; Johannsen 2003; Smith 1997; Stern 1997; Tenenbaum 1995; Waverman and Koutroumpis 2011; OECD 2000).

A series of often similar principles and recommendations on how to achieve and sustain regulatory independence has been developed from this literature (see, for example, Brown et al. 2006; Estache 1997; Johannsen 2003; OECD 2000, 2013, 2014a, 2015, 2016b, 2016c, 2017a, 2017b; Smith 1997; Tenenbaum 1995), bringing together many of the findings in the form of advice for regulators and is drawn on significantly in this manual.

The OECD's 2015 study *Being an Independent Regulator* (OECD 2016b), which combines a literature review with the results of a survey of 48 regulators, identifies the key points where undue influence can be exercised and suggests ways of developing a culture of independence. Key strategies proposed include expanding interactions with stakeholders, addressing staffing issues, and ensuring adequate and independent financing sources. The OECD study (2017a), as noted above, draws heavily upon OECD (2015), which provided the analytical background for the guidance offered and should be referred to for more in-depth analysis of the rationale for, and evidence of, the benefits of ensuring the independence of regulators.

The regulatory capture literature has its origins in the economic theory of regulation. Capture can be thought of as an extreme version of the loss of regulatory independence. Dal Bó's 2006 survey of the literature regarding capture has been particularly influential. Of special relevance to this manual is Dal Bó's highlighting of the very high cost of regulatory capture in developing countries. Carpenter and Moss (2014), focus on how to reduce or prevent capture with a series of case studies. Key strategies highlighted include: encouraging the media to inform the public and hold policymakers accountable; developing rules of administrative procedure; using cost-benefit analysis to help query the supposed costs and benefits of proposals put forward; drawing upon the expertise and involvement of subnational officials; creating consumer empowerment programs linked to regulators; cultivating the development of diverse and independent experts and institutionalizing "devil's advocates," within regulatory agencies.

Roles, functions, and relationships

Much of the work on the roles, functions and relationships of regulatory institutions is included in works that focus on particular themes and challenges, such as regulatory capacity, independence and capture, decision-making bodies and decision processes, and accountability and transparency. However, a number of studies have focused specifically on roles, functions and relationships. One of the most influential is Smith's 1997 study of the roles of utility regulators, which focuses on defining their responsibilities, particularly in developing countries, and considers the scope of agencies' industry coverage and their relationship to ministers and to other regulatory bodies and objectives. Smith proposes a "transition path" of organizational forms leading, eventually, to a truly independent agency. The key steps are 1) establishing a dedicated regulatory unit within a department; 2) creating an agency with many of the attributes of an independent agency, but with one or more ministers taking part in its decision-making; and 3) empowering a more truly independent agency, though with some or all of its powers limited to making recommendations to a minister.

Groom, Halpern, and Ehrhardt (2006) outline a set of principles and practices to guide the design of a system of regulation in the developing world. Their specific focus is on water supply and sanitation, although their content is largely applicable to other infrastructure industries. They cover the selection and design of organizations and instruments, the use of contracts and public-private partnerships, prices and tariffs, and the major issues and challenges faced.

A very recent OECD study (2017c) examines the role of economic regulators in encouraging the efficient delivery of infrastructure services and considers whether the approach that economic regulators take to applying tariff and access regulation has implications for the governance of infrastructure more generally. As well as looking at the roles and functions of economic regulators, the report examines how economic regulators are involved in the infrastructure life cycle; the infrastructure needs of the industries they regulate; how they use data to support the delivery of their mandate; the extent to which their roles and functions have changed; the involvement of economic regulators in the policy process; and the challenges that economic regulators are currently facing in fulfilling their mandate.

The study concludes that since economic regulators in different sectors face similar challenges, there is scope for them to work together to address them. Other findings include: flexibility can help economic regulators adapt to change; and the knowledge and experience of economic regulators should be used to develop and refine legislative frameworks for the regulation of infrastructure.

Decision-making bodies and decision processes

In many respects the literature on regulatory governance in relation to decision-making bodies and decision processes overlaps with that on roles, functions and relationships, but with a greater emphasis on the design and evaluation of organizations and their internal decision processes. It varies in content from studies of whole-of-system bodies and processes to narrower, more in-depth studies of specific issues and challenges.

Recuero Virto, Gasmi, and Noumba Um (2008) discuss the relationship between the quality of political and economic institutions and the performance of the reform process for infrastructure industries in developing countries. They examine the impact of the quality of institutions on the performance of regulation, finding that the political accountability of institutional systems is a key determinant of regulatory performance. Secondly, they examine the factors that shape sectoral reforms and the impact of these reforms on the development of the infrastructure industry. Their main conclusion is that countries' institutional environment and the cost of public funds are among the major factors that explain which reforms are actually implemented.

Berg, Memon, and Skelton (2000) discuss the design and reform of independent regulatory commissions, setting out general guidelines and recommendations framed as a series of nine principles: communication, consultation, consistency, predictability, flexibility, independence, effectiveness/efficiency, accountability and transparency. It is argued that these principles can guide decisions on the basic design and structure of an independent commission, its jurisdiction and its key regulatory functions. The paper focuses on the electricity sector, highlighting the ongoing nature of reform and the consequent need for adaptive regulatory agency structures to underpin long-term good practice. It draws on a wide range of country examples.

The OECD's study of regulatory enforcement and inspections (2014c) is part of a developing body of literature addressing the administration and enforcement stages of the regulatory cycle. It seeks to develop a framework to support improved regulatory enforcement, arguing that better-designed and targeted inspections processes make them more effective and efficient, less burdensome and less resource-demanding. It includes 11 principles to guide the design of the policies, institutions and tools to promote effective compliance and the process of reforming inspection services to achieve results. The principles are: evidence-based enforcement; selectivity; risk-focus and proportionality; responsive regulation; long-term vision; coordination and consolidation; transparent governance; information integration; clear and fair process; compliance promotion; and professionalism.

A second OECD study (2014b) has a broader scope, aiming to develop general governance principles applicable to a wide variety of regulators, whatever the breadth of their responsibilities. The focus of the study is on the effect of external governance arrangements on the performance of regulators, but some issues of internal governance are also addressed as the two aspects necessarily overlap. The study identifies seven principles of good governance: role clarity; preventing undue influence and maintaining trust; the structure of decision-making and governing bodies; accountability and transparency; engagement; funding; and performance evaluation. These principles have been widely accepted and adopted and are used as a core element informing Parts B and C of this manual.

Appeals and reviews of decisions

Much of the research related to appeals and reviews of regulatory decisions is found in the legal literature, rather than that specifically addressing regulatory governance. It springs from the view that, while the independence of regulatory agencies is important to their credibility and performance, there is a clear need for a process of appeal from their decisions which is itself independent, to ensure they act lawfully and appropriately and within their legal mandate. This literature argues that regulation is more credible where political and legal institutions are seen to be able to oversee and control the regulator's exercise of discretion.

Baldwin and Cave (1999) conduct a wide-ranging examination of the roles of legislative bodies, courts, central government departments, and local authorities in this regard, while Albon and Decker (2015), describe and assess the major issues related to the design of appeal and review processes, drawing on a literature relating to 15 OECD members and their infrastructure industries. In particular, they consider types of appeal mechanisms and forms of appeal. They find that rights to appeal regulatory decisions are common but that the design of such arrangements varies widely. While neither Baldwin and Cave (1999), nor Albon and Decker (2015) provide much in the way of direct advice and recommendations, the OECD (2014b) study noted above provides useful recommendations, drawn upon in the manual, regarding appeals and reviews.

Accountability, transparency, credibility, and engagement

The literature bearing on the four closely related topics of accountability, transparency, credibility, and engagement often also addresses regulatory appeal and review mechanisms. A small but growing element examines these issues in the regulatory governance context. In essence, accountability and transparency is the obverse of regulatory independence, so that greater independence for regulators calls for more robust accountability and transparency mechanisms. Several studies argue for comprehensive accountability and transparency measures that enable the regulator's performance to be assessed by the legislature or some other body, thus providing incentives for better regulatory performance. It is also argued that transparent accountability processes help boost regulated entities' confidence in the regulatory regime, thereby leading to greater *voluntary* compliance. Greater trust and confidence in the regulatory environment can also reduce administrative costs for regulators and compliance costs for regulated entities.

This literature also suggests several means for achieving and sustaining accountability, including:

- publishing annual reports on performance, provided to the legislature;
- publication of clear operational policies covering compliance, enforcement and decision reviews and guidance material;
- disclosure by the regulator of what rules, data and other inputs are used to make decisions (other than where disclosure might lead to the "gaming" of the regulatory system by regulated entities); and
- publication of the reasons for regulatory decisions in a timely, accessible manner.

The OECD's study of accountability and transparency (2016c) incorporates detailed case studies of four regulatory agencies. It recommends that governments should be clear and transparent about what they expect of regulators, and what the latter can do to meet these expectations. Similarly, clarity as to the respective roles of ministries, other government agencies and regulators can help avoid coordination issues. Importantly, management must be committed to ensure that accountability and transparency are accepted throughout the organization and to make coordination arrangements work in practice. The report concludes with nine "guiding lessons" for reformers.

Deighton-Smith (2004) considers transparency as a core governance value and highlights the increasing recognition of its importance in OECD countries. However, the article concludes that, despite many new initiatives intended to enhance transparency, results have often fallen short of expectations. It examines the reasons for the poor performance and suggests some solutions. These include focusing on the quality of individual transparency initiatives as well as on the level of integration of the different moves pursued, and the links between transparency initiatives and the regulatory process more broadly. In addition, attention must be paid to potential conflicts between transparency and other regulatory quality values, such as timely and responsive regulation, and any such conflicts should be managed to achieve a balanced outcome.

There is a rapidly growing literature related to credibility and engagement, though little relates directly to countries in fragility (see, for example, Alemanno 2014; Balla and Daniels 2007; Balla and Dudley 2014; Bertot et al. 2010; Cass 2006; Coglianese 2006; Grimmelikhuijsen and Meijer 2014; Lavrijssen and Vitez 2015; OECD 2001, 2009). Nash and Walters (2015) provide a useful review of much of that literature and the options available to regulators. The main conclusion reached is that there are no fixed formulae for success, as public engagement and transparency depend not just on the intrinsic characteristics of the methods used but also on external and internal factors that shape the context in which regulators act.

Nonetheless, the authors propose five key principles:

1. Regulators can maximize the benefits and minimize the costs of public engagement and transparency if they apply these principles at the earliest stages of their decision-making, including the priority-setting stage.
2. Regulators can enhance the public's perception of their legitimacy by actively listening to the public's voice, showing respect, and providing reasons for their actions.
3. Regulators should be attentive to disparities in participation, and always strive to achieve a diversity of viewpoints and experience.
4. Regulators should be purpose-driven in choosing from among the options available to them, seeking to find the option that best suits those purposes and fits the context in which they will be applied; and
5. Regulators should seek to learn from their use of public engagement and transparency, investing in evaluation of their practices so as to facilitate an ongoing project of pragmatic experimentalism.

In sum, there is a large literature related to accountability, transparency, credibility, engagement and the relationship between them. Most is general in nature, but there is a growing focus on the regulatory governance context, especially as regards the use of internet. The extent of the literature in relation to fragile states is far more limited and care has to be taken in drawing lessons for such situations.

Funding

Little research addresses the interaction between funding and regulatory governance. What does exist is largely based on the assumption that inadequate funding will lead to greater dependence on the few available funding sources, leading to undue influence being exercised and poorer regulatory governance. The Academy for Educational Development (2003), for example, summarizes essential elements of the relationship between fiscal autonomy and the decision-making and planning independence of an energy regulatory authority. It makes several practical recommendations to promote fiscal autonomy, including: the use of a hybrid mechanism for funding; ensuring a correlation between the funding mechanism and future plans; ensuring the hybrid mechanism has a sound legal basis; allocating funds to the agency on a predictable and stable basis and ensuring funding levels are free from outcome-based decision-making to ensure funding levels do not fluctuate.

Kelley and Tenenbaum (2004) studied eight new regulatory commissions in the energy sector that were intended to encourage private investment in previously largely state-owned infrastructure entities. It found the objectives of independence and accountability proved difficult to achieve in practice, leading the authors to recommend a number of principles for the funding of such commissions, including: the level of funding should allow commissions to perform their assigned tasks; commissions should receive their funding from fees, charges and specific utility taxes rather than from general government budget allocations; the executive and legislative branches of the government must have the right to review the funding levels of commissions, which must be protected from political budget cuts motivated by unpopular commission decisions; commissions should have the legal right to impose penalties on regulated power enterprises, but should not be allowed to use penalties to augment their own budgets; and, in return for receiving greater financial independence than a normal government agency, commissions must be held accountable for their expenditures and performance.

The OECD's 2014b report provides a summary of the major issues related to the funding of regulatory governance and a detailed list of principles for establishing a sound funding model, derived from a survey of regulators. The proposed principles provide a basis for evaluating existing funding structures and, importantly, provide guidance on how to remedy identified deficiencies. In summary, they are that: funding levels should be sufficient to enable the regulator, operating efficiently, to fulfill the objectives set by government, including obligations imposed by other legislation; they should be transparent, efficient and as simple as possible; regulators should not set the level of their fees without arm's-length oversight; and regulators should follow a defined process to obtain funding for major unanticipated court actions.

Measuring and evaluating performance

In this manual the terms evaluate, review and appraise are used as synonyms to refer to both *ex ante* and *ex post* examinations of systems of regulatory governance. Such systems should be evaluated to see if they achieve their objectives effectively and efficiently. Performance evaluations can be conducted on a system-wide basis, or at a more targeted level. System-wide evaluations are costly and demanding, as well as time-consuming. They are also politically sensitive as, if successful, they provide detailed information, both positive and negative, on the performance of organizations and systems for which ministers and senior officials are responsible and accountable. Conversely, they can provide strategic insights and understanding of the interaction of different system elements that more piecemeal, or targeted, reviews are less likely to identify. The choice as to which type of review is required must take account of these characteristics.

There is an extensive general literature on performance evaluation, but much of it focuses on the performance of employees, rather less on organizations and still less on system-wide regulatory governance. However, the assumptions underlying any form of performance evaluation are similar, regardless of the specific focus of the evaluation.

The literature on measuring regulatory governance performance has grown rapidly over the last 20 years, in part due to growing dissatisfaction with the increasingly market-based regulatory reform efforts introduced in the 1980s and 1990s, and has a particular focus on regulatory governance in relation to infrastructure industries. Stern and Holder (1999) discuss the main issues affecting the regulatory governance of infrastructure industries and their implications for regulatory practice. They derive six criteria for appraising performance. Among the main conclusions are the importance of structural liberalization as a catalyst for developing effective regulation as well as of transparency. The authors also identify six core elements which, they argue, affect the governance properties of regulatory frameworks: clarity of roles and objectives; autonomy; participation; accountability; transparency; and predictability. The authors further provide a list of questions to be used to evaluate whether or not a regulatory system displays the six core elements.

Brown et al. (2006) produced a detailed and widely cited World Bank handbook on evaluation for regulators with responsibility for infrastructure. They authors argue that regulatory systems require effective performance evaluation and the handbook provides detailed, step-by-step, practical guidance as to how to conduct basic, mid-level and in-depth evaluations of processes, institutions and regulatory content. Chapter 6 examines regulatory governance, with a major focus on the development and use of the independent regulator model to provide a set of criteria to guide evaluation. It notes, however, that the model is not necessarily the best in all situations. In common with Stern and Holder (1999) and Stern and Cubbin (2005), they also argue that any model adopted should closely align with the three "meta-principles" of credibility, legitimacy and transparency.

Minogue and Cariño (2006) review regulatory reforms in developing countries and argue that existing policy models of regulatory reform are inappropriate, ineffectual, and too narrowly conceived. Similarly, IFC (2010) reviewed the evidence for the impact of regulatory governance initiatives, and how regulatory governance tools had been applied in developing countries. They find that, for the most part, there is a lack of convincing evidence as to the impact of regulatory governance reforms in developing countries.

Effective systems of evaluation depend upon the development, implementation and monitoring of appropriate performance indicators. The challenges of developing such indicators are considerable, but usefully reviewed by Kaufmann and Kraay (2008). OECD (2014c) also outlines a framework for regulatory policy evaluation, providing an overview of evaluation practices in OECD countries and a variety of examples. It is similar in its aims to Stern and Cubbin (2005), forming a part of the OECD program on Measuring Regulatory Performance, which aims to help countries demonstrate how improvements to regulatory governance deliver actual benefits to businesses and citizens. It describes how different types of indicators can be used to create a broad measure of regulatory policy performance.

CONCLUSIONS

What can be learned from the literature in relation to regulatory governance? This review finds, first, that the empirical literature on the subject is limited, far smaller than that on governance in general, though rapidly growing. There is currently relatively little cross-fertilization between the more general governance literature and that more specifically related to regulatory aspects. Second, the conceptual and theoretical literature on regulatory governance is also limited, though growing and, while initially dominated by the economics of regulation, has grown to include a variety of inter-disciplinary perspectives. A great deal of the literature has been developed by the World Bank and the OECD.

The third finding is that the literature on regulatory governance in fragile states and conflict-affected states is very limited, with the literature on regulatory governance and infrastructure being the major focus of attention, particularly in World Bank studies. Fourth, the literature on what are appropriate systems of regulatory governance for fragile and conflict-affected states is largely nonexistent, and there is also relatively little detailed work on the importance of socio-economic, political and security issues in this context. Fifth, there is a small but growing, and highly interdependent literature that offers guidance principles for regulatory governance, notably from the OECD and World Bank.

Sixth, for the most part, the guidance principles offered in the literature are based on independent regulator models of regulatory governance operating in market-based economies. Seventh, the guidance principles for regulatory governance found in the literature are suggested for use, primarily, as a set of criteria against which to measure regulatory governance practice. However, they can also be used to help guide the implementation of reforms to regulatory governance systems.

Finally, and of particular importance to this manual, there is significant evidence that effective systems of regulatory governance have a positive impact on economic development. A growing number of sets of principles for improving regulatory governance is being developed, and although there is currently a limited empirical base for this work, it is largely emerging in particular from the experiences of more developed states, notably OECD members. There have been very few evaluations of the impact or usefulness of the various principles found in the literature, yet there is a high degree of convergence in the advice provided and a clear congruence between that advice and the features of regulatory governance systems found in the most successful economies. While care is needed in translating this material into advice that is relevant to developing countries—and particularly to the fragile context—it provides a sound basis for assessing the reform experience of countries that have had success in exiting situations of fragility and are seeking to develop more specifically tailored advice that will meet needs of fragile countries more effectively.

NOTE

1. The study was based on mixed-method empirical research carried out on nine public agencies in Lao People's Democratic Republic, Sierra Leone, The Gambia, and Timor-Leste.

REFERENCES

Academy for Educational Development. 2003. *Fiscal Autonomy Review: Comparative Study of Regulatory Fiscal Autonomy Around the World.* Prepared for the Philippine Energy Regulatory Commission. http://regulationbodyofknowledge.org/wp-content /uploads/2013/03/AcademyforEducationalDevelopment_Fiscal_Autonomy_Review.pdf.

Albon, R., and C. Decker. 2015. "International Insights for the Better Economic Regulation of Infrastructure." Australian Competition and Consumer Commission (ACCC)/Australian Energy Regulator (AER) Working Paper Series, Working Paper 10. https://www.accc.gov .au/system/files/International%20Insights%20for%20the%20Better%20Economic%20 Regulation%20of%20Infrastructure.pdf.

Alemanno, A. 2014. "Stakeholder Engagement in Regulatory Policy." Prepared for the 11th Meeting of the Regulatory Policy Committee, OECD Conference Centre, Paris, 3–4 November.

Andrés, L. A., J. L. Guasch, and S. Lopez Azumendi. 2008. "Regulatory Governance and Sector Performance: Methodology and Evaluation for Electricity Distribution in Latin America." Policy Research Working Paper 4494, World Bank, Washington, DC.

Andrés, L. A., J. L. Guasch, and S. Straub. 2007. "Do Regulation and Institutional Design Matter for Infrastructure Sector Performance?" Policy Research Working Paper, World Bank, Washington, DC.

Andrés, L. A., J. Schwartz, and J. L. Guasch. 2013. *Uncovering the Drivers of Utility Performance: Lessons from Latin America and the Caribbean on the Role of the Private Sector, Regulation, and Governance in the Power, Water, and Telecommunication Sectors*. Washington, DC: World Bank.

Baldwin, R., and M. Cave. 1999. *Understanding Regulation: Theory, Strategy and Practice*. Oxford: Oxford University Press.

Balla, S. J., and B. M. Daniels. 2007. "Information Technology and Public Commenting on Agency Regulations." *Regulation & Governance* 1 (1)1: 46–67.

Balla, S. J., and S. E. Dudley. 2014. *Stakeholder Participation and Regulatory Policymaking in the United States*. Report for the OECD. Washington, DC: The George Washington University Regulatory Studies Center.

Barma, N. H., E. Huybens, and L. Viñuela, eds. 2014. *Institutions Taking Root: Building State Capacity in Challenging Contexts*. Washington, DC: World Bank.

Bartle, I., and P. Vass. 2007. "Independent Economic Regulation: A Reassessment of its Role in Sustainable Development." *Utilities Policy* 15 (4): 261–69.

Baudrier, A. 2001. "Independent Regulation and Telecommunications Performance in Developing Countries." Paper prepared for the Annual ISNIE Conference: Institutions and Governance, Berkeley, California, USA, September 13–15.

Berg, S. V., A. N. Memon, and R. Skelton. 2000. "Designing an Independent Regulatory Commission." Working Paper 00-17, Public Utility Research Center, University of Florida.

Bertot, J. C., P. T. Jaeger, S. Munson, and T. Glaisyer. 2010. "Engaging the Public in Open Government: Social Media Technology and Policy for Government Transparency." http://tmsp.umd.edu/TMSPreports_files/6.IEEE-Computer-TMSP-Government-Bertot-100817pdf.pdf.

Branch, D., and N. Cheeseman. 2009. "Democratising, Sequencing and State Failure in Africa: Lessons from Kenya." *African Affairs* 108 (430): 1–26.

Brown, A. C., J. Stern, B. Tenenbaum, and D. Gencer. 2006. *Handbook for Evaluating Infrastructure Regulatory Systems*. Washington, DC: World Bank. http://documents.worldbank.org/curated/en/428111468177849284/pdf/364990Handbook101OFFICIAL0USE0ONLY1.pdf.

Carment, D., Y. Samy, and J. Landry. 2013. "Transitioning Fragile States: A Sequencing Approach." *Fletcher Forum of World Affairs* 37 (2): 125–51.

Carothers, T. 2007. "How Democracies Emerge: The 'Sequencing' Fallacy." *Journal of Democracy* 18 (1): 12–27.

Carpenter, D., and D. A. Moss, eds. 2014. *Preventing Regulatory Capture: Special Interest Influence and How to Limit It*. Cambridge: Cambridge University Press.

Cass, N. 2006. "Participatory-Deliberative Engagement: A Literature Review." Working Paper 1.2, School of Environment and Development, Manchester University, Manchester. https://core.ac.uk/download/pdf/16285075.pdf.

Christoplos, I., K. Engstrand, and A. L. Hedqvist. 2014. "Capacity Development Literature Review." UTV Working Paper 2014:1, Sida, Stockholm. http://www.sida.se/contentassets/e152ed3b81ab4b9ebaf51362cc2721ea/capacity-development-literature-review_3761.pdf.

Coglianese, C. 2006. "Citizen Participation in Rulemaking: Past, Present, and Future." *Duke Law Journal* 55: 943–68.

Cordova-Novion, C., and S. Jacobzone. 2011. "Strengthening the Institutional Setting for Regulatory Reform: The Experience from OECD Countries." OECD Working Papers on Public Governance 19, OECD Publishing, Paris.

Cubbin, J., and J. Stern. 2006. "The Impact of Regulatory Governance and Privatization on Electricity Industry Generation Capacity in Developing Economies." *World Bank Economic Review* 20 (1): 115–41.

Dal Bó, E. 2006. "Regulatory Capture: A Review." *Oxford Review of Economic Policy* 22 (2): 203–25.

Deighton-Smith, R. 2004. "Regulatory Transparency in OECD Countries: Overview, Trends and Challenges." *Australian Journal of Public Administration* 63 (1): 66–73.

Diamond, J. 2012. "Guidance Note on Sequencing PFM Reforms." EC (European Commission), IMF (International Monetary Fund), PEFA (Public Expenditure and Financial Accountability). PFM (Public Financial Management Blog). https://blog-pfm.imf.org/files/guidance-note-on-sequencing-pfm-reforms.docx.

Estache, A. 1997. "Designing Regulatory Institutions for Infrastructure: Lessons from Argentina." In *Public Policy for the Private Sector*, Note 114. World Bank, Washington, DC.

Estache, A., A. Goicoechea, and L. Trujillo. 2009. "Utilities Reforms and Corruption in Developing Countries." *Utilities Policy*, 17 (2): 191–202.

Estache, A., and L. Wren-Lewis. 2010. "On the Theory and Evidence on Regulation of Network Industries in Developing Countries." In *The Oxford Handbook of Regulation*, edited by Robert Baldwin, Martin Cave, and Martin Lodge, 371–406. Oxford: Oxford University Press.

Gilardi, F. 2002. "Policy Credibility and Delegation to Independent Regulatory Agencies: A Comparative Empirical Analysis." *Journal of European Public Policy* 9 (6): 873–93.

———. 2008. *Delegation in the Regulatory State: Independent Regulatory Agencies in Western Europe*. Cheltenham: Edward Elgar Publishing.

Grimmelikhuijsen, S., and A. Meijer. 2014. "Effects of Transparency on the Perceived Trustworthiness of a Government Organization: Evidence from an Online Experiment." *Journal of Public Administration Research and Theory* 24 (1): 137–57.

Groom, E, J. Halpern, and D. Ehrhardt. 2006. "Explanatory Notes on Key Topics in the Regulation of Water and Sanitation Services." Water Supply and Sanitation Sector Board Discussion Paper Series, Paper No. 6, World Bank, Washington, DC.

Gutiérrez, L. H. 2003. "The Effect of Endogenous Regulation on Telecommunications Expansion and Efficiency in Latin America." *Journal of Regulatory Economics* 23 (3): 257–86.

Gutiérrez, L. H., and S. V. Berg. 2000. "Telecommunications Liberalization and Regulatory Governance: Lessons from Latin America." *Telecommunications Policy* 24 (10–11): 865–84.

Herbert, S. 2014. *Sequencing Reforms in Fragile States: Topic Guide*. Birmingham, UK: GSDRC, University of Birmingham.

IFC (International Finance Corporation). 2010. *Regulatory Governance in Developing Countries*. Better Regulation for Growth: Governance Frameworks and Tools for Effective Regulatory Reform. Washington, DC: IFC. https://openknowledge.worldbank.org/bitstream/handle/10986/27881/556450WP0Box0349461B0GovReg01PUBLIC1.pdf?sequence=1&isAllowed=y.

Jacobzone, S., F. Steiner, E. L. Ponton, and E. Job. 2010. "Assessing the Impact of Regulatory Management Systems: Preliminiary Statistical and Econometric Estimates." OECD Working Papers on Public Governance 17, OECD Publishing, Paris.

Johannsen, K. S. 2003. *Regulatory Independence in Theory and Practice–A Survey of Independent Energy Regulators in Eight European Countries*. Copenhagen: AKF Forgalet.

Kaufmann, D., and A. Kraay. 2008. "Governance Indicators: Where Are We, Where Should We Be Going?" Policy Research Working Paper 4370, World Bank, Washington, DC.

Kelley, E., and B. Tenenbaum. 2004. "Funding of Energy Regulatory Commissions." Energy and Mining Sector Board Working Notes 30525, World Bank, Washington, DC.

Kirkpatrick, C. 2014. "Assessing the Impact of Regulatory Reform in Developing Countries." *Public Administration and Development* 34 (3): 162–68.

Laffont, J.-J. 2005. *Regulation and Development*. Cambridge: Cambridge University Press.

Lavrijssen, S., and B. Vitez. 2015. "The Principles of Good Regulation in the Water Sector." TILEC Discussion Paper 2015-002. Tilburg Law and Economics Center (TILEC), Tilburg.

Maiorano, F., and J. Stern. 2007. "Institutions and Telecommunications Infrastructure in Low and Middle-Income Countries: The Case of Mobile Telephony." *Utilities Policy* 15 (3): 165–81.

Minogue, M. and L. Cariño. 2006. "Introduction: Regulatory Governance in Developing Countries." In *Regulatory Governance in Developing Countries*, edited by M. Minogue and L. Cariño. Cheltenham: Edward Elgar Publishing.

Nash, J., and D. E. Walters. 2015. "Public Engagement and Transparency in Regulation: A Field Guide to Regulatory Excellence." Research Paper Prepared for the Penn Program on Regulation's Best-in-Class Regulator Initiative, University of Pennsylvania Law School, Philadelphia. https://www.law.upenn.edu/live/files/4709-nashwalters-ppr-researchpaper 062015.pdf.

OECD (Organisation for Economic Co-operation and Development). 2000. "Telecommunications Regulations: Institutional Structures and Responsibilities." OECD Digital Economy Papers 48, OECD Publishing, Paris.

———. 2001. *Citizens as Partners: Information, Consultation and Public Participation in Policy -Making*. Paris: OECD Publishing.

———. 2009. *Focus on Citizens: Public Engagement for Better Policy and Services*. OECD Studies on Public Engagement. Paris: OECD Publishing.

———. 2013. "OECD Principles on Transparency and Integrity in Lobbying." OECD, Paris. http://www.oecd.org/gov/ethics/oecdprinciplesfortransparencyandintegrityinlobbying.htm.

———. 2014a. *The Governance of Regulators*. OECD Best Practice Principles for Regulatory Policy. Paris: OECD Publishing. http://dx.doi.org/10.1787/9789264209015-en.

———. 2014b. *OECD Framework for Regulatory Policy Evaluation*. Paris: OECD Publishing. http://dx.doi.org/10.1787/9789264214453-en.

———. 2014c. *Regulatory Enforcement and Inspections*. OECD Best Practice Principles for Regulatory Policy. Paris: OECD Publishing. https://www.oecd-ilibrary.org/governance/reg ulatory-enforcement-and-inspections_9789264208117-en.

———. 2015. *Policy Framework for Investment*. Paris: OECD Publishing. http://dx.doi .org/10.1787/9789264208667-en.

———. 2016a. *Driving Performance at Latvia's Public Utilities Commission*. The Governance of Regulators. Paris: OECD Publishing. http://dx.doi.org/10.1787/9789264257962-en.

———. 2016b. *Being an Independent Regulator*. The Governance of Regulators. Paris: OECD Publishing. http://dx.doi.org/10.1787/9789264255401-en.

———. 2016c. *Governance of Regulators' Practices: Accountability, Transparency and Co-ordination*. The Governance of Regulators. Paris: OECD Publishing. http://dx.doi .org/10.1787/9789264255388-en.

———. 2017a. *OECD Integrity Review of Mexico: Taking a Stronger Stance Against Corruption*. OECD Public Governance Reviews. Paris: OECD Publishing. https://www.oecd-ilibrary .org/governance/oecd-integrity-review-of-mexico_9789264273207-en.

———. 2017b. *Creating a Culture of Independence: Practical Guidance against Undue Influence*. The Governance of Regulators. Paris: OECD Publishing. https://www.oecd-ilibrary.org /governance/creating-a-culture-of-independence_9789264274198-en.

———. 2017c. *The Role of Economic Regulators in the Governance of Infrastructure*. The Governance of Regulators. Paris: OECD Publishing. http://dx.doi.org/10.1787 /9789264272804-en.

Painter, M. 2014. "Governance Reforms in China and Vietnam: Marketisation, Leapfrogging and Retro-Fitting." *Journal of Contemporary Asia* 44 (2): 204–20.

Rao, S. 2014. "Prioritising and Sequencing Public Sector Reform." Helpdesk Research Report. GSDRC Applied Knowledge Services. http://gsdrc.org/docs/open/hdq1080.pdf.

Recuero Virto, L., F. Gasmi, and P. Noumba Um. 2008. "The Role of Institutional Design in the Conduct of Infrastructure Industry Reforms: An Illustration through Telecommunications in Developing Countries." MPRA Paper 28253. *Southern African Journal of Information and Communication* 9 (1): 4–16. https://mpra.ub.uni-muenchen.de/28253/.

Rihani, S. 2002. *Complex Systems Theory and Development Practice: Understanding Non-Linear Realities*. London/New York: Zed Books.

Roll, M. 2013. "Pockets of Effectiveness: Why Do Strong Public Institutions Exist in Weak States?" Paper prepared for the American Political Science Association (APSA) Annual Meeting, Chicago, August 29–September 1.

Ros, A. J. 2003. "The Impact of the Regulatory Process and Price Cap Regulation in Latin American Telecommunications Markets." *Review of Network Economics* 2 (3):1–17.

Smith, W. 1997. "Utility Regulators: The Independence Debate." In *Public Policy for the Private Sector*, Note 127. World Bank, Washington, DC.

Stern, J. 1997. "What Makes an Independent Regulator Independent?" *Business Strategy Review* 8 (2): 67–74.

Stern, J., and J. Cubbin. 2005. "Regulatory Effectiveness: The Impact of Regulation and Regulatory Governance Arrangements on Electricity Industry Outcomes." Policy Research Working Paper 3536, World Bank, Washington, DC.

Stern, J., and S. Holder. 1999. Regulatory Governance: Criteria for Assessing the Performance of Regulatory Systems: An Application to Infrastructure Industries in the Developing Countries of Asia. *Utilities Policy*, 8 (1): 33–50.

Tenenbaum, B. 1995. "The Real World of Power Sector Regulation." *Public Policy for the Private Sector*, Note 50. World Bank, Washington, DC.

Trillas, F., and M. A. Montoya. 2013. "Independent Regulators: Theory, Evidence and Reform Proposals." *Info* 15 (3): 39–53.

Wallsten, S. 2002. "Does Sequencing Matter? Regulation and Privatization in Telecommunications Reforms." Policy Research Working Paper 2817, World Bank, Washington, DC.

Waverman, L., and P. Koutroumpis. 2011. "Benchmarking Telecoms Regulation: The Telecommunications Regulatory Governance Index (TRGI)." *Telecommunications Policy* 35 (5): 450–68.

Developing a Government-Wide Regulatory Policy

Gaining investor confidence in key infrastructure sectors requires establishing the credibility of the legal and regulatory system across a number of fields and adopting key reforms to infrastructure regulation. Where reform is needed, it is likely to be required across several infrastructure sectors in which many of the key challenges and priorities will be similar. Accordingly, the reform agenda is likely to be more effectively and rapidly implemented if it is guided by a consistent set of principles and approaches—in other words, a government-wide policy for regulatory governance. As well as helping to provide a template for implementing a reform agenda in various sectors, such a policy will send a strong signal about the government's commitment to reform to investors and businesses, particularly if they are given an opportunity to participate in the process of developing and implementing this policy.

REGULATORY POLICIES AND INFRASTRUCTURE IN DEVELOPING COUNTRIES

Regulatory policies have been adopted by all OECD countries in one form or another but are less common in developing countries and are rare in low-income and post-fragile contexts. This likely reflects the fact that developing and implementing a fully developed regulatory governance policy requires relatively high-level capacities within government, which are unlikely to be present in an immediate, post-fragile context. However, while capacity constraints are likely to prevent a fully-articulated regulatory governance policy being implemented effectively in these situations, there are strong arguments for countries to adopt at least some of the key elements of regulatory governance policy at an early stage in the process of exiting situations of fragility. Indeed, there are specific elements of the post-fragile context that suggest that the potential benefits of adopting the key principles of a regulatory governance policy may be particularly significant. In particular:

- A regulatory governance policy provides a template that can be used in the wide-ranging task of regulatory reconstruction/reform required in most post-fragile contexts.

- General agreement on broad principles and approaches to making and assessing regulation can support reformers in their attempts to apply these in specific sectors—like infrastructure—in which there is likely to be self-interested opposition. In essence, reformers, if challenged, can refer to the agreement to support their decisions and activities.
- Using a regulatory governance policy as a reform template helps promote consistency in regulatory approach between sectors, thus helping to minimize economic distortions.
- Regulatory governance policy focuses on improving the policy development process, making it more systematic and efficient and minimizing reworking abandoned policy initiatives. As the system begins to become effective, it can often yield net *cost savings* in ministries, as well as improve policy outcomes. This is likely to be particularly important in an environment of very constrained government budgets, as noted in box C.1.

While relatively rare, as noted above, some post-fragile countries have adopted government-wide policies as the foundation for their regulatory reform activities. While few include a substantial focus on regulatory governance, they do as a rule address the question of how governments will make, assess and revise regulation, usually with an emphasis on Regulatory Impact Assessment (RIA). These policies therefore represent an attempt to establish a policy framework that will systematically ensure high-quality regulation, thus supporting sector-specific reforms and contributing to good economic and social outcomes. Two recent examples are Georgia[1] and Kosovo[2] (see box C.2).

The costs of adopting a regulatory governance policy

While regulatory governance policies seek to fundamentally change the way that governments make laws, countries have usually found the direct costs of implementing them to be relatively modest.

The main direct costs involved are:

1. the development of the policy, including the establishment and operation of a small, central unit to oversee and report on policy implementation;
2. the work involved in training staff in departments and agencies;
3. the work in implementing the policy as part of regulatory development in departments and agencies.

While the first two costs are necessary investments in achieving better regulatory outcomes, the medium-term outcome can be that regulatory development costs in departments actually fall, rather than rise, as suggested above. This stems from the gains in effectiveness and efficiency achieved by the policy.

Specific process requirements, such as the need to prepare written regulatory impact assessments and ensure they meet relevant quality standards do have resource implications, but these have been found to be relatively small. For example, one study found that, in Australia, the average labor cost to departments and agencies preparing RIA for decision-makers averaged around US$3,500 per RIA (World Bank 2010, 9), equivalent to less than 2 weeks of a policy official's time. Moreover, these costs are offset by the wider efficiency gains that the RIA process enables.

Better policy planning and Regulatory Impact Assessment in Georgia and Kosovo

Recognizing the need for more evidence-based policymaking and improved legislative drafting standards, the Government of Georgia approved the *Policy Planning System Reform Strategy 2015–17.* This required the introduction of a more systematic process of policy and regulatory development, including Regulatory Impact Assessment into the Georgian legislative process. The Department of Policy Analysis, Strategic Planning and Coordination in the Prime Minister's Office requested USAID's assistance in designing a national RIA framework. The Government also established the Investors' Council, which is expected to help develop a more business-friendly regulatory framework over time by acting as a systematic consultation and cooperation mechanism, ensuring that private-sector views are heard and taken into account in developing reforms.

The Government of Kosovo adopted a Better Regulation Strategy in 2014 but experienced serious issues with regards to its implementation. Problems were caused by a lack of resources and overly ambitious assumptions as to how the policy should be designed and implemented. After a period of review, the Government decided to restructure the strategy in a more realistic fashion by:

1. adopting a program of continuous reduction of administrative burdens, using the Standard Cost Model (SCM) methodology and the Doing Business indicators;
2. adopting a systematic process to identify priority reforms of existing regulation, emphasizing the use of *ex post* RIA;
3. introducing RIA by integrating the requirement with the established system for developing "concept documents" (or explanatory memoranda), for which policy development capacities will be significantly increased;
4. improving stakeholder consultation through effective outreach (including internationally) and providing incentives for stakeholders to participate;
5. improving policy communication based on in-depth analysis of the current situation, to be presented in a concept document combined with a specific action plan;
6. improving incentives for institutional compliance with administrative procedures; and
7. developing more realistic work planning that takes into account the time needed to conduct policy analysis and stakeholder consultation and is based on a concept document in which the design is elaborated.

Sources: Republic of Kosovo 2014; USAID 2015.

IMPACT ON INFRASTRUCTURE SECTOR REFORM EFFORTS

Thus, a regulatory governance policy can play an important part in supporting national and/or sectoral infrastructure policies and plans, while streamlined versions of regulatory governance policy, such as that outlined in box C.3, can feasibly be implemented in post-fragile contexts, as the examples of Kosovo and Georgia demonstrate. Adopting this approach will:

- enhance confidence among investors as to the government's commitment to regulatory integrity;
- promote consistency in regulatory approach between infrastructure sectors, thus helping to minimize economic distortions; and
- provide a public statement of principles and approaches to making and assessing regulation that can support reformers in their attempts to apply these in infrastructure sectors.

Elements of a basic, national regulatory governance policy statement

1. Adopt a whole-of-government policy on regulation which recognizes that:
   a. Regulation has numerous unintended and often negative consequences. Accordingly, governments must carefully consider proposals to regulate before adopting them.
   b. Taking account of this, regulation should only be adopted where there is a substantial problem to be addressed and other actions by government or private players are unlikely to address it.
2. A small, expert advisory body should be established at the center of government to provide expert advice on new regulatory proposals, priorities for reforming existing regulation and assessments of regulatory governance. This body should report to a senior minister with specific responsibility for regulatory governance policy.
3. Where regulation is to be used, government should adopt a systematic approach to identifying and weighing its likely benefits and costs.
   a. This should take account of environmental and social benefits and costs that cannot easily be weighed in cash terms, as well as economic costs.
   b. The distribution of these costs should also be considered.

c. Consultation should be undertaken with those likely to be affected. This will both help governments obtain a better understanding of the impacts of regulating and clarify what support regulatory intervention would have.
d. Consideration should be given to the use of international standards and/or policy transfer in areas covered by the regulations and to whether these are appropriate for use in a low-income country context.
e. The expert advisory body should review regulatory proposals and provide its opinion before they are considered for adoption by the government. Opinions should address both the specific merits of the proposal and its implications for regulatory governance.
4. Government should endorse a set of regulatory governance principles that apply to all independent and arm's-length regulators such as those outlined in in Part B of this manual.
5. The expert advisory body on regulation should periodically assess the performance of sectors where regulation has been recently reformed.
6. Governments should adopt a basic regulatory governance policy in the early post-fragile context and should regularly consider the scope to expand it to include other relevant elements as circumstances change.

DEVELOPING A REGULATORY GOVERNANCE POLICY STATEMENT FOR THE WHOLE OF GOVERNMENT

In fragile or post-fragile countries, reforms to the civil service, financial management, procurement, decentralization and anti-corruption policies and programs are often underway at the same time, so the policy agenda is crowded as governments try to rebuild the economy with very limited resources. Adopting a strategic approach is therefore vital if support for a regulatory governance policy is to be obtained. The following steps can help do that.

Gain high level support and formal endorsement for the policy

It is vital to gain high-level political and administrative support and formal policy endorsement if reform is to be achieved. It may be more feasible and appropriate to seek endorsement for the more limited goal of establishing a regulatory governance policy for the infrastructure sector as a whole, or for specific infrastructure industries, rather than for government as a whole.

This support should, if possible, be formalized in legislation. If this is not possible, it should be specified in a Presidential Decree, Prime Ministerial Instruction, Cabinet Handbook or other significant policy document. Whatever form it takes, it should prescribe the core elements of the regulatory governance policy, such as those listed in box C.2, although there should be a degree of flexibility so as to allow the policy to be amended if circumstances change.

Develop the content of the policy for submission

Box C.2 provides an indication of what a basic, national regulatory governance policy suitable for adoption in low-income and post-fragile contexts could include. It is based on the recommendations of the OECD and Asia-Pacific Economic Cooperation (APEC) in relation to regulatory governance policy, and the regulatory reform policies adopted by countries such as Malaysia, Georgia, Rwanda and Kosovo. Even where agreement to adopt whole-of-government policy cannot be obtained, consideration should be given to adopting a basic set of regulatory governance *principles*, such as those outlined in Part B of this manual, which can function as a source of inputs for reformers in designing regulatory governance models (including governance models for regulators) in specific sectors.

At the very least, a regulatory governance policy statement should indicate:

- the aims of the policy and its relation to the government's policy agenda;
- which minister is to be responsible for the policy;
- the regulatory principles for government;
- the establishment of a small, expert unit of government responsible for administering the policy, its governance and reporting arrangements. Ideally it should be placed in the prime minister's office, or that of another senior minister;
- where it is not a fully national policy, which sectors are within scope;
- a list of planned reforms with a brief explanation of their relationships to the overall objectives of the policy;
- the estimated implementation capacity for each reform with associated costs and benefits;
- the expected commitment to, support for, and opposition to, each reform;
- the foreseeable risks involved;
- a list of the major phases and timelines;
- the deliverables to be achieved in each phase;
- the major activities necessary for each deliverable;
- the key milestones;
- a list of who is to be responsible for the delivery of each major activity.

As noted, the policy should also include the establishment of a small, expert body at the center of government to guide and support its implementation, particularly by undertaking the following tasks:

- provide expert advice to cabinet on new regulatory proposals;
- provide advice to cabinet on reforming existing regulation;
- provide cabinet with assessments of regulation and regulatory governance, using a prescribed but flexible methodology for estimating costs, benefits and likely environmental impacts, following systematic consultation with all relevant parties;

- have responsibility for gradually integrating the regulatory assessment process into the established, departmental policy and decision processes, as resources permit.

This body should report to the senior minister with specific responsibility for regulatory governance policy.

While statements of regulatory governance policy can have significant benefits, even in the low-income country context, it is important to recognize practical constraints and avoid unrealistic expectations about the benefits of such policies. While broad policy statements can be expected to yield benefits over the medium- and long-term, it will often be difficult to point to major, concrete gains in the short term. Moreover, while these policies provide a sound template for improving the body of regulation and its administration by government over time, these benefits will only be obtained if the broader political and economic environment is characterized by at least basic levels of stability, capacity and government commitment to reform.

Develop an implementation plan

A broad implementation plan will be required to support any proposal to develop a regulatory governance policy and demonstrate the feasibility of the proposal. It should explain the relationship between the government's objectives and the proposed regulatory governance policy outcomes, showing how the policy will help achieve the objectives. It should also identify:

- the major implementation challenges;
- timeframes and broad project phases;
- the relationship, if any, between the regulatory governance policy and other policies, regulations and projects;
- the likely resources needed;
- governance arrangements that indicate who will be responsible for what major decisions; and
- the consultations undertaken with stakeholders and their support for the project.

Developing and putting into practice an implementation plan is a complex and challenging task that will be examined in more depth in the next chapter.

THE ROLE OF A PERMANENT POLICY ADVISORY UNIT

A permanent regulatory oversight (or regulatory policy advisory) unit is a key institution underpinning successful regulatory policy. The roles that these bodies typically perform, and their importance, were discussed in general terms above and in chapter 12. Such bodies should ideally be established at the earliest stages in the reform process, since their contributions are often particularly significant then. However, their importance during the policy implementation, review and revision stages is also crucial.

A key role of these units is to help to maintain a strategic, whole-of-government view of the reform agenda's progress, assessing the performance of sectoral reforms, such as those relating to infrastructure industries, in the light of the government's overall priorities, including those identified in the general regulatory policy (if one has been adopted). This focus on the government's strategic objectives and on coordination between the reforms being adopted in related sectors should help to establish and maintain consistent policy approaches and prevent distortions arising due to regulatory differences in related sectors (e.g., where gas and electricity are in competition).

More generally, regulatory oversight bodies can act as champions of reform and strengthen the influence of pro-reform forces addressing individual-sector reform issues. This can include helping to further develop or refine sectoral reform policies and assist in achieving effective implementation (e.g., by providing training to officials in key organizations), as well as strengthening the authority of sectoral regulators in their dealings with government and stakeholders.

In a post-fragile environment, where newly adopted reforms may be undercutting long-established systems of rent extraction, there will often be strong and sustained opposition lobbying. In the early stages of reform, in particular, where widespread benefits are not yet visible, such lobbying risks undermining the reform program. This makes the role of center-of-government oversight bodies in providing ongoing support for the reform agenda particularly important. Ensuring that these bodies are located at the center of government (e.g., in the President/Prime Minister's Office or the Ministry of Finance) helps to maximize their effectiveness. Appointing a board with significant nongovernmental representation and explicitly empowering the oversight body to speak publicly on reform priorities are also key strategies to maximize their influence in this area.

In post-fragile contexts in particular, capacity development will be a key determinant of the success of reform programs over time. Capacity development is a primary need, as the progressive expansion of the reform agenda will impose continually increasing requirements in this area. As suggested above, regulatory oversight units typically take a lead role in developing capacity by offering training to officials across government, developing guidance materials and undertaking quality control in relation to Regulatory Impact Assessment.

NOTES

1. Policy Planning System Reform Strategy 2015–17, which prescribes the introduction of RIA into the Georgian legislative process. Additionally, the Government proposed to establish an Investors Council in 2017, which is expected to serve as a high-level cooperation platform for the public and private sectors in shaping a better and more business-friendly regulatory framework. http://gov.ge/files/425_49310_540377_PolicyPlanningSystemReform StrategyandActionPlan.pdf.
2. *Better Regulation Strategy 2014–2020*, outlining a revised strategy (Republic of Kosovo 2014).

REFERENCES

Republic of Kosovo. 2014. *Better Regulation Strategy 2014–2020: Regulatory Impact Assessment*. http://kryeministri-ks.net/repository/docs/Better_Regulation _Strategy_2014_-_2020.pdf.

USAID (United States Agency for International Development). 2015. *Recommendations on RIA National Framework of Georgia*. USAID, Governing for Growth (G4G) in Georgia. https://pdf.usaid.gov/pdf_docs/PA00KVD5.pdf.

World Bank. 2010. *Making It Work: 'RIA Light' For Developing Countries*. Better Regulation for Growth: Governance Frameworks and Tools for Effective Regulatory Reform. Washington, DC: World Bank. http://documents.worldbank.org/curated/ en/184141468167049021/pdf/55636-WP-REPLACEMENT-RIALightNov2009.pdf.

Checklist of Anti-Corruption Risks[1]

1. **Ambiguity**
   a. Language
      i. Does the draft law choose the most precise word in all cases? (Word choice).
      ii. Do sentences and half-sentences relate to each other in a way that leaves no room for ambiguity? (Construction of sentences).
   b. Legal coherence
      i. Are there provisions in other laws that might conflict with the draft law? (Conflicting provisions).
      ii. Does one term have different meanings throughout the draft law or other laws? (Inconsistent terminology).
      iii. Is any reference to another law or instance possibly unclear to the reader? (Unclear references).
      iv. Did the drafters "forget" to cover all necessary aspects requiring regulation? (Regulatory gaps).
      v. Does the draft law deviate from the uniform structure of laws for no reason? (Uniform structural laws).
2. **Prevention gaps (public laws)**
   a. Competencies
      i. Did the draft law "forget" to define a competent body for any of the tasks described? (Unidentified competencies).
      ii. Did the law "forget" to furnish the government body with any competencies?
      iii. If the law delegates the identification of the responsible government body to another regulation or instance—is there a clear timeline and is it clear which other official body exercises the tasks until the new body is identified? (Delayed identification).
      iv. If the draft introduces a new government body or new competencies—is it clear which other body exercises the tasks until the new entity is set up? (Delayed setting up).
      v. Does the draft delegate the regulation of central points to another body, which should actually be in the draft law itself? (Competency for further regulation).
      vi. Does the law create powers for one state body that overlap with the powers created by another law? (Overlapping competencies).

    vii. If several state bodies have powers in implementing the law, are all competencies fully allocated to one of them and are no competencies "forgotten"? (Split competencies).

    viii. Does the draft touch on situations where the private interest of a public official may conflict with his/her official duties and, if so, do provisions on managing this conflict of interest apply under this or another law? (Conflict of interest).

  b. Powers and resource. It is important that a public body should have all the powers and resources needed to carry out its tasks.

  c. Procedures

    i. Are all steps of the procedure defined, not leaving their definition to the arbitrariness of a public official? (Undefined steps).

    ii. Is it unclear to citizens when they can claim their rights or when a public official has to fulfill his/her obligations? (Unidentified timelines).

    iii. Are fees undefined or not clearly calculable? (Unidentified fees).

    iv. Can a public official arbitrarily harass citizens with repeated inspections for no clear reason? (Repetition of inspection).

    v. Does the law require citizens to seek approval from many different state bodies, thus increasing the chance of facilitation payments being sought? (Multi-stop procedures).

    vi. Does the law cover the distribution of limited state resources (jobs, subsidies, etc.) and are the criteria and procedures fully transparent? (Competitions for limited state resources).

  d. Decisions. Does the law provide for excessive, unnecessary discretion? (Excessive discretion).

  e. Oversight

    i. Does the law provide for transparency in procedures and results, allowing citizens and the media to scrutinize them? (Transparency and civil society oversight).

    ii. Does the law avoid unnecessary concentration of power in one government body, one department or unit, or one public official? (Separation of tasks).

    iii. Does the law (or another applicable law) foresee rotation of staff in high-risk areas (e.g., procurement)? (Rotation).

  f. Sanctions. Are effective, proportionate and dissuasive sanctions available?

  g. Judicial review. Does the draft law make available to citizens clear, comprehensive appeals procedures covering all possible grievances?

  h. Sector-specific safeguards. What risks specific to the particular sector covered by the draft law might not have been fully mitigated by the draft?

3. **Addendum. Corrupted legislation**—are there indications that a stakeholder has unfairly distorted free political competition in order to bend the wording of the draft law to his/her advantage?

  a. Illegal activities

    i. violation of lobbying rules by interest groups;

    ii. political finance violations by anybody profiting from a law;

    iii. procedural violations during the legislative process in particular on transparency;

    iv. ethical violations of legislators (such as provisions on conflict of interest);

    v. instances of bribery.

b. Legal activities (that can still point to hidden corruption in the legislative process)
   i. suspicious privileges contained within a law (for certain interest groups);
   ii. large (but legal) financial donations by any individual or group profiting from a law;
   iii. extraordinary (legal) lobbying activities by interest groups;
   iv. lack of transparency of the legislative process (even if formally within legal limits);
   v. ethical challenges (despite compliance with rules);
   vi. obvious detriment to, or waste of, public funds.

NOTE

1. Source: Hoppe 2017.

REFERENCE

Hoppe, T. 2017. *Methodology for Corruption Proofing in Montenegro*. Sarajevo: Regional Anti-Corruption Initiative (RAI). http://www.antikorupcija.me/media/documents/CP_Methodology_ENG.pdf.

www.ingramcontent.com/pod-product-compliance
Lightning Source LLC
Chambersburg PA
CBHW080545220326
41599CB00032B/6362